What Do You
Have To Lose?

What Do You Have To Lose?

The Pillars of a Republic
Conceived in Liberty and
Dedicated to the Rule of Law

David L. Nelson
and
Mary Margaret Serpento

To order additional copies of this book, contact:
Xlibris
844-714-8691
www.Xlibris.com
Orders@Xlibris.com
861827

DEDICATION

This book is dedicated to Capitol and District of Columbia policemen and policewomen who taught us what true patriotism means by guarding the citadel of democracy on January 6, 2021, and establishing order in the chambers of that citadel where our vice president, senators, and representatives opened, tabulated, counted, and certified the votes cast by the Electoral College.

*It is for us, the living rather to be dedicated here to the unfinished work which they who fought here have thus far so nobly advanced. It is rather for us to be here dedicated to the great task remaining before us – that from these honored dead we take increased devotion to that cause for which they gave the last full measure of devoti*on *– t*hat *we here highly resolve that these dead shall not have died in vain that this nation under God shall have a new birth of freedo*m an*d that government of the people by the people for the people shall not perish from the earth.*

Closing remarks of Abraham Lincoln at
Gettysburg on November 19, 1863

CONTENTS

ACKNOWLEDGMENTS

Coauthor David L. Nelson thanks his elementary school teachers who introduced him to Abraham Lincoln's Gettysburg Address while teaching him penmanship and cursive handwriting. He gripped a pen and dipped it in an inkwell to write its opening sentences again and again on white lined paper. His wife Judy reintroduced him to Lincoln when upon returning from the battlefield at Gettysburg she told of the immense calm that permeated that battlefield at sunrise as she stood at the place where Lincoln gave that address.

Coauthor Mary Margaret Serpento wishes to thank her husband Stan, who has stood by her side for over forty-four years. She also thanks the staff on 77 Mich. L. Rev. no. 1, November 1978. The secretary position was her first job in the legal world, at the dawn of word processing on an amazing IBM Selectric typewriter. They gave her the opportunity to see firsthand what thorough research, meticulous documentation, and clear writing can do. She also thanks all the librarians who track down the answers to obscure reference requests and preserve the world's knowledge for the generations who follow us.

MISSION STATEMENT

This book was written prior to November 5, 2024, to consider events surrounding the 2020 presidential election. The threats to our right to vote, the stability of our republic, our inalienable rights, and the rule of law remain regardless of which side won the 2024 election. During the 2016 presidential campaign then-candidate Donald Trump, while seeking the support of skeptical low-income voters, asked, "What the hell do you have to lose?"[1] Having observed his campaign statements, his conduct in office, and the events and aftermath of January 6, 2021, this book is the authors' response. Voters still have skin in the game.

The US Constitution places the ultimate responsibility for protecting our Republic on American voters. If our republic falls, an autocrat will step forward and all other rights in the Constitution will fall like a row of dominos. Yet the voters' ability to vote intelligently depends on the integrity of news providers, our elected officials, and other public sources of information.

Today, a flood of information saturates the news outlets and social media, and it is critical that voters keep things in perspective and review what's at stake. Cascading events, legal experts and public officials confirm that our republic, the rule of law and the rights of Americans created by the US Constitution are now at their greatest risk since the Civil War. One example—an editorial by Charles M. Blow published in the *New York Times*, "America's Thirst for Authoritarianism,"[2] considered a recent remark by Donald Trump that if reelected he would not be a dictator, "except for Day 1."[3] The *New York Times* reported on March 16, 2024, that Trump predicted to a crowd in Ohio: "Now, if I don't get elected, it's going to be a blood bath for the whole—that's going to be the least of it. It's going to be a blood bath for the country."[4]

This book does not establish or evaluate whether assertions in the news media, books, or other sources are true. The authors make no accusations or recommend indictments for alleged crimes. Those functions belong to the Department of Justice (DOJ) at the federal level, to state law enforcement, and to our courts. All charged and prosecuted because of those events are entitled to the protection of all constitutional safeguards outlined in Chapter 12—for example: the right to a verdict based on proof beyond a reasonable doubt. Until adjudicated otherwise, all who acted are presumed innocent. That is the way it must remain.

But voters do not sit as a judge or jury, nor do these authors. When a candidate files for public office, they ask the voters to hire them. Voters need not find a candidate possessed criminal intent or decide whether they have been proven unworthy beyond a reasonable doubt. Instead, they must decide if the candidate will fulfill their obligations to the office they seek and if their "job history" reveals anything of concern. A candidate applying for private sector employment could not blow off an interviewer by refusing to supply their résumé or by laying down a litany of lies. The interviewer would close the file, open the door, wish the candidate a nice day, and invite in the next candidate.

The mission here is to analyze the evolution of our rights under the US Constitution and to explore the risk to those rights revealed by recent events. It explores that risk by reviewing the words and actions of candidates and public officials published in hearing transcripts and court decisions, and reported and analyzed in the news media from the viewpoint of an American voter.

The Founding Fathers warned that the republic might succumb to the machinations of an autocrat, but—they also assured that the American people, armed with the right to vote in free and fair elections, are the defenders of our republic and our rights. Yet it isn't clear that voters *will* defend that right.

INTRODUCTION

Those who do not remember the past are condemned to relive it.

—George Santayana

Our republic has faced many attacks: August 24, 1814—the British capture and burning of Washington, DC; April 12, 1861—Fort Sumter; December 7, 1941—Pearl Harbor; and September 11, 2001—the World Trade Center and the Pentagon. We remember these attacks because they were existential and repelling them exacted a heavy price. But January 6, 2021, was different. As shown in live television coverage and reported in the news media, January 6 was a savage assault *by Americans* on our right to vote for our leaders as set down in the Constitution. It exposed our republic's fragility and imperiled all our rights.

The House of Representatives Select Committee to Investigate the January 6th Attack on the United States Capitol (herein the Select Committee or the Committee) reported its findings from its eighteen-month investigation. The DOJ investigated criminal responsibility arising out of the attack, and as of December 2023 over 1,237 people were charged with federal crimes, 714 pled guilty, and 723 received sentences.[1] Criminal investigations continue, and several cases are awaiting trial or are on appeal. (See criminal cases listed in Chapter 4 "Major Investigations and Indictments.")

News reports continue to document how the Trump presidency drove our nation into political chaos as it confronts reproductive rights, climate change, gun violence, and other urgent dilemmas. They assert autocrats in other nations threaten our ability to promote peace and financial stability. Hard questions have been left unanswered. Will our republic fall? Will our right to vote survive? Will our Constitution and our inalienable rights prevail?

Coauthor Nelson has in his study over 500 books. Many concern politics and governance. One has a brown, leather-like plastic cover. It is four inches wide, six and a half inches tall, a quarter inch thick, and weighs three ounces.* Its title reads *The Constitution of the United States 1787–1987*. All rights we now have are derived from the document printed in that tiny book. When he received it from Lexis, he presented it to his wife Judy with the inscription, "To Judy with all my love." She placed it on their étagère among family treasures. Later, as he returned to the family room to retrieve it, she told him to keep it in his study. Many take it for granted and haven't read it since school, if then. But Americans can no longer ignore the clarion call in its first three words—"We the People" created it and, by it, placed the ultimate responsibility for answering hard questions like those above on us all.

Any critique of Donald Trump must acknowledge that many Americans support him despite his reported lack of truthfulness, his unproven claims of voter fraud, and the televised events of January 6, 2021. Intelligent, hardworking Americans continue to back him even though many of his statements and actions challenge provisions of the Constitution. His loyal followers cheer him on no matter what he says or what criminal investigations reveal. Why? What do they seek to change? Are they asking that we abandon the Constitution?

Many express a fear of the *deep state,* a concept pervasive in the far-right press and on social media. Supposedly within the federal bureaucracy, a cabal of government workers runs the nation—and elected officials have failed to disband that cabal. But who are its members? Where do they labor and assert their control? Do they have an "Overlord"? Do they keep records? If so, who has them? And what do Trump's supporters recommend be done about this alleged deep state?

No one has brought forth tangible evidence that a deep state cabal exists within our government. There is ample evidence it does not. Federal agencies are authorized by the Administrative Procedure Act (44 U.S.C. § 3501) to adopt administrative rules and regulations to implement programs and policies enacted into law by Congress. These

---

* For comparison, a US first-class letter can weigh up to 3.5 ounces.

agencies can only create regulations and enforcement procedures pursuant to Congressional statutes. Laws are published in Statutes at Large as enacted by Congress. Public laws* become codified in the fifty-four titles of the U.S. Code (U.S.C.) as federal statutory law. For example, Title 52 codifies voting and elections statutes. Agency regulations to enforce them are published in the Federal Register for public review and comment before codification in the fifty titles of the Code of Federal Regulations (CFR) as federal administrative law. Title 11 regulations administer federal elections law. Federal regulations are subject to congressional oversight and statutory amendment as necessary. The president also issues executive orders to direct or restrict agency activities. The Government Publishing Office's govinfo.gov website has the full text of the Federal Register, CFR, Statutes at Large, and USC for free online (see Appendix B).

To be sure, thousands of workers toil within the federal government, make policy decisions, and administer the law. And it is undoubtedly true that some of them make bad decisions, exceed their authority, or violate laws enacted by Congress. But Congress can enact new legislation, and perpetrators can be taken to court – that's how the rule of law works. No one has produced credible evidence that a deep state cabal has wrested control of our government from our elected officials or from our courts. But on the contrary, aggressive political factions have vigorously employed fear of a deep state conspiracy. Those deep-seated fears planted in the minds of many have created a genuine threat to the continuation of our republic.

That was driven home on January 6, 2021, when on live television, a mob broke through defensive barricades, battered police officers, ransacked the Capitol, threatened to kill its leaders, and forced our elected representatives and their staffs to flee and hide. The mob intended to block Congress from performing its constitutional duty to certify the votes of duly selected presidential electors for the 2020

---

* Public laws ("Pub. L. Congress number-law number") apply to society as a whole. Private Laws ("Pvt. L. Congress number-law number") apply to an individual, family, or small group, and are enacted to assist citizens injured by government programs or who are appealing an executive agency ruling such as deportation.

election. Their attack delayed the certification for several hours, but the election result was certified the next morning because Vice President Pence rejected President Trump's proposal that he rig the count of Electoral College votes in Trump's favor, or return the certification process to state governments. January 6 brought us face to face with the fragility of our Constitution and our institutions.

News reports that followed magnified the danger to voting rights with descriptions of Republican officials and their supporters orchestrating a nationwide program to restrict voting rights through the enactment of laws at the state level and to block all efforts to stop those restrictions. Restricting voting rights violates the principle that "all men (and all women and racial groups we might add) are created equal and endowed by their Creator with unalienable* rights."[2] The rule of law, representative government, and the balance of power concepts that undergird them are besieged. The time has come for all who believe in the Constitution, contained in coauthor Nelson's little brown book, to stand up and defend it.

To find a way forward, we must take a critical look back at the nation our Founding Fathers established in very trying times. They set out to create a nation founded on individual rights when slavery had begun to split that new nation in two. The fragility inherent in a representative democracy plagued them from the start. Consider that in 1796 our first president, George Washington, expressed deep concern that despotism could destroy the new nation in his "Farewell Address," an address Alexander Hamilton helped to write:

> Friends & Fellow-Citizens ... The alternate domination of one faction over another, sharpened by the spirit of revenge natural to party dissension, which in different ages & countries has perpetrated the most horrid enormities, is itself a frightful despotism. But this leads at length to a more formal and permanent despotism.

---

* Unalienable (also, inalienable. adj.: incapable of being alienated, surrendered, or transferred [rights]). See Endnote 5 for a fuller discussion of *unalienable* vs. *inalienable*.

The disorders & miseries which result, gradually incline the minds of men to seek security & repose in the absolute power of an individual: and sooner or later the chief of some prevailing faction more able or more fortunate than his competitors, turns this disposition to the purposes of his own elevation, on the ruins of Public Liberty.[3]

As early as 1787, Alexander Hamilton had already expressed similar concerns over the "extremes of tyranny and anarchy" and "tempestuous waves of sedition and party rage" in *Federalist* No. 9, which he titled, "The Utility of the Union as a Safeguard Against Domestic Faction and Insurrection":

A FIRM Union will be of the utmost moment to the peace and liberty of the States, as a barrier against faction and insurrection. It is impossible to read the history of the petty republics of Greece and Italy without feeling sensations of horror and disgust at the distractions with which they were continually agitated, and at the rapid succession of revolutions by which they were kept in a state of perpetual vibration.... If momentary rays of glory break forth from the gloom, while they dazzle us with a transient and fleeting brilliancy, they at the same time admonish us to lament that the vices of government should pervert the direction and tarnish the luster, of those bright talents and exalted endowments for which the favored soils that produced them have been so justly celebrated.[4]

Abraham Lincoln put it this way in his address to the Young Men's Lyceum of Springfield, Illinois, in 1838:

Is it unreasonable then to expect that some man possessed of the loftiest genius, coupled with ambition sufficient to push it to its utmost stretch, will at some time, spring up among us? And when such a one does, it will require *the people* to be united with each other, attached to the government and laws, and generally intelligent, to successfully frustrate his designs[5] (emphasis added).

The same agitations for "frightful despotism" that concerned Washington, Hamilton, and Lincoln now emanate from government leaders, news outlets, and social media. In litigation concerning a plan by John Eastman, a Trump attorney, to overturn the votes of presidential electors for the 2020 presidential election, US District Judge David O. Carter (Central District of California) wrote in one of his orders, "It was a coup in search of a legal theory."[6] He also said that Messrs. Trump and Eastman had, "more likely than not," broken the law.[7] (See discussion in Chapter 5 First Hearing.)

Later, retired Federal Appeals Court Judge J. Michael Luttig testified before the Select Committee that if Vice President Pence followed Trump's demands that he rig the count of the electoral votes for president in the 2020 election, it would have amounted to "a revolution within a constitutional crisis." (See Chapter 5 Third Hearing.) He also testified that Trump's continuing efforts to upset the results of the 2020 election posed a "clear and present danger" to the republic.[8] The concerns of Judges Carter and Luttig demand that Americans recognize and expose those threats for what they are.

Our Founders wrote inalienable rights into our organic law.* They include our very lives and the lives of family and loved ones. Many were written into the original Constitution; some grew from Amendments; and others are derived from statutes enacted pursuant to the Constitution. The Constitution grants our courts power to enforce those rights through due process of law. Citizens of other nations don't have these rights. If they don't get in line, autocrats eliminate them by

---

* organic law (n.): the body of laws (as in a constitution or charter) that form the original foundation of a government. Also: one of the laws that make up such a body.

intimidation, imprisonment, disappearance, or assassination. Here's a short list.

A. **Enumerated Constitutional Rights**
    - The right to select our representatives by voting them into office
    - Freedom to speak
    - Freedom to assemble
    - Freedom to petition our government for redress of grievances
    - Freedom to pray or not to pray as we choose
    - Freedom of the press
    - Freedom to seek due process and equal protection of the law
    - Freedom from arbitrary or political imprisonment
    - Freedom to file claims in federal or state court
    - Freedom to contract

B. **Statutory Rights Created under the Constitution**
    - Freedom to own private property
    - Freedom to seek medical care for ourselves and our family
    - Freedom to will or pass our assets on to our heirs or devisees (See statutes summarized in Appendix A)

C. **Unenumerated, Implied, Derivative, and Aspirational Rights**
    - The right of privacy
    - Freedom to express our opinions
    - Freedom to attend schools of our choice
    - Freedom to select, train in, and practice our employment
    - Freedom of enterprise
    - Freedom to travel about our nation and indeed the world
    - Freedom to think, explore, work, create, pursue happiness, meditate on, and to seek the fullness of life.

The January 6 attack and its aftermath reminded coauthor Nelson of an incident at his law firm. A secretary, Jackie, had placed a note on the paper cutter. "When you are finished, PLEASE, leave the handle down. The fingers you slice off may be your own." Jackie's notes got her in trouble with the office manager. But she wasn't wrong about the paper cutter. January 6, 2021, sounded a warning: if you don't protect the voting process, the rights you cut off may be your own.

For years, the principle that each citizen's vote should carry the same weight has been under attack by gerrymandering politicians, filibustering senators, reactionary Supreme Court justices, and scheming partisans. But the events of January 6 came close to eliminating the right of all Americans to cast their vote for president and vice president and have it counted. That is as basic as it gets.

There is no way to sugar coat it. The primary thing we have that we may lose, Mr. Trump, is the balanced representative government our Founders created at both the federal and state levels. President Biden confirmed that fact in a speech to the nation, when he stated that, "I revere this office, but I love my country more,"[9] and selflessly abandoned his reelection campaign because the nation needed younger voices to save the republic.

CHAPTER 1

What's at Stake—A Review of the Basics and a Historical Overview

Our children learn the general framework of their government and then they should know where they come in contact with the government, where it touches their daily lives and where their influence is exerted on the government. It must not be a distant thing, someone else's business, but they must see how every cog in the wheel of a democracy is important and bears its share of responsibility for the smooth running of the entire machine.

—Eleanor Roosevelt

The first three Articles of the Constitution protect all rights we have as a free people. It is there that our Founders delegated legislative, executive, and judicial powers into equal branches that check and balance each other as opposed to a government where a dictator decrees, administers, and judges without "the consent of the governed."[1] Then in Article IV Section 4, they guaranteed each state a republican form of government. Later in Amendments IX and X they reserved undelegated powers to the states or to the people.

Many may say it is trite, even jingoistic, to wrap oneself in the flag. But you can see it in Americans' faces when they sing of our republic. They love their freedoms and our flag. Francis Scott Key wrote the poem that became the "Star-Spangled Banner" we sing at sports events after he witnessed the British cannonading of Fort McHenry during the War of 1812 while he was held captive. Key's poem "Defence* of Fort

---

* Alternate spelling for "defense" in use at the time of original writing. Several words are spelled using British conventions in the original text. For a fuller discussion, see https://www.usconstitution.net/constmiss.html.

McHenry" described the flag with bright stars and broad stripes that he saw flying over the Fort at the twilight's last gleaming. He watched that flag through the night by the light of bombs bursting in the air and of rockets that were streaming over the ramparts of the fort. Then by dawn's early light, he saw the proof he yearned to see. The flag was still there. In his poem, Key asked future generations whether that flag still flies over the land of the free and home of the brave. Francis Scott Key knew that not only our flag was waving over the ramparts at Fort McHenry—so was our Constitution. When we stand with our hands over our hearts and pledge our allegiance to our flag, we pledge allegiance to the republic for which that flag was unfurled and to the Constitution which created it. But the pride that surges through us as we give voice to our anthem is not enough.

More than a million service men and women have given their lives in defense of that flag and the Constitution it represents.[2] They did so because they understood that our Founding Fathers created a new kind of government in Philadelphia. While many have not studied what was done there, they know in their gut that the gift of freedom the Founding Fathers gave us is precious. Like another patriotic song we sing (as Dr. Martin Luther King reminded us) our Constitution shouts out, "From every mountainside, let freedom ring."[3] It is through that gift of freedom that we express our humanity. But the roots of our republic run far deeper than our National Anthem, the Pledge of Allegiance, or our flag.

Throughout history when dictators took over a nation, they took over the entire government—its courts, its legislative halls, and its military forces. Their edicts became the nation's laws. Thus, if an authoritarian regime ever casts our Constitution aside, Congress's power to enact laws would be nullified. There would no longer be checks and balances on executive power. The Constitution created the Supreme Court in Article III and provided Congress with the power to create lower courts to enforce our laws. John Marshall, our first Supreme Court chief justice, told us that "it is emphatically" the province and duty of the judiciary to tell us what our laws are. That function does not belong to the president and must never be given to an autocrat—we'd have no redress for injuries inflicted by the dictator's edicts.

Our state governments would become rubber stamps. The Constitution is the document that established a republican form of representative government at both the federal and the state levels. But that requirement would disappear.

Left unsaid in the document itself, the Constitution imposed obligations on the citizens of our republic. After the Founding Fathers completed their work at the Philadelphia Constitutional Convention of 1787, Benjamin Franklin was asked what kind of government had been created. He answered, "A republic if *you* can keep it"[4] (emphasis added). Note that Franklin, in answering Mrs. Powel, the lady questioning him, identified "you" as the one obligated to "keep" the new government. Note as well that the Preamble to the US Constitution drives that same point home:

> *We the People* of the United States, in Order to form a more perfect Union, establish Justice, insure domestic Tranquility, provide for the common defence, promote the general Welfare, and secure the Blessings of Liberty to ourselves and our Posterity, do ordain and establish this Constitution for the United States of America[5] (emphasis added).

Later, at Gettysburg, Abraham Lincoln described our government as being "of the people by the people and for the people." With these words, Franklin, the Constitution itself, and Lincoln told us that self-governance was a bedrock principle upon which our Founding Fathers grounded our nation.

From their experience with the British monarchy and their knowledge of the history of other nations, the Founding Fathers understood that the new government would fail and that an autocrat would usurp it unless they found a way to clearly define, separate, and balance the powers of the new government among legislative, executive, and judicial functions, and establish the rule of law. Americans today are both the beneficiaries and the guardians of what they did. To be sure, the continued vitality of our republic depends on the officials we vote into office, the judges, and justices they appoint to sit in our courts, their oaths of office, and on our free press, but in the last analysis, it rests on the people themselves to keep it. They are the heart and soul of our government.

Current events discussed in the following chapters have brought these truths into sharp focus. They tell us, as Shakespeare wrote in *The Tragedy of Julius Caesar*, "The fault, dear Brutus, is not in our stars / But in ourselves that we are underlings."[6] The events that led up to and exploded on January 6, 2021, and reverberated thereafter, demonstrated that the issue we face today isn't just bad politicians. It is whether the American people have the fortitude to preserve our freedoms by asserting their power to hold our officials to their oaths of office under our Constitution.

As the authors watched American citizens in MAGA* caps lunging at police officers with flagpoles, smashing the windows of the Capitol building to gain entry, and threatening to hang the vice president, unfold on their television screens, they became increasingly alarmed. Didn't this mob realize what it was doing? Was Congress about to trash the Constitution and simply name a new president? Later, when reports appeared concerning a Capitol attacker wearing an animal skin and horns, the threat to our Constitution became even more alarming. The mob did *not* realize or care what it was doing. The attacker said, after his sentencing to several years in prison, that he was sorry he participated in the riot of January 6. Really? Considering the enormity of the insurrection and possible coup, how could he *not* admit he was sorry? Later, as the authors inventoried the rights our Constitution provides to all Americans and discussed them in the chapters below, the guy with the horns kept coming back.

The overthrow of our republic and of our Constitution, had that happened on January 6, 2021, would have constituted a replay of the

---

* MAGA: acronym for the "Make America Great Again" slogan associated with Donald Trump beginning with his 2016 presidential campaign. Like other phrases and symbols (ex.: the swastika), its meaning has shifted from its original usage. Ronald Reagan and Bill Clinton had used similar slogans in their presidential campaigns.

demise of the Weimar Republic in Germany in 1933. Hitler arranged to have the Weimar Republic abolished and himself named Chancellor of Germany. Later, it was written that the German people themselves allowed that to happen.

> But the Third Reich owed nothing to the fortunes of war or to foreign influence. It was inaugurated in peacetime, and peacefully, by the Germans themselves, out of both their weaknesses and their strengths. The Germans imposed the Nazi tyranny on themselves. Many of them, perhaps a majority, did not quite realize it at that noon hour of January 30, 1933, when President Hindenburg, acting in a perfectly constitutional manner, entrusted the chancellorship to Adolf Hitler.

> But they were soon to learn.[7]

Based on the Select Committee's exposure of attempts to unravel our republic, it now appears that we did not learn a whole lot from Nazi Germany. The events of January 6, 2021, came at a time when our nation faced enormous threats to its existence from around the world. We cannot meet those threats unless we realize that they emanate from the same concerns expressed by Washington, Hamilton, and Lincoln. Autocracies are expanding worldwide. We can't ignore that reality. It *can* happen here.

Following World War II (WW2), international organizations were formed with high hopes and at great expense to rebuild areas and populations devastated by that war. The Marshall Plan,[8] Point Four,[9] and the United Nations (UN) were promoted to carry out the rebuilding and to promote peace. But despite the urgent need for new international policies that moved humanity forward, tyranny and war soon reemerged and threatened to destroy democracies and human rights around the world. What followed became a struggle for dominance between nations committed to freedom and democracy and those ruled by autocrats.

The USSR* was organized in 1922 following the Bolshevik (Communist) Revolution in Russia. It produced Joseph Stalin and later Mao Zedong (f.k.a. Mao Tse-tung) in the People's Republic of China. During WW2, it should be noted the United States through Lend Lease[10] helped the Soviet Union acquire the armament it needed to repel the Nazi German Army.

The Yalta agreement at the close of WW2 divided Germany and Berlin into sectors. The USSR was given East Germany and East Berlin, and the Western Allies were given West Germany and West Berlin.[11] West Berlin, however, was situated in East Germany. That arrangement contributed to later conflicts.

Soon after Yalta, instead of thanking us for our assistance, the Soviet Union broke with its former allies. "From Stettin in the Baltic to Trieste in the Adriatic an Iron Curtain … descended across the Continent."[12] Behind that Iron Curtain, the USSR incorporated East Germany and seven other countries into the Eastern Bloc.† The Cold War began in earnest in June 1948 when the Soviet Union blocked access to West Berlin in what became known as the Berlin Blockade. To counter the blockade, the United States and its Western Allies organized the Berlin Airlift to carry supplies to West Berlin until September 1949. To meet the growing threat posed by the Soviet Union, in 1949 twelve nations allied with the United States created the North Atlantic Treaty Organization (NATO) to defend each other against attack. The European Allies also established political and economic ties to counter the Eastern Bloc. The Council of Europe (1949) and the European

---

* The Union of Soviet Socialist Republics: initially Russia, Ukraine, Belorussia, Transcaucasia (present-day Armenia, Georgia, and Azerbaijan). Also known as the Soviet Union.

† Eastern Bloc: the Soviet Union, Poland, East Germany, Albania, Bulgaria, Yugoslavia, Romania, Czechoslovakia, and Hungary. NATO coined the term after the USSR did not withdraw completely after WW2.

Economic Community (1958)* led to the European Union (EU) in 1993.[13]

Meanwhile in Cuba, Fidel Castro overthrew the government of Fulgenci Batista in 1959 and established a communist government ninety miles off the shore of Florida aligned with the Soviet Union. To combat that threat, in 1961 the United States, through the Central Intelligence Agency (CIA), funded a group of Cuban exiles who landed at the Bay of Pigs with the intent to overthrow Castro. The operation failed.[14] Later in the summer of 1962, the Soviet Union began to establish bases for ballistic nuclear missiles in Cuba to deter any future invasion attempts. The Cuban Missile Crisis ended in November of 1962 when the US Navy blocked the shipment of missiles to Cuba, and the Soviet Union agreed to withdraw its missiles from Cuba in exchange for a secret assurance from the United States, later fulfilled, that it would withdraw its Jupiter nuclear missiles from Turkey.[15]

But the Cold War continued apace. The Soviet Union and the Eastern Bloc formed the Warsaw Pact† in 1955 to counter NATO.[16] Both sides began to stockpile nuclear bombs in what became known as the Balance of Terror. The superpowers also engaged in proxy wars (the Korean and Vietnam wars for example) and supported insurgencies in lieu of direct confrontation.[17] Other nations began to assemble and test fire ballistic missiles designed to carry nuclear warheads. According to the Union of Concerned Scientists,

> Nine countries possess nuclear weapons: the United States, Russia, France, China, the United Kingdom, Pakistan, India, Israel, and North Korea. In total, the global nuclear stockpile is close to 13,000 weapons.

---

* Also known as the European Common Market until the Maastricht Treaty in 1993. Original members: Belgium, France, (West) Germany, Italy, Luxembourg, and the Netherlands (1958). Twenty-two other countries later joined the EU. Great Britain joined in 1973 but has since left the EU.

† The Warsaw Pact was a collective defense treaty established by the Soviet Union and seven satellite states in the Eastern Bloc: Albania (until 1968), Bulgaria, Czechoslovakia, East Germany, Hungary, Poland, and Romania.

While that number is lower than it was during the Cold War—when there were roughly 60,000 weapons worldwide—it does not alter the fundamental threat to humanity these weapons represent.[18]

Mikhail Gorbachev, General Secretary of the Communist Party from 1985 to 1991, attempted to open the Soviet Union through his twin programs of Perestroika (reconstruction) and Glasnost (openness). Gorbachev won the Nobel Peace Prize in 1990 for his leading role in proposing radical changes to East-West Relations, but his programs failed. On December 31, 1991, the Soviet Union dissolved into fifteen independent countries*.[19] The two Germanys reunited. Many Eastern Bloc countries eventually joined the EU and NATO.

That lasted for three decades until Russian Federation President Vladimir Putin began a campaign to take over Ukraine. First Russia annexed the Crimea from Ukraine in 2014. Then Putin recognized two regions of Ukraine as "independent."[20] In February of 2022, he launched a military invasion of Ukraine. In September of 2022, Putin announced that Russia was annexing additional swaths of Ukrainian territory. The invasion not only revealed Russia's intent to reestablish the Soviet Union, but it also laid before the whole world the vast difference between a republic structured to protect freedom and the rule of law and an autocratic regime. In a speech to the US Congress by video link, President Volodymyr Zelensky of Ukraine made a powerful defense of democracy that was printed in full in the *New York Times*:[21]

> Russia has attacked not just us, not just our land, not just our cities. It went on a brutal offensive against our values, basic human values. It threw tanks and planes against our freedom, against our right to live freely in our own country, choosing our own future, against our

---

* The fifteen former Soviet Socialist republics: Armenia, Azerbaijan, Belarus, Estonia, Georgia, Kazakhstan, Kyrgyzstan, Latvia, Lithuania, Moldova, the Russian Federation, Tajikistan, Turkmenistan, Ukraine, and Uzbekistan.

desire for happiness, against our nation dreams, just like
the same dreams you have, you Americans.

Across the border, the Russian government ordered its citizens not
to describe the military operations against Ukraine as a "war," the police
brutally rounded up and incarcerated Russian anti-war protesters, and
the Russian news media was forthwith silenced.[22]

In 1938 Adolf Hitler undertook the liquidation of Czechoslovakia,
and WW2 exploded across Europe despite appeasement. Beginning in
2014, Vladimir Putin has undertaken the liquidation of Ukraine and
threatens neighboring countries not to interfere. We now confront the
economic and humanitarian disaster that Russia ruthlessly inflicted.
Putin and the oligarchs who support him initiated the war to suit their
own interests. At stake are the rule of law and possibly civilization itself.

The swift course of the events taking place in Ukraine make it
indelibly clear that now is not the time for internal attacks on our
Republic. As Senator Arthur H. Vandenberg (R-Michigan) warned in
a speech reprinted in the Congressional Record in January of 1947, "In
any event, partisan politics, for most of us, stopped at the water's edge."[23]
Even with the peril to both our Republic and our allies, it is not clear
that we are prepared to stop partisan politics at the water's edge.

CHAPTER 2

A Framework for Representative Democracy That Has Endured for 237 Years

The Founding Fathers undertook to put in place a government based on self-governance. To achieve that goal, they grounded our republic on principles of divided power, individual freedoms, an independent judiciary, and the rule of law. The balance of power concepts that undergird our republic were uniquely different from those of any other nation. The Founders removed all governmental power from the autocrat formerly governing them, transferred that power to the people as a representative democracy, and instilled in its citizens inalienable rights. It is true, as shown below, that the government the Founders created was hardly perfect. It did not grant the freedoms that it established to all residents of the new nation. It did, however, contain a framework for its government and a blueprint for the protection and later expansion of fundamental human rights.

The Declaration of Independence had already described the "unalienable rights" of Americans violated by the British monarch as self-evident truths and inscribed them into that document out of "a decent respect to the opinions of mankind." We revere our Founding Fathers for greatly valuing honesty, civility, and decency, and for expressing their concerns to England that way—even as they set out to break away from her. It's a concept some of our current leaders ought to study. Recall that at the time we broke from England there was no constitution, no republic, and no body of national law. The Continental Congress, a loose confederation of the colonies that met in Philadelphia, ran the Revolutionary War. It was only after the Articles of Confederation failed, that our rights were set forth in our Constitution, Bill of Rights, Amendments to the Constitution, and in statutes enacted pursuant to the Constitution. Our courts then elaborated and articulated those rights in their decisions. Though they are fragile, they are today taken for granted or, worse, deliberately ignored by many Americans—some in high places.

In the hurly burly of today's political challenges, we don't sit down and quietly reflect on what our lives would be like if our inalienable rights were taken from us. Put yourself back in the years leading up to the revolution. What rights did the colonists have before our Constitution was adopted? Think about it. What were they complaining about in 1776? What did they do about it?

> We hold these truths to be self-evident, that all men are created equal, that they are endowed by their Creator with certain unalienable Rights, that among these are Life, Liberty, and the pursuit of Happiness.—That to secure these rights, Governments are instituted among Men, deriving their just powers from the consent of the governed,[1]

That is the most profound statement of human rights and governance ever uttered. In succinct and eloquent language, it states that equality and our inalienable rights are self-evident truths. Studying Greek philosophers, the Romans, and philosophers like John Locke and Jean Rousseau, our Founding Fathers set out to replace the British monarchy. In terse and straightforward language, they stated their concept to be a new nation derived *from its people and grounded on the freedom of its people.* From their experience, they understood that the new government would fail unless they found a way to ensure liberty and freedom by separating and balancing the powers of government among legislative, executive, and judicial functions.

At the time of the American Revolution, about 3 million persons resided in the thirteen colonies. Today, the nation's population exceeds 331 million in fifty states, five (inhabited) territories,* and the District

---

* American Samoa, Guam, Northern Mariana Islands, Puerto Rico, and the US Virgin Islands.

of Columbia. Its citizens confront an unstable economy, toxic social media, civil unrest, challenges to voting rights, and global climate change that challenge the ability of that gift to deliver on its promise.

We read and hear the words of the Founding Fathers, but do not take time to reflect on the profound truths their words expressed and how they relate to the challenges we face today. Very few take time to read *The Federalist*[2] to understand the thinking that lay behind our Constitution or even read the Constitution itself. Exactly how do we preserve our inalienable rights in today's political climate? Who protects them? Why should we take time to think about any of that anymore? Isn't the existence of our republic and our rights a given?

No. It is not. Our Founding Fathers were well-to-do New England lawyers and bankers, New York and Pennsylvania businessmen, a newspaper man, and wealthy southern plantation owners (slave owners). No working class, Blacks, First Peoples, or women are depicted in John Trumbull's *The Declaration of Independence* painting in the Capitol Rotunda.* But we should not throw the baby out with the bath water. To understand the words they gave us more fully, we must focus on the time in which they lived and the place where they lived. They were struggling to establish independence on the eastern shore of a continent contested by the First Nations† and European colonial powers.‡ Their very lives were at stake. Doing *whatever he wanted to do* the British king was running roughshod over the colonists. He impressed American sailors into his navy, quartered his troops in their homes, taxed them without representation in parliament, threatened their right to speak freely, and censored their press. The Founding Fathers were as mad

---

* Image and more details available here: https://www.aoc.gov/explore-capitol-campus/art/declaration-independence.

† Originally known as American Indians. There are 574 federally recognized tribal entities living within the fifty states. Alaska Natives (f.k.a. Eskimo) are not First Nation (Indians). For more information, see https://www.bowmanvillerotaryclub.org/sitepage/a-note-on-terminology-for-indigenous-peoples/a-note-on-terminology-inuit-m%C3%A9tis-first-nations-and-aboriginal.

‡ The Iroquois Confederacy for example. European colonial powers included France, England, Spain, the Netherlands, and Russia (Alaska).

as hell. Thomas Jefferson, the principal author of the Declaration, provided a detailed description of the reasons why the colonies issued it. The date on which it was ratified, July 4, 1776, is now our foremost national holiday. But freedom is never a given. It is a challenge.

1776 was a dangerous time to be alive in America. Franklin drove that point home when he stated that if the leaders of the American Revolution "did not all hang together they most assuredly would all hang separately."[3] Thankfully, the Founding Fathers did hang together regardless of the risk to their own lives, families, and fortunes.

Our Constitution has endured for over 237 years because it is the most masterful statement of self-governance and human rights ever conceived. We kept their creation through slavery, Civil War, Jim Crow, territorial conflicts with the First Nations, world wars, economic depressions, the labor movement, the pursuit of women's suffrage and economic rights, the civil rights movement, urban riots, the Cold War, internal migration, and foreign immigration, to name a few.

The Constitution created in Philadelphia was hardly perfect, however. It protected only the freedoms, rights, and privileges of free, white, male property owners. This is seen in part in Article I, Section 2 of the Constitution:

> Representatives and direct Taxes shall be apportioned among the several States which may be included within this Union, according to their respective Numbers, which shall be determined by adding to the whole Number of *free Persons*, including those bound to Service for a Term of Years, and excluding Indians not taxed, *three fifths of all other Persons* (emphasis added).

Section 2 reveals on its face that the new Constitution expressly discriminated against Blacks living here as slaves as well as the First Nations and women ("other persons"). Later, in *Scott v. Sandford* (*Dred Scott*),[4] the US Supreme Court held that Blacks were not United States citizens because their ancestors had been brought here from Africa as slaves. The Constitution did not grant Blacks full citizenship, the right to vote, own property, obtain due process, and achieve equal protection of the law until a brutal civil war spawned in part by *Dred Scott*, resulted in the adoption of the Thirteenth, Fourteenth, and Fifteenth Amendments. But discrimination persisted. The Civil Rights Act of 1964[5] was passed to end racial discrimination, but it continues to this day as revealed in the Black Lives Matter movement, the controversy over teaching critical race theory,[6] and other current events.

First Nations people and Alaska Natives (Inuit) also have faced voting and other legal restrictions. Excluded from birthright citizenship until passage of the Indian Citizenship Act in 1924, no naturalization process applied to them because they were not considered "foreigners."[7] Alaska Natives only gained US citizenship with the Immigration and Nationality Act of 1952.[8] The Voting Rights Act of 1965 (VRA) aimed to eliminate many impediments imposed by the states, such as literacy tests (see Chapter 6 for a fuller discussion).

Further, though considered among the persons to be counted as described in Article I Section 2, the original Constitution did not extend to women the right to vote, contract, or own property in their own names. Their right to vote did not come into being until a massive suffrage movement (begun in the 1840s) resulted in the ratification of Amendment XIX on August 18, 1920.[9] The right of citizens eighteen years of age or older to vote came with the ratification of Amendment XXVI on July 1, 1971.

To mitigate these gaping holes, the Constitution and Bill of Rights have been amended to make *all* persons born on United States soil or naturalized here citizens who are entitled to exercise the freedoms it protects. Yes, we are flawed, but America became the greatest nation in the world and a thriving industrial society with sound financial institutions and a free press. Immigrants flocked here. It became the arsenal of democracy, a helping hand to and leader of the free world and gave millions of people around the globe insights into democracy, freedom, and balanced power. Even more, it gave them hope.

America is an idea we must build on but never relinquish. It is time to reflect not only on the rights and privileges our Constitution protects, but on the obligations it imposes on all Americans. It is time to reacquaint ourselves with the principles that undergird the republic.

The term *republic* has historically described various forms of government that upon inspection radically differ from one another. It is not a matter of linguistics. It is a matter of power to govern. It is not enough to describe the United States as a republic or a democracy. It has elements of each. In other nations, the term *republic* has a much different meaning. The People's Republic of China and the Democratic People's Republic of Korea (North Korea) have forms of government that markedly differ from the form adopted in the US Constitution. Some definitions include governments with elected representatives, even though their citizens' eligibility to choose their representatives may or may not be democratic.[10] The concept that our representatives be freely elected by the people in open and fair elections is another pillar of our Republic.

Citing *In re Duncan*,[11] *Black's Law Dictionary* is very terse. It defines "Republican Government" to be a "government of the people, a government of representatives chosen by the people." One of our Founders, James Madison, described the "republic" the US Constitution created as a representative democracy in Essay No. 10 of *The Federalist* as follows:

> The two great points of difference, between a democracy and a republic are: first, the delegation of the government, in the latter, to a small number of citizens elected by the rest; secondly, the greater number of citizens, and greater sphere of country, over which the latter may be extended.[12]

Our Constitution provided not only the elected, representative democracy envisioned by Madison but enshrined the personal rights of its citizens into enforceable organic law. Should a dictator ever take over our government and dissolve our Constitution, our rights as American citizens would disappear. We've seen that movie before. The German Reich (Nazi Germany) is the foremost example. The Union of Soviet

Socialist Republics (Communist Russia) is another. It is happening today in other nations as this is written.

As discussed earlier, Article IV Section 4 of the Constitution guaranteed a republican form of government to every state in the Union. Amendment X provides that powers not delegated to the United States, nor prohibited by it to the states, are reserved to the States respectively or to the people. When political ideas and misinformation threaten our republic, we must recognize them for what they are and reject them. If we do not, the concept that "We the people" are the source of the nation's laws would crumple and coauthor Nelson's little brown book would be cast on the trash heap of history.

Our republic and the Constitution that created it lie at the very core of the things that we stand to lose, Mr. Trump.

CHAPTER 3

Donald Trump's 2016 Campaign and His Presidency—What the Prelude to Autocracy Might Look Like

Though Americans have frequently been disappointed in our leaders, we have always valued decency, righteousness, and truthfulness as bedrock qualities that we seek in them. It was said of our first president, George Washington, for example, that "he could not tell a lie." Our sixteenth president, Abraham Lincoln, was known as Honest Abe. The monuments later erected for them in Washington, DC stand on the National Mall as forceful expressions of their character. Then Donald Trump came down the escalator and announced his candidacy for president in 2016. It soon became clear that his interpretation of presidential power greatly exceeded the description of those powers in Article II of the Constitution and vastly differed from that of his predecessors.

Trump had hosted *The Apprentice*, a reality television show, from 2004 to 2015. Reality television has been criticized because, while presented as reality, it is not. Like Alice's trip through the looking glass, it presents artificial scripted events created as it goes along to bring the narrative to predetermined conclusions. Reality, no matter how fervently a particular conclusion is scripted or prayed for, is never predetermined. But *The Apprentice* blew up Trump's image and made him "a big star." When the Access Hollywood tape was released during Trump's 2016 campaign, it revealed Mr. Trump stating that when one is a big star, they can do whatever they want. "You can grab (women) by the pussy." That may be "boy talk" as his wife later claimed[1] that society laughs at, but it is not the kind of attitude or language that we expect from a president. It considers women to be second-class citizens and reduces them to objects.

While his opponents and others insisted that Trump was not fit by temperament, training, or experience to be president, he was elected in 2016 by the Electoral College even though he did not win a majority of the popular vote recorded across the nation.[2] Many of his supporters continued to support him and ignored reports in the *Washington Post*,[3] *Politico Magazine*,[4] and elsewhere alleging his campaign failures to tell the nation the truth persisted throughout his presidency. His alleged lies continued through his campaign for reelection and the insurrection of January 6 (according to the *Washington Post* tally, 30,573 lies in four years).[5] That disturbing tally tells us that in today's America, political ethics standards are eroding and that too many citizens don't care.

Except in a few instances like Theodore Roosevelt's Progressive (Bull Moose) Party of 1912 and the Dixiecrats of 1948, candidates vying for a party's nomination traditionally agreed to support their party's nominee. But at one of the first Presidential Debates for Republican candidates in 2016, the moderator asked the twelve candidates to step forward if they would not pledge to support the party's nominee. Donald Trump was the only one who stepped forward on the debate stage. His doing so told us who he was right then and there. Also, in those debates, he criticized Senator Marco Rubio's (R-Florida) height; he described Senator Ted Cruz (R-Texas) as "lying Ted;" and he derided Carly Fiorina, a former Hewlett Packard CEO. He shouted, "Look at that face! Would anyone vote for that? Can you imagine that the face of our next president?"[6] In August of 2016, he awkwardly waved his arms and mocked Serge Kovaleski, a reporter for the *New York Times*, who suffers from arthrogryposis, a congenital condition affecting the joints. Who does things like that? Trump later said he thought Carly Fiorina's face was beautiful, and that he did not intend to mock Mr. Kovaleski. But his performances, both televised, revealed his intent to do *exactly* that.

At the Republican National Convention in 2016, Trump's supporters began to chant "Lock Her Up" at every mention of the name Hillary Clinton, the Democratic nominee. The chant was repeated at campaign rallies during Trump's 2016 presidential campaign. Trump later suggested at one of the presidential debates that a special prosecutor be appointed to prosecute Mrs. Clinton and allegedly stated, "She has to go to jail."[7]

This statement along with his tacit support of the chants displays a willful ignorance of the judicial process and contempt for the rule of law. If Mrs. Clinton had committed any criminal acts as Secretary of State in the Obama administration in relation to the Benghazi matter*, or otherwise, she would have been presumed innocent until proven guilty beyond a reasonable doubt in a court of law. It violates the Constitution and the rule of law to slander others with claims they are criminals who should be "locked up" *before* they are accused, tried, and convicted. The novel (and later film) *The Ox-Bow Incident*[8] dramatized that tagging folks with guilt and stringing them up before they have been proven guilty of a crime is contrary to our system of justice and is itself criminal. Threats of using bills of attainder† and "lock her up" chants as campaign slogans should sound the alarm.

During the 2016 Campaign for the Presidency, Trump was asked to produce his federal tax returns. Traditionally, presidential candidates have done so. Trump refused, claiming he was being audited by the IRS. Pursuant to its 1977 mandatory audit policy, the IRS has audited presidential and vice-presidential returns while they were in office. But in Trump's case, the IRS failed to do so.[9] No existing federal statute requires the IRS to audit presidential or vice-presidential federal tax returns. The policy of doing so is based on Internal Revenue Manual Part 3, chapter 28, section 3, which states, "Individual income tax returns for the president and vice president are subject to mandatory examinations."[10]

---

* The attack in the US diplomatic mission in Benghazi, Libya, on September 11, 2012, and subsequent investigation into Hillary Clinton's role.

† Bill of attainder (n.): a legislative act that imposes any punishment (including death) on a named or implied individual or group without a trial. Note: Article I Section 9 of the US Constitution prohibits bills of attainder. See Chapter 12 for further discussion.

During his presidency a district attorney for the Southern District of New York subpoenaed Trump's tax returns claiming they were relevant to an investigation of possible criminal fraud committed in the business activities of Trump's companies. Trump again refused to produce his returns and appealed all the way to the US Supreme Court, claiming that he had immunity from state subpoenas by virtue of his position as president. The Supreme Court denied his claim and sent the case back to the state court. Ultimately, Trump's tax returns were delivered to a Manhattan grand jury.[11] Allen H. Weisselberg, CFO for the Trump Organization, pled guilty to fifteen felonies involving tax fraud[12] and received a sentence of five months. The Trump Organization was fined $1.6 million.

The House Ways and Means Committee also subpoenaed Trump's tax returns. On August 9, 2022, the US Court of Appeals for the District of Columbia Circuit ruled that Trump's federal income tax returns and those of his businesses must be furnished to the Ways and Means Committee.[13] Later, the Ways and Means Committee released a report on Trump's tax returns for years 2015–2020 which was published in the *New York Times*.[14]

The purpose here is not to audit or judge Trump's tax returns or those of his companies. Those issues are for the IRS and the DOJ. The purpose here is to demonstrate that the verdict and punishments meted out in the New York tax fraud case and the report published in the *New York Times* show on their face why Trump's tax returns and those of his corporations should have been disclosed to the voters prior to the 2016 and 2020 presidential elections. Had they been released earlier, the voters could have decided for themselves whether improprieties or misdeeds occurred. Recall that when Trump was asked about his tax returns during the Clinton debates in 2016, he cavalierly stated his payment of low taxes for some of the years reported in the media "makes me smart."[15]

After he became president, Donald Trump criticized the press and called their reports "fake news." A vigorous, independent free press is one of the pillars of our republic. To resist that power, Kellyanne Conway, a counselor to the president, used the phrase "alternative facts" during a *Meet the Press* January 2017 interview to defend White House Press Secretary Sean Spicer. Conway used the phrase regarding exaggerations Trump made concerning the crowd size of those attending his inauguration. The sizes of crowds at Trump's inauguration were certainly not secret—they had been televised. To adopt Trump, Spicer, and Conway's version of the size of the crowds at President Trump's inauguration as an "alternative fact" was to enter the world of the Looking Glass. But that is where Mr. Trump was headed, and through the looking glass he went, where everything becomes "curiouser and curiouser" and words mean what he wants them to mean.

We were reminded daily from his conduct as president that Trump did not accept the constraints of Article II, his oath of office, or the rule of law. He boasted while in office that Article II of the Constitution authorized him as president to do "whatever he wanted to do," even though the Constitution *expressly separates* legislative, executive, and judicial powers and provides that all powers not delegated by that document to the three departments of the national government be reserved to the states or to the people. Nowhere does it state that presidents or any other national official can do whatever they want to do.

As president, he issued written directives and displayed them to the television cameras as edicts issued by the president. While other presidents have issued presidential executive orders, they did so to interpret or enforce a law enacted by Congress. When Congress failed to adopt a second package of laws to confront the health and economic effects of COVID-19, President Trump took it upon himself to issue executive orders purportedly granting some of the relief that Congress was considering.[16] But Article I of the Constitution grants "*all* legislative powers" to Congress (emphasis added).While he did have power to veto laws enacted by Congress, Article II gave him *no* power to create laws on his own, and his vetoes could be overridden by Congress.

When the coronavirus (COVID-19) pandemic emerged as a menace to our nation in early 2020, President Trump played it down as a hoax perpetrated by the Chinese. He did this to protect his candidacy for reelection. Later, Bob Woodward's book *Rage* disclosed (based on taped interviews Woodward had with Trump) that when he gave assurances to the public Trump knew they were false and he had been notified that the coronavirus was deadly.[17] When it became clear that the coronavirus was not going away and posed a genuine danger to the nation and its economy, he opined without medical evidence that hydroxychloroquine, a drug used to treat malaria, could be used to treat COVID-19, and went so far as to state that since bleach and rubbing alcohol were used to disinfect, they could be injected to combat COVID-19. He later tried to downplay it,[18] but medical advice from Alice's mushroom caterpillar rarely has a good outcome.

Trump's absurd assertions should not be dismissed as comic hyperbole. During so-called briefings on the activities of the Presidential Task Force appointed by Trump to combat COVID-19, the president chaired the briefings and upstaged recommendations of Dr. Anthony Fauci, Director of the National Institute of Allergy and Infectious Diseases, and Dr. Deborah Birx, the White House Coronavirus Response Coordinator. In the face of the dire threat posed by COVID-19, the "briefings" became reality shows that Trump scripted as he went along. They morphed into campaign events to promote his reelection. A blog post by Representative Lloyd Doggett (D-Texas), "Timeline of Trump's Coronavirus Responses" lists by date over 200 statements that Trump made from May 2018 through January 20, 2021, that his administration had the coronavirus under control.[19] But no national plan to control the virus was developed, and it proceeded to ravage the nation. *JAMA*, the journal of the American Medical Association, portrayed the toll thus:

> The daily US mortality rate for COVID-19 deaths is equivalent to the September 11, 2001, attacks, which claimed 2988 lives, occurring every 1.5 days, or 15 Airbus 320 jetliners, each carrying 150 passengers, crashing every day.[20]

Instead of presenting a role model for the nation, Trump conducted a campaign rally in Tulsa, Oklahoma, on June 20, 2020, where an estimated 6,000 followers sat shoulder to shoulder, most of them unmasked,[21] to cheer him on. Herman Cain, who had also been a presidential candidate in 2016 for the Republican nomination, was televised unmasked and ignoring social distancing while attending the Tulsa rally. Cain died of COVID-19 on July 30, 2020. It is uncertain if Cain contracted COVID-19 at the rally, though the timing suggests it, or if other attendees contracted it, or if they spread it to others. Reportedly, Trump himself contracted COVID-19 and needed treatment at Walter Reed Medical Center in October 2020.

While the coronavirus spread out of control, Trump opened the country in a grandiose plan to return the nation and its economy back to what it had been before the pandemic. But without necessary safety measures, it resulted in a coronavirus surge across every state in the union. His words and actions recklessly left the impression for millions of Americans that the president considered the COVID-19 threat to be over. He did ask that vaccination serums be produced with "warp speed," but developed no national plan or funding to distribute them or to vaccinate the population, leaving that to the states. Consider that other nations were experiencing COVID-19 deaths at far lower rates[22] than in the United States where COVID-19 became the third leading cause of death in both 2020 and 2021.[23]

The power to pardon should *not* be a means of avoiding the rule of law, rewarding political cronies, or obstructing justice. It was never intended to be a device to seek campaign contributions or reelection. But Trump pardoned or commuted sentences to benefit political operative Roger Stone, former Arizona Sheriff Joseph M. Arpaio, financier Michael R. Milken, and former Governor of Illinois, Rod R. Blagojevich.[24]

At the Republican Convention in August of 2020, speakers referred to President Trump as the "bodyguard of Western civilization,"[25] even though that acclaim flew in the face of Trump's criticism of our allies, his disdain for international treaties like NATO and the Paris Accords on Climate Control, and his own assertions that he believed in "America First."

On the final day of the 2020 Republican Convention, President Trump used the White House as a prop to support his campaign. Over

600 of his supporters, including members of Congress and Executive Department officials, sat on folding chairs on the South Lawn. With American flags displayed in a neat row behind him, the president concluded the Republican Convention with a speech right there on the South Lawn excoriating Joe Biden and Kamala Harris as leftist extremists who would, if elected, destroy the nation. It was wrongly asserted that blatantly using the White House for private political purposes by conducting the convention on the White House grounds violated the Hatch Act[26], which prohibits government employees from using the property and employees of the federal government (i.e., the White House and its staff) for political purposes.[27] The president and vice president are expressly exempt from its provisions.[28]

Following the eruption of the Black Lives Matter protests in the summer of 2020, federal agents in camouflage gear with no identifying insignia began to arrest protestors on the streets of Portland, Oregon, and force them into unmarked vehicles. The Trump Administration announced that it intended to dispatch similar forces to other cities, including Chicago.[29] These threats echo the Cheka (KGB predecessor) of Stalin's Terror and the Gestapo of Hitler's Nazi Germany.

According to reports on June 1, 2020, Trump publicly demanded that state governors call up their National Guard units and "dominate the streets." He then staged a walk from the White House Rose Garden to St. John's Church via Lafayette Square. The square was full of peaceful Black Lives Matter protesters, whom US Park Police forcibly removed using tear gas before Trump's walk. Later reports differed whether the order was given to clear a path for the president or whether it had been planned in advance of his appearance at the church. After arriving unannounced, Trump stood in front of St. John's Church where he held up a Bible and used it and the church as a backdrop photo op for his political campaign for reelection in 2020. St John's Church staff were outraged* to have their church used in that way, especially after having ministered to the protesters outside.[30] The Constitution does *not* authorize a president to violate the First Amendment rights of those peacefully assembled to petition for redress of their grievances for his own election campaign activities.

Trump's statements that as president he could do "whatever he wanted to do" laid bare his autocratic tendencies. His public criticism of court personnel and witnesses displayed his disdain for due process and the rule of law. His statements that he will seek retribution from his enemies foretell what his master plan may be on resuming office. In his guest essay in the *New York Times*, Donald P. Moynihan, a professor of Public Policy at Georgetown University, quoted him as saying, "Either the deep state destroys America, or we destroy the deep state." Moynihan also stated Trump has, "a real and plausible plan to utterly transform American government."[31] By his words and actions, and his conduct of the presidency as reported in the media, Donald Trump has proven that his rivals and critics were right. It is no longer unfathomable that our republic may share the fate of the Weimer Republic of Germany in the 1930s. It *can* happen here as Sinclair Lewis' dystopian novel[32] foretold. That stark reality makes it imperative that Americans realize that if our republic and our rights were lost, they might never get them back.

---

* Former St. John's minister Gini Gerbasi posted in Facebook (https://www.facebook.com/gini.gerbasi/posts/10157575422089624): "WE WERE DRIVEN OFF OF THE PATIO AT ST. JOHN'S - a place of peace and respite and medical care throughout the day - SO THAT MAN COULD HAVE A PHOTO OPPORTUNITY IN FRONT OF THE CHURCH!!! PEOPLE WERE HURT SO THAT HE COULD POSE IN FRONT OF THE CHURCH WITH A BIBLE! HE WOULD HAVE HAD TO STEP OVER THE MEDICAL SUPPLIES WE LEFT BEHIND BECAUSE WE WERE BEING TEAR GASSED!!!!"

CHAPTER 4

The 2020 Election—"Stop the Steal," Insurrection, and Two Impeachment Acquittals—a Brush with Disaster

Following the presidential election of November 2020, Trump refused to accept news reports that Biden had won the presidency by almost seven million votes. He made numerous declarations that the election had been rigged, that massive fraud had occurred, and that he had in fact won the election "in a landslide." His subsequent statements and actions and those of his supporters cast doubt on the validity of the election, and more critically put the continued existence of our republic at risk.

Except for 1860[1], presidential candidates historically accepted a peaceful transfer of power following even hotly contested elections. Recall that after the 2000 election Al Gore conceded the election after the US Supreme Court ordered that the counting of popular votes in Florida stop, no matter how bitter it was for him and his supporters to do it. Gore did not launch a Constitutional attack on the Supreme Court or on that election. In considering the many unsubstantiated claims of fraudulent ballots and compromised voting machines Trump and his followers made regarding the 2020 election, one should note that in the Florida 2000 presidential election defective ballots were shown to exist. Voters punched out a chad to leave a rectangular hole in the ballot card opposite their chosen candidate's name to facilitate the computer vote tally. But the styluses often failed to completely punch out the chads from the computer card ballots. Televised scenes of Florida election workers staring at hanging chads and dented chads through magnifying glasses stirred the nation to laughter. When *Bush v. Gore*[2] was appealed to the US Supreme Court, it found that Florida's statutes and regulations failed to provide guidance as to how, or if, such votes should be counted. It stopped the count.

There are other wide differences between the 2020 presidential election and the Florida experience in 2000. In 2000 Al Gore and George W. Bush were separated by only 537 popular votes in the state of Florida, and the national election of a new president hinged on Florida's twenty-five electoral votes. But there was no claim or evidence of widespread voter fraud in the Florida case. The result in Florida decided the national election of a new president, and a peaceful, though disputed, transfer of power took place.

But in 2020 there were several hotly contested key states; the parties were separated by close to a reported seven million popular votes nationally and by an anticipated seventy-four electoral votes in the Electoral College.* Before the election even occurred Trump asserted to his followers that the only way he could lose the election would be if election fraud occurred. Then, alleging that fraud had occurred, he brazenly asked on the night of the election to stop counting the votes before the count was completed.

No evidence of ballot defects, voting irregularities or fraud of a sufficient size to upset the election was pled or proven in the sixty or so lawsuits that Trump and his supporters later filed in courts across the nation.[3] Trump still refused to concede the 2020 election even after he and his supporters continued to lose their court challenges. The *New York Times* later reported that Trump's lawyers knew as early as November 12, 2020, that there was no credible evidence that election fraud or irregularities had occurred in the 2020 election adequate to reverse the result that Trump had lost the election.[4]

Bear in mind that presidential and vice-presidential candidates' names appeared on the *same* ballots that listed senatorial and House of Representatives candidates, state and local candidates, as well as state and local ballot proposals across the nation. Yet there were no

---

* The Electoral College refers to the process by which the United States elects the president, although the term does not appear in the US Constitution. In this process, set forth in Article II Section 1 of the Constitution, Electors chosen by the States (and the District of Columbia just for this process) elect the president and vice president.

news reports that other listed candidates asserted claims of election fraud or abusive counting practices. Inexplicably, as we shall see, many elected to Congress by votes for them recorded on the very same ballots that elected the president, later vigorously joined the "Stop the Steal" movement, participated in attempts to decertify the election, and voted against impeachment.

Defeated in recounts and court cases Trump supporters went into high gear after the election and proceeded to organize political rallies to "Stop the Steal." Their opponents dubbed that slogan the "Big Lie."* A Million MAGA March on the Capitol was quickly put together to take place on November 14, 2020. It brought groups like the Proud Boys[5] and the Oath Keepers[6] to Washington, DC. They collaborated with Women for America First[7] in planning and conducting a rally to "Stop the Steal" at Freedom Plaza. Some estimates stated that more than a million Trump supporters attended. A smiling President Trump was televised through the rear window of the presidential limousine driving by in support of the rally. On nationwide television, a sitting president was out on the street encouraging a mob to contest a presidential election. Nothing like it had ever happened over the 237 years since our Constitution was ratified. No one realized that it was a dress rehearsal for January 6.

In the weeks following the election, all the rallies, court challenges, recounts, and attacks that Trump and his supporters made on the validity of the 2020 election failed to change the result or to even present credible evidence it should be changed. The so-called audit later conducted by Republicans in Arizona came up empty as well. A cybersecurity company with no prior elections auditing experience conducted an "audit" of the results in Maricopa County, the largest Arizona county and which Democratic candidates had won. After several months, the "auditors" reported no significant problems, but instead found that the Biden total should have had ninety-nine more

* Critics began using the term "Big Lie" after the January 6, 2021, insurrection to convey the idea that one has to disregard ample evidence and believe in a preposterously large conspiracy theory to accept Trump's claims. For a fuller explanation, see https://www.cnn.com/2021/05/19/politics/donald-trump-big-lie-explainer/index.html.

votes and Trump 261 fewer votes than the totals certified. The certified count had reported that Biden won by over 10,000 votes. Trump-supporting groups had paid over $5.7 million for the "audit."[8]

Fox News aired reports alleging that Dominion Voting Systems machines had changed thousands of Trump votes to Biden votes even though audits indicated otherwise. Dominion sued for defamation and demanded $1.6 billion in damages. Fox settled "on the courthouse steps" to avoid a very public and very damaging trial, issued a statement acknowledging their news reports were indeed false, and settled for $787.5 million.[9] The amount "represents vindication and accountability," said Dominion lawyer Justin Nelson. "Lies have consequences."[10]

But Trump and his supporters continued to spout a torrent of spurious claims of widespread fraud and irregularities. One of the over sixty cases[11] Trump's lawyers filed attacking the 2020 election was in the Federal District Court for the Eastern District of Michigan.[12] It was filed after Michigan certified the result of the election in Michigan but before the December 8, 2020, "safe harbor" deadline.[13] Trump's lawyers asserted election fraud and asked that Michigan's governor, Gretchen Whitmer, be ordered to award Michigan's sixteen electoral votes to Trump even though Trump had lost the election in Michigan by 154,000 votes. US District Judge Linda Parker dismissed the Michigan case on the grounds that the pleadings and affidavits submitted by the plaintiff's lawyers failed to provide specific evidence of fraud or other election irregularities to support the relief sought. Judge Parker's order dismissing the case was appealed all the way to the US Supreme Court, but never overruled. Later, Judge Parker sanctioned the nine attorneys who filed the Michigan case.[14] Judge Parker wrote in her order,

> This lawsuit represents a historic and profound abuse of the judicial process. It is one thing to take on the charge of vindicating rights associated with an allegedly fraudulent election. It is another to take on the charge of deceiving a federal court and the American people into believing that rights were infringed, without regard to

whether any laws or rights were in fact violated. This is what happened here.[15]

In November of 2020, with the Electoral College vote set for December 14, 2020, attorneys supporting Trump abruptly filed a lawsuit directly in the US Supreme Court with Texas as the plaintiff. They asserted that enough irregularities and fraud had occurred to permit Republican-controlled legislatures in swing states to summarily declare the popular vote invalid even though no credible evidence of any significant voter fraud was shown to exist. The lawsuit asked the Supreme Court to determine as a matter of law that the legislatures of these states could send slates naming Presidential Electors of their own choosing to the Electoral College. It was an entirely preposterous claim, yet Representative Mike Johnson (R-Louisiana) asked other Republican Representatives to join in an amicus brief supporting the lawsuit. 126 Republican House members signed the amicus brief, including their caucus leader, Kevin McCarthy* (R-California). Eighteen Republican state attorneys general also filed an amicus brief supporting the Texas lawsuit.[16] On December 11, the US Supreme Court declined to hear the case on grounds that the State of Texas had no right under the Constitution to challenge the votes of other states and therefore no standing to make that claim.[17] That decision was seen as the death knell of efforts to overturn the 2020 election, but Trump's supporters, including Republican congressional representatives, vowed to fight on.[18]

Before the ink was dry on the Supreme Court's rejection of the Texas lawsuit, two rallies took place on December 12, 2020, at Freedom Plaza and at the Capitol in Washington, DC. Thousands of Trump's supporters crowded together to oppose the Electoral College's certification of the election results on December 14. Televised conduct of Trump's supporters at this rally warned that the "Stop the Steal" campaign would employ violence to stop certification of the results.[19]

---

* On January 6, 2023, Kevin McCarthy was elected Speaker of the House of Representatives after fifteen rounds of voting over five days, the greatest number of rounds since 1923. His party had a majority in the House, but he lacked support from the ultra-conservative representatives.

Notwithstanding all these attacks on the validity of the election, on December 14, 2020, the Electoral College certified the Electors' votes for president and vice president and sealed their votes in envelopes addressed to Vice President Pence as required by the Constitution. That event was taken by many as the final nail in the coffin that would end Trump's efforts, but Trump and his supporters didn't concede. It was instead reported that Michael T. Flynn, a former national security advisor pardoned by Trump for his conviction for lying to the FBI about his contacts with Russia, publicly suggested that the president use martial law to force a revote in the swing states.[20]

Then, reportedly, at a White House meeting of Congressional Republican Trump supporters on December 18, 2020, it was suggested that they concentrate their efforts on the Joint Session of the Vice President, Senators, and Representatives (herein Joint Session of Congress or Joint Session) to open, count, and certify the election results reported by the Electoral College.[21] That session was set to take place on January 6, 2021, at the Capitol in Washington, DC. Some Trump supporters argued that Vice President Pence had power to stop the certification of the Electoral College votes and discard any electoral votes he deemed fraudulent. Ignoring the advice of other members of Trump's team that Pence had no such power, his do-or-die supporters proceeded to organize rallies regardless.

By mid-December 2020, escalating failures to change the results of the 2020 presidential election had frustrated Trump and his supporters. On December 19, 2020, Trump asked his followers through social media to assemble on the Ellipse, a park adjoining the White House, on January 6, 2021, promising that it "will be wild!"[22]

Trump personally phoned the Georgia Secretary of State, Brad Raffensperger, on January 2 and asked that he "find" the 11,780 popular votes Trump needed to overturn the result in Georgia and to win that state's electoral votes. Raffensperger refused.[23] Fulton County, Georgia, superior court judges authorized the District Attorney to impanel a special grand jury to investigate allegations of fraud in the Raffensperger matter.[24] After its dissolution, the grand jury's final report came before Judge McBurney on January 24, 2023, who determined it would not immediately be made public. (See Major Investigations and Indictments section below.) The *New York Times* reported on January 22, 2021, that an attorney in the DOJ, Jeffery Clark, had suggested to Trump in relation to the Georgia incident that he use the DOJ to force Georgia lawmakers to reverse the result of the 2020 election.[25] This incident is explored in Acting Assistant Attorney Donoghue's testimony in Chapter 5 Fifth Hearing.

Efforts to seat fake presidential electors were pursued in several states besides Georgia. According to an audio obtained by CNN, the Michigan Republican Party Co-chair Meshawn Maddock, stated that the Trump presidential campaign directed Republicans in Michigan to name unelected Electoral College delegates for the 2020 presidential election.[26] The Select Committee subpoenaed fourteen people who falsely claimed to be electors for Trump and submitted Certificates for Trump electors in seven states won by Biden: Arizona, Georgia, Michigan, New Mexico, Nevada, Pennsylvania, and Wisconsin.[27]

In their book *Peril*, Bob Woodward and Robert Costa report that on January 2, 2021, Trump attorney John Eastman drafted a memo in which he stated that "seven states have submitted dual slates of electors to the president of the Senate." The Eastman memo went on to state that because there were dual slates no Electors had been validly appointed in the seven states which would, he opined, reduce the number of Electors needed to form a majority and allow Pence to announce that President Trump had been reelected.[28] No evidence that any states *had officially submitted dual slates* was produced, and no procedure for reducing electoral votes is in the Constitution.

Thousands of Trump's supporters, including right-wing militia groups, attended a warmup rally held at Freedom Plaza on the evening of January 5, 2021. Also, on that evening, Woodward and Costa report in their book that Trump made several attempts to convince Pence in a meeting at the White House that Pence did have power to throw out the votes of Biden Electors at the Joint Session, and that if he did not do so, he did not want Pence to be his friend anymore. When Pence refused on grounds that he had no power to do that under the Constitution,

Woodward and Costa report, Trump told Pence that he was being weak, that he lacked courage and that he had betrayed Trump.[29]

Woodward and Costa also report in *Peril* that Boris Epshteyn, an advisor to the Trump Campaign, Rudy Giuliani, Trump's legal counsel, and Steve Bannon, a former Trump chief White House strategist and outside adviser, were meeting on the evening of January 5, 2021, at the Willard Hotel. Their suite (later dubbed the War Room) was across the street from the White House and within earshot of the warmup rally. They asked Republicans in Congress by phone to join forces with Trump on January 6 and block Biden's certification.[30]

Notwithstanding Trump's entreaties, Pence stuck with his position that the Constitution only empowered him to open the ballots of the Electors, count the Electoral College votes for each candidate and then announce the result. Article I Section 3 of the Constitution fully supports Pence's position. It provides that the vice president (Pence's term did not expire until January 20) shall be president of the Senate. Then, with respect to opening, tabulating, counting, and certifying the votes of the Electoral College, Article II Section 1 of the Constitution provides

> The Electors shall meet in their respective States, and vote by Ballot for two Persons, of whom one at least shall not be an Inhabitant of the same State with themselves. *And they shall make a List of all the Persons voted for, and of the Number of Votes for each, which List they shall sign and certify, and transmit sealed to the Seat of the Government of the United States, directed to the President of the Senate. The President of the Senate shall, in the Presence of the Senate and House of Representatives, open all the Certificates, and the Votes shall then be counted.* The Person having the greatest Number of Votes shall be the President, if such Number be a Majority of the whole Number of Electors appointed (emphasis added).

Trump's supporters assembled on the Ellipse the following day at noon—the very date and time that the vice president, US senators, US representatives, and their staffs were assembling to meet in the Joint Session to count the votes of the Electors in the Electoral College, to certify the result of the 2020 presidential election, and for no other purpose. Giuliani addressed the rally held on the Ellipse and using military language, said to them, "Let's have trial by combat."[31]

When Trump spoke to those assembled on the Ellipse, he asked, among other things, that they proceed to the Capitol, and stated that unless they were willing to "fight like hell" they could lose their country. Even as his speech continued, his amassed followers began to leave for the Capitol which was about a mile away.

Once at the Capitol, Trump's supporters invaded the Capitol, broke the defense line of Capitol Police, terrorized everyone there, and overran and ransacked the Capitol. Over one hundred Capitol and District of Columbia Police officers were injured. One Capitol Police officer died shortly afterward. The medical examiner later determined that he died of natural causes although the events of January 6 played a role in his condition.[32] Several police officers traumatized by the event later committed suicide. Many huddled in the Capitol phoned or texted family members to convey final messages to them in the belief they would be killed in the violent insurrection. Pundits described the 2021 insurrection as the worst since the British burned Washington, DC, during the War of 1812.[33]

The Joint Session of Senators and Representatives to count the votes of the Presidential Electors was debating objections to Arizona's electoral votes, but it was called to recess at 2:30 p.m. when the insurrectionists stormed into the Capitol.[34] After the insurrectionists had been cleared out, the Joint Session resumed meeting at 8:00 p.m., and took up the challenge to Pennsylvania's electoral votes. Contrary to their oath to support the Constitution, 139 Republican representatives, including Minority Leader Kevin McCarthy, and eight Republican senators voted to discard the Presidential Elector votes received from Texas and Pennsylvania. They did not prevail.[35]

After the senators and representatives finished counting and certifying the votes of the Electors, Biden and Harris became the president and vice president elect, respectively, of the United States, and it appeared that the Constitutional procedure for electing the nation's president and vice president had held.

Following the insurrection at the Capitol, the House of Representatives adopted Articles of Impeachment on January 11, 2021, while Trump was still president.[36] At the impeachment trial in the Senate after Trump's term as President ended, the House of Representatives Managers[37], who prosecuted Trump, presented evidence in support of their allegations that Trump had not only incited the January 6, 2021 insurrection by the actions he took and the statements he made, but had done nothing to protect the elected officials and others in the Capitol once the violent insurrection began, all in violation of his oath under Article II Section 1 to "faithfully exercise the Office of President of the United States," and protect and defend the Constitution.

At the impeachment trial, fifty-seven senators voted Trump "guilty" of an impeachable offense (inciting an insurrection against the United States), and forty-three found him "not guilty." A legal finding that an impeachable offense had occurred required a two-thirds vote by the senators (67), so Trump was acquitted. Mitch McConnell (R-Kentucky), who had by then become Minority Leader of the Senate, made a statement immediately following the verdict that the House of Representatives Managers had proven the existence of an impeachable offense, but that he voted Trump not guilty because he believed it was unconstitutional to impeach an office holder after the office holder had left office. With no suggestion that a president might be immune from criminal prosecution, the minority leader also stated that Trump remained subject to criminal prosecution and civil liability litigation based on the evidence presented at the impeachment trial. This from a Senate leader who had supported Trump throughout his campaign for reelection.[38]

The *New York Times* reported on October 19, 2021, that Trump filed a lawsuit to block release of White House papers concerning the January 6, 2021, insurrection. When Trump left office, his presidential papers were transferred to the National Archives and Records Administration. Later, the Select Committee issued a subpoena to the National Archives to produce detailed records concerning Trump's movements, phone calls, and meetings on January 6, 2021. When Trump claimed executive privilege, President Biden's White House lawyer, Dana Remus, issued a letter stating Trump's claim of executive privilege was "not in the best interests of the United States and therefore is not justified as to any of the Documents," and was asserted "to shield from Congress or the public, information that reflects a clear and apparent effort to subvert the Constitution itself."[39] Trump's lawsuit followed, claiming executive privilege.[40] On January 25, 2022, the US Supreme Court refused to block the release of White House records concerning the attack. The order was a major victory for the Select Committee.[41]

Step back and examine what the House Managers established at the impeachment trial. All of Trump's efforts and those of his followers to change the result of the 2020 election before the Joint Session of Congress certified the election on January 6 failed for lack of merit. Yet it remained clear from his many statements and actions that President Trump intended to soldier on and block certification of the election. He called his supporters to meet in Washington on the Ellipse near the White House on January 6, 2021, the day designated for counting the ballots of the Electors for the 2020 presidential election.

The January 6 event was not a campaign rally nor was it ever billed as or intended to be one. The election was over. Those who assembled in response to Trump's call included members of right-wing militia groups like the Proud Boys and the Oath Keepers. Many had arrived in buses supplied by Trump's supporters and were housed in hotels near the Ellipse. It hasn't yet been established who paid for all of that although news reports claimed two donors of millions of dollars around that time have been identified.[42] Trump addressed the mob on the Ellipse immediately before they marched to the Capitol on that day, breached security, and stormed the Capitol. He reportedly watched the violence at the Capitol on television back at the White House as did the entire nation. He did not ask his supporters to "go home" until late that afternoon. Then he appeared on a taped video and stated to his supporters, who had just savagely violated the Capitol, "We love you."[43] Based on those words, what on earth could be clearer?

Had Pence complied with Trump's request that he reject the votes of some of the presidential Electors and declare Trump the winner of greatest number of the votes of the Electors sent to the president of the Senate, the votes of the millions of voters who elected the presidential Electors as well as the votes of the Electors themselves would have been unlawfully cast aside.

Worst of all, a candidate who did *not* receive the greatest number of electoral votes would have illegally taken charge of the entire executive branch of our national government, including the US Treasury and intelligence services, and as Commander in Chief of our military forces would possess the nation's nuclear weapons codes. The *New York Times* reported on April 19, 2022, that Trump's allies were *still* seeking state legislative resolutions and court orders to overturn the 2020 presidential election in key states.[44]

The following section provides a chronological summary of the investigations and indictments stemming from Trump's alleged 2020 election activities and mishandling of classified documents. These investigations and indictments took place at both the federal and state levels. The New York business records investigation occurred at the same time as the other investigations and appears in the list for reference only. It has no bearing on the other matters.

Major investigations and indictments that followed the events of January 6

- Select Committee to Investigate the January 6th Attack on the United States Capitol.
  Final Report (House Report 117–663) issued December 22, 2022.
  (4 criminal referrals sent to the DOJ)

- Investigation by Manhattan District Attorney Alvin Bragg into alleged felony falsification of business records.
  Indictment filed in the Supreme Court of the State of New York County of New York on April 4, 2023 (34 counts).
  IND-71543-23. On May 30, 2024, a jury returned a verdict finding Trump guilty on thirty-four felony counts of falsifying business records. The case is awaiting sentencing and an appeal is expected.

- Investigation by DOJ special counsel Jack Smith into alleged mishandling of classified documents.
  Grand Jury Superseding indictment filed in the US District Court for the Southern District of Florida on July 27, 2023 (42 counts).
  (Trump and 3 other defendants) Case 9:23-cr-80101-AMC. The trial judge entered an order dismissing the case holding that the appointment of Jack Smith as special counsel violated the US Constitution. Smith has appealed that order.

- Investigation by DOJ special counsel Jack Smith into alleged interference with the lawful transfer of power following the 2020 presidential election.
  Grand Jury Indictment filed in the US District Court for the District of Columbia on August 1, 2023 (4 counts).
  United States v Trump Case 1:23-cr-00257-TSC. Trump claimed absolute immunity for all acts charged in the indictment. On appeal, the Supreme Court ruled some acts charged in the indictment were absolutely immune and sent the case back to the trial court to determine if other acts charged were "presumptively" immune. See discussion of *Trump v. United States* later in this section.

- Investigation by Fulton County District Attorney Fani Willis into alleged violations of the Georgia RICO act and other charges.

Indictment filed in the Fulton County Superior Court on August 14, 2023 (41 counts).
(Trump and 18 other defendants) Case 23SC188947.
Trump moved to dismiss, claiming Willis's affair with an associate attorney she hired to prosecute the case prejudiced the prosecution. A Georgia appeals court set a December hearing for arguments on the appeal of a lower court ruling allowing Willis to continue to prosecute the case.

Concurrent with the Select Committee's work discussed in the next chapter, the DOJ under Attorney General Merrick Garland had continued its own investigation into Trump's alleged actions to overturn the 2020 election. Federal prosecutors issued over thirty subpoenas for Trump associates to testify before a grand jury. On November 18, 2022, Attorney General Garland appointed Jack Smith as special counsel to investigate the January 6 riot and Trump's alleged mishandling of classified documents at his Mar-a-Lago resort.

As part of its investigations into matters concerning Trump's presidency, on August 8, 2022, the FBI executed a search and seizure warrant issued by the US District Court for the Southern District of Florida. The affidavit for the warrant established probable cause to search Trump's Mar-a-Lago residence in Palm Beach, Florida, and seize classified materials unlawfully taken there.[45] The residence lacked secure storage for classified documents, which posed a national security risk. The FBI inventory for items seized during the search lists over one hundred classified documents, including TS/SCI* documents.[46] The inventory also shows forty-three empty folders with classified labels and no indication of the whereabouts of their original contents.[47] Trump's attorney had represented before the search warrant was issued, that

---

* Three security levels—confidential, secret, and top secret—refer to the clearance needed to access documents and other assets. TS/SCI (top secret/sensitive compartmented information) further restricts access to specific documents or information. See Wynne Davis, "TS/SCI: What an abbreviation reveals about the files seized from Mar-a-Lago," NPR, August 16, 2022, https://www.npr.org/2022/08/16/1117455322/trump-mar-a-lago-documents-fbi-ts-sci.

all classified materials held by Trump had been delivered.[48] On July 27, 2023, the federal grand jury's indictment was unsealed.[49] Special counsel Smith said, "This indictment was voted by a grand jury of citizens in the Southern District of Florida, and I invite everyone to read it in full, to understand the scope and the gravity of the crimes charged."[50]

Smith then filed his indictment of Trump in the Federal District Court for the District of Columbia (herein DC District Court) on August 1, 2023, based on the findings of the DC grand jury.[51] The counts focused on conspiracy charges rather than incitement to avoid free speech claims, or a claim of insurrection per se. Smith's indictment also referenced evidence uncovered after the Select Committee concluded its investigation, including a secret internal memo about the plot to use false slates of electors (August 1 Indictment paragraph 54). The December 6, 2020 "Fraudulent Elector Memo"[52] by Kenneth Chesebro, ("Co-Conspirator 5") a Wisconsin attorney with the Trump campaign, had constructed a detailed plan to prevent Biden electors' votes from being counted. Trump-Pence electors would meet in six contested states, vote, and send in their certificates to Congress on December 14. Vice President Pence would count them during the January 6, 2021, Joint Session. Whether or not the slates were contested, the plan would allow more time for voter fraud litigation to proceed. The pro-Trump electors would assert that their meetings were a normal measure to ensure that Congress counted the slates of electors.[53] (See further discussion in Chapter 5 Fourth Hearing.)

On August 14, 2023, a Georgia grand jury unveiled its own indictment. In forty-one counts, it charged a criminal enterprise had committed 161 predicate acts* that violated Georgia's statutes, including its RICO statute, forgery, impersonating public officers, influencing witnesses, election fraud, defrauding Georgia, computer tampering,

---

* predicate act (n.): 1) a crime composed of some of the elements of a more serious crime and which is committed for carrying out the greater crime. 2) under RICO (Racketeer Influenced and Corrupt Organizations Act), one of two or more related acts of racketeering necessary to establish a pattern.

soliciting violations of oaths by public officials, and false statements and writings. It named Trump and eighteen others as codefendants.

These investigations and indictments were placed in doubt on July 1, 2024, when the Supreme Court in *Trump v. United States*,[54] using vague definitions and failing to cite a specific constitutional provision, held the Constitutional structure of separated powers provided presidents with absolute immunity from criminal prosecution for actions within their "conclusive and preclusive" constitutional authority and presumptive immunity from prosecution for "official acts." No prior opinion had found such immunities. Some acts charged in the January 6 indictment were held absolutely immune and others sent back to the trial court to determine if immunity applied.

As of August 1, 2024, none of the pending criminal cases against Trump were expected to go to trial before the 2024 presidential election. As pointed out in the Mission Statement, however, elections are not criminal trials. Trump's "job history" remains before the electorate even if courts later apply the ruling in *Trump v. United States* and grant him immunity from criminal prosecution or if Special Prosecutor Jack Smith and the DOJ follow past practice and not indict or try a sitting president. But if those two principles apply to a sitting president, then the principle that no man is above the law, the presidential oath, and the supremacy clause are meaningless, and pertinent federal criminal statutes and Section 3 of the Fourteenth Amendment are unenforceable.

CHAPTER 5

The Select Committee Investigation of the January 6 Attack on the US Capitol

To say of what is that it is not, or of what is not that it is,
is false, while to say of what is that it is, and of what is not
that it is not, is true.

—Aristotle, *Metaphysics*

The US House of Representatives established the Select Committee to Investigate the January 6th Attack on the United States Capitol by adoption of H. Res. 503 on June 30, 2021. It was formed to investigate the attack, attempts to interfere with the peaceful transfer of power, the response of the law enforcement agencies, as well as other factors that influenced or fomented the attack. The committee's public hearings, aired live, starkly portrayed the chaos created by the attack on the Capitol and events surrounding it. While the following recap of the hearings repeats some material considered in previous chapters and widely covered in the news media, the committee organized the facts and sworn testimony into a compelling narrative that was presented in the committee's final written report.[1]

First Hearing—June 9, 2022

The Select Committee began its public hearings with opening statements by Representatives Bennie Thompson (D-Mississippi) and Liz Cheney (R-Wyoming). Thompson described the attack on the Capitol as an attempted coup. "The violence was no accident. It represents seeing Trump's last stand, most desperate chance to halt the transfer of power."[2] In her statement, Representative Cheney called attention to an order by US District Judge David O. Carter (Central

District of California) that concerned a memo written by a former President Trump attorney, John Eastman, in which Eastman proposed a plan to have Vice President Pence rig the certification of electoral votes in Trump's favor. Judge Carter stated it "likely furthered the crimes of obstruction of an official proceeding and conspiracy to defraud the United States."[3]

The Committee pursued its investigation into Eastman and his communications, and Eastman filed suit to bar them as privileged. In an order issued October 19, 2022, Judge Carter directed Eastman to turn over thirty-three more emails to the Committee, as they contain possible evidence of criminal behavior.[4]

> President Trump, moreover, signed a verification (in a Georgia state action) swearing under oath that the incorporated, inaccurate numbers "are true and correct" or "believed to be true and correct" to the best of his knowledge and belief.
>
> The emails show that President Trump knew that the specific numbers of voter fraud were wrong but continued to tout those numbers, both in court and to the public. The Court finds that these emails are sufficiently related to and in furtherance of a conspiracy to defraud the United States.[5]

The Committee opened with a video recorded at the Capitol on January 6, 2021. Previously unseen publicly, this video of the attack rendered wildly absurd Trump supporters' earlier claims that the breach was a customary tourist visit.[6] Violent Trump supporters wielded bicycle racks and flag poles to ram police officers defending the Capitol, smashed windows and climbed through them, erected gallows, and shouted they were going to "take out" Speaker Nancy Pelosi (D-California) and Senate Majority Leader Chuck Schumer (D-New York), and "hang Mike Pence."[7] Footage of the insurrection showed congressional leaders in a secure location seeking to demonstrate that the government still functioned and that the transfer of presidential power would take place.[8]

The violence, which continued for several hours as shown by time stamps on the video, was punctuated by Capitol Police Officer Caroline Edwards' testimony.

> I felt the bike rack come on top of my head and I was pushed backwards and my foot caught the stair behind me I—my chin hit the handrail. And then I—at that point I had blacked out. But my—the back of my head clipped the concrete stairs behind me.

After she regained consciousness,

> what I saw was just a—a war scene ... I was slipping in people's blood ... it was carnage. It was chaos ... And that day, it was just hours of hand-to-hand combat, hours of dealing with things that were way beyond any—any law enforcement officer has ever trained for.[9]

Officer Edwards recounted how the attack traumatized those who experienced it in a *New York Times* opinion piece. "For me, this story cannot end overnight, because the riot itself was an attack not just on an essential American institution but also on the people who live and serve to protect it."[10]

Second Hearing —June 13, 2022

At the second hearing, the Committee documented that Trump and his advisors knew there was no evidence of significant fraud but continued to promote the "Big Lie" that the election had been stolen from Trump. Former Attorney General William Barr's videotaped testimony accentuated the issue. He told Trump and his supporters that their claims of election fraud were "bull——" and that he thought Trump had become "detached from reality." Barr added, "when I went into this and would, you know, tell him how crazy some of these allegations were … there was never an indication of interest in what the actual facts were."[11]

Third Hearing—June 16, 2022

On June 16, 2022, the Committee considered evidence that Trump and Eastman pressured Vice President Mike Pence to reject the electoral votes from seven states that Joe Biden had won even though they knew their actions were illegal. The testimony of Pence's counsel, Greg Jacob, confirmed:

> I told the Vice President that … our review of text, history, and frankly just common sense all confirmed the Vice President's first instinct on that point. There is no justifiable basis to conclude that the Vice President has that kind of authority (to unilaterally decide the outcome of an election).[12]

At this hearing former Federal Appeals Court Judge, J. Michael Luttig discussed his statement posted on Twitter* the day before the attack, "The Constitution does not empower the Vice President to alter in any way the (electoral) votes that have been cast, either by rejecting them or otherwise."[13] Judge Luttig also described the events of January 6 in a twelve-page statement obtained by CNN:

> The war on democracy … was the final fateful day for the execution of a well-developed plan by the former president to overturn the 2020 presidential election at any cost, so that he could cling to power that the American People had decided to confer upon his successor.[14]

---

* Cited publications and hearing transcripts use "Twitter" as the platform's name. The Twitter name and branding change to X occurred in July 2023 after the events discussed here.

He also testified that "today, almost two years after that fateful day in January 2021, that still Donald Trump and his allies and supporters are a clear and present danger to American democracy."[15]

Fourth Hearing—June 21, 2022

The Select Committee next heard riveting testimony from Representative Rusty Bowers, the Republican speaker of the Arizona House of Representatives, that President Trump and his associates made repeated attempts to get him to illegally change Arizona Biden Electors to Trump Electors. He told Trump and his associates, "look, you are asking me to do something that is counter to my oath when I swore to the Constitution to uphold it, and I also swore to the Constitution and the laws of the state of Arizona … and I will not break my oath."[16] He testified he asked Rudy Giuliani to provide him with names and ballot descriptions to prove illegal voting had occurred in Arizona, and that Giuliani never did. Giuliani later told him, "We've got lots of theories, we just don't have any evidence."[17]

Following his refusal to alter Arizona's electoral votes, Bowers testified:

> we have various groups come by, and they have had video panel trucks with videos of me proclaiming me to be a pedophile and a pervert and a corrupt politician and blaring loudspeakers in my neighborhood and leaving literature both on my property, and—but arguing and threatening with neighbors and with myself.[18]

He said his daughter who was gravely ill later died. The harassment didn't appear to have caused her death, but she had been disturbed by it.[19] It was reported the next day, however, that after his testimony, Bowers stated he would vote for Trump in 2024 if he became the Republican candidate.[20] But his own reelection bid failed after he recanted his statement, and a backlash defeated him in the Arizona primary election for state senate.[21]

Brad Raffensperger, Secretary of State and Gabriel Sterling, Deputy Secretary of State of Georgia, also testified before the Select Committee concerning the pressure Trump, his chief of staff Mark Meadows, Guiliani, and other Trump associates exerted against them to alter the results of the 2020 election. Raffensperger described the January 3, 2021, phone call he received from then President Trump during which he was asked about late-delivered ballots, votes from dead people and other irregularities. Raffensperger refuted all of Trump's allegations. They had counted ballots three times with very close results each time. Trump then asked him to "find 11,780 votes" that would flip the State of Georgia's electoral votes from Biden to Trump. Raffensperger testified he refused to do so "Because I knew that we had followed the law, we had followed the Constitution ... You're doing your job. And that's all we did ... And at the end of the day, President Trump came up short."[22]

A video of a press conference Sterling held on December 1, 2020, was played in which he told Trump, "What you don't have the ability to do, and you need to step up and say this, is stop inspiring people to commit potential acts of violence." Sterling testified that claims of Mr. Trump and his allies that Georgia election workers had been caught on video pulling thousands of ballots out of a suitcase taken from underneath a table and fed into election counting machines multiple times had been investigated and debunked. Sterling said,

> They're putting ballots that are prepared to be scanned into ballot carriers that are then sealed with tamper proof seals so that you — they can — you know they're not messed with ... That if there is a missed scan if there's a misalignment ... You have to delete that batch and put it back through again. And by going through the hand tally ... we showed that if there had been multiple ballots scanned without a, you know, corresponding physical ballot, your counts would have been a lot higher than the ballots themselves.[23]

BJay Pak, US Attorney for the Northern District, who had investigated the alleged suitcase full of ballots, testified that his investigation did not find any irregularity concerning the allegation.[24] Sterling testified that even after the allegation was debunked, Mr. Trump and his allies pushed false claims in statements and on social media. Fighting back against this flood of misinformation he said was like "a shovel trying to empty the ocean."[25]

The Select Committee considered evidence that shortly after the election, Cleta Mitchell, a Trump lawyer, suggested a plan to have state lawmakers create a second set of elector ballots from swing states like Georgia, Pennsylvania, Michigan, and Wisconsin. Mitchell wrote in an email to Eastman, "A movement is stirring … But needs constitutional support."[26]

Casey Lucier, investigative counsel for the committee, testified regarding a memo that Kenneth Chesebro wrote on November 18, 2020[27] (the Wisconsin Memo). His memo suggested that the Trump campaign organize its allies in Wisconsin and draft a Trump-Pence slate of electors. The memo said the real deadline wasn't December 14 but January 6, 2021. Later, a December 6, 2020, memo that Chesebro also wrote surfaced, stating, "Important that all Trump-Pence electors vote on December 14 … *in all six contested States*." (emphasis added) (The Fraudulent Elector Memo discussed in Chapter 4 Major Investigations and Indictments.) Both Chesebro memos were cited in the August 1, 2023, Smith indictment. Giuliani and Meadows supported the plan later known as the fake elector plan.[28]

Ronna Romney McDaniel, former Michigan party chairwoman and current Republican National Committee chairwoman, testified by video that Trump called her about the fake elector certificate plan. McDaniel said Eastman

> proceeded to talk about the importance of the RNC helping gather these contingent electors in case any of the legal challenges that were ongoing changed the result of any of the states. I think more just helping them reach out and assemble them.[29]

The fake elector certificate plan went forward even though lawyers for the Trump campaign, including some in the White House Counsel's Office, believed it was illegal.[30]

By a video played at the hearing Laura Cox, a former state Republican Party chairwoman, testified concerning the plan to submit fake Michigan Electors. She testified, "I told him (a Trump supporter) in no uncertain terms that that was insane and inappropriate."[31]

Michigan Senate Majority Leader Mike Shirkey (R-16th District) testified by video before the Select Committee that he and former Michigan House Speaker Lee Chatfield (R-107th District) discussed overturning the results of the Michigan election with Trump and Giuliani. Shirkey testified "we are going to follow the law."[32] Later Trump posted personal contact information for both Shirkey and Chatfield on social media, "demanding that the Michigan Legislature meet and decertify the vote." Later, Shirkey received "just shy of 4,000 text messages ... calling to take action. It was a loud noise, loud consistent cadence ... the Trump folks are calling and asking for changes in the electors and you guys can do this."[33] Michigan never changed its electors.

Ms. Wandrea "Shaye" Moss, a former local elections worker in Fulton County, Georgia, also testified at the hearing. She had processed votes in Atlanta, Georgia, for the 2020 election with her mother Ruby Freeman. When he spoke to the Georgia state legislature in December 2021, Giuliani accused Ms. Moss and her mother of taking allegedly illegal ballots from a suitcase under a table and running them through voting machines several times. Moss testified that after these baseless accusations were later repeated by Trump and took off on right wing media outlets, the women endured unrelenting harassment. Moss testified, "Yes, a lot of threats wishing death upon me, telling me that, you know, I'm — I'll be in jail with my mother, and saying things like be glad it's 2020 and not 1920."[34] Moss described a call from her grandmother:

> she called me screaming at the top of her lungs, ...
> Just freaking me out saying that there are people at

her home … And they just started pushing their way through, claiming that they were coming in to make a citizen's arrest. They needed to find me and my mom. … And she was just, like, screaming and didn't know what to do.[35]

The Committee then played a video clip of Moss's mother, Ruby Freeman. She testified, "I've lost my name, and I've lost my reputation." Freeman added, "There is nowhere I feel safe. Nowhere. Do you know how it feels to have the President of the United States target you?"[36]

In 2023, a federal jury awarded $148 million in damages to Moss and Freeman in their lawsuit for Giuliani's defamation and infliction of emotional distress over his claims. The judge also ruled that, under a theory of civil conspiracy, Giuliani was liable for Trump's statements about the election workers.[37]

Fifth Hearing—June 23, 2022

On June 23, 2022, the Select Committee took the testimony of three witnesses who served in the DOJ during Trump's presidency: Jeffrey A. Rosen, Richard P. Donoghue, and Steven Engel. When Attorney General William Barr resigned after telling Trump there was no evidence of election fraud to support Trump's claims, Rosen became acting Attorney General. Donoghue served as Acting Deputy Attorney General, and Engel served as Assistant Attorney General for the Office of Legal Counsel. Their testimony described the pressure Trump exerted on the DOJ to overturn the 2020 election. Donoghue testified,

> the president essentially said, Ken*, I'm sitting here with the Acting Attorney General … He just told me it's your job to seize machines and you're not doing your job."
> Donoghue continued, quoting Trump, "What I'm just

* Kenneth Thomas Cuccinelli II, Senior Official with the Department of Homeland Security

asking you to do is to say it (the election) is corrupt and leave the rest to me and the Republican Congressmen."[38]

Jeffrey Clark, an assistant attorney general in the DOJ Environment and Natural Resources Division with no criminal practice experience, had been introduced to Trump as someone who would pursue Trump's election fraud claims. Ken Klukowski, who had worked with Eastman, had recently joined the DOJ. He also worked with Clark and helped draft a proposed "Georgia Letter" addressed to the Georgia Governor, Speaker of the Georgia House, and President Pro Tempore of the Georgia Senate. The letter stated among other things that "the Department (DOJ) believe [*sic*] that in Georgia and several other States, both a slate of electors supporting Joseph R. Biden, Jr. and a separate slate of electors supporting Donald J. Trump,… have been transmitted to Washington, DC, to be opened by Vice President Pence." The letter also stated that the DOJ believed that Georgia's governor or its General Assembly had power to call for a special session to consider issues pertaining to the appointment of presidential electors.[39] The letter was to be sent under the imprimatur of the DOJ and signed by Rosen, Donoghue, and by Clark as (Acting) Assistant Attorney General. Rosen and Donoghue refused to sign the letter, and it was never sent.

When Rosen and Donoghue refused to comply with Trump's requests, the disagreement came to a head three days prior to the attack of January 6, 2021. Trump called for a meeting with Rosen, Donoghue, and Clark. At that meeting, Rosen tried to convince Trump not to follow the path Clark advocated. Trump responded that he would appoint Clark to replace him. Rosen and Donoghue both testified they informed Trump that Clark was clearly not qualified to be the Acting Attorney General. Donoghue then testified,

> And I said, Mr. President, I would resign immediately. I'm not working one minute for this guy, who I had just declared was completely incompetent … You're going to lose your entire department leadership. Every single AAG will walk out on you … within 24, 48, 72 hours,

you could have hundreds and hundreds of resignations of the leadership of your entire Justice Department because of your actions. What's that going to say about you?[40]

Despite evidence that Clark had already been recognized at the White House as Acting Attorney General, Trump did not pursue the plan to replace Rosen with Clark. On June 23, 2022, the FBI searched Clark's home, indicating in the warrant that prosecutors were investigating Clark on charges that include conspiracy to obstruct the certification of the presidential election.[41]

Sixth Hearing—June 28, 2022

Cassidy Hutchinson, an aide to Mark Meadows, provided devastating testimony to the Select Committee regarding events and conversations she observed and heard while serving as Meadows's aide, including events surrounding the insurrection. She said that Giuliani told her on January 2 that Trump would go to the Capitol and "look powerful." Alarmed, Hutchinson spoke to Meadows. "I just had an interesting conversation with Rudy, Mark. It sounds like we're going to go to the Capitol. He ... said something to the effect of, there's a lot going on, Cass ... Things might get real, real bad on January 6."[42]

Hutchinson testified that Anthony "Tony" M. Ornato, former White House Deputy Chief of Staff, warned Meadows on January 6 that the crowd

> had weapons and other items that were confiscated: pepper spray, knives, brass knuckles, tasers, body armor, gas masks, batons, blunt weapons. And those were just from the people who chose to go through the security for the President's event on the Ellipse, not the several thousand ... (who) watched from the lawn near the Washington Monument.[43]

She added, "And I looked at Tony and I was like, Sir he just told you about what was happening down at the rallies. And he was like yeah, yeah. I know. And then he looked up and said have you talked to the President? And Tony said yes, Sir. He's aware. And he said Alright. Good."[44] Hutchinson said she was at the Ellipse when she texted Ornato, "(Trump) wanted the arena that we had on the ellipse to be maxed out at capacity for all attendees … Everybody who wanted to come in had already come in. But he still was angry about the extra space and wanted more people to come in."[45] Televised scenes of Trump's followers on the Ellipse presented during Hutchinson's testimony showed several carrying firearms.

Hutchinson testified that Trump demanded that security checkpoints be removed from his rally on the Ellipse on January 6, 2021: "I don't effing care that they have weapons. They're not here to hurt me … Take the effing mags (metal detectors) away. Let my people in. They can march to the Capitol from here."[46]

Hutchinson heard Trump insist on going to the Capitol to join his supporters there and testified that when Pat A. Cipollone, the White House counsel, heard of that prospect, "(He) said … please make sure we don't go up to the Capitol, Cassidy … We're going to get charged with every crime imaginable if we make that movement happen."[47] Hutchinson testified she heard of the incident in the presidential limousine from Ornato. Following the rally on the Ellipse, Trump insisted his security detail drive him to the Capitol.

> So once the president had gotten into the vehicle with Bobby,*… when Bobby had relayed to him we're not,… it's not secure, we're going back to the West Wing … The president said … I'm the f'ing president, take me up to the Capitol now… The president reached up toward the front of the vehicle to grab at the steering wheel. Mr. Engel grabbed his arm, said, sir, you need to take your hand off the steering wheel.… Mr. Trump

---

* Robert "Bobby" Engel, Special Agent in Charge of Trump's security detail

then used his free hand to lunge toward Bobby Engel. And Mr. — when Mr. Ornato had recounted this story to me, he had motioned toward his clavicles.[48]

Trump later denied he had done so. He said he did not know who Hutchinson was, but labeled her a "whacko," "total phony," "social climber," and a "leaker."[49] Secret Service officials later said that the two agents with Trump were prepared to state under oath that neither was assaulted, and that Trump did not reach for the steering wheel, but other reports indicated an incident did happen.[50]

Hutchinson testified that Trump did not heed recommendations by aides and family members, including his daughter Ivanka to tell the mob to stand down.[51]

> I remember Pat (Cipollone) saying … They're literally calling for the vice president to be f'ing hung. And Mark had responded something to the effect of "you heard him (Trump), Pat. He thinks Mike deserves it. He doesn't think they're (the rioters) doing anything wrong, to which Pat said something, this is f'ing crazy, we need to be doing something more.[52]

Hutchinson confirmed seeing a tweet that Trump issued at 2:24 p.m. on January 6, 2021, that stated,

> Mike Pence didn't have the courage to do what should have been done to protect our Country and our Constitution, giving States a chance to certify a corrected set of facts, not the fraudulent or inaccurate ones which they were asked to previously certify. USA demands the truth! — Donald J. Trump (@realDonaldTrump) January 6, 2021)[53]

Hutchinson testified after seeing Trump's tweet attacking Pence she felt,

As an American, I was disgusted. It was unpatriotic … It was un-American. We were watching the Capitol building get defaced over a lie, and it was something that was really hard in that moment to digest, knowing what I've been hearing down the hall and the conversations that were happening.[54]

Seventh Hearing—July 12, 2022

At its July 12, 2022, hearing Chairman Bennie Thompson placed the blame for the riot of January 6 on Trump. "Donald Trump summoned a mob to Washington, DC, and ultimately spurred that mob to wage a violent attack on our democracy."[55]

Video depositions and live testimony covered an unscheduled White House meeting that occurred on December 18, 2020. US Representative Jamie Raskin (D-Maryland), a member of the committee, presented text messages from Hutchinson reporting that the meeting in the West Wing was "unhinged."[56] The meeting continued over six hours and extended past midnight.[57]

Three of Trump's outside advisors (Sidney Powell, a former lawyer for the Trump campaign who had accused voting software company Dominion Voting Systems of altering the tallies to rig the election; Michael T. Flynn, a National Security adviser Trump had fired; and Patrick Byrne, former CEO of Overstock.com and a proponent of Trump's false election claims) had been let into the White House. Alarmed that unscheduled outside advisors were meeting with Trump, Cipollone, Eric Herschmann, a senior advisor to Trump, and Derek Lyons, the White House Staff Secretary, broke into the meeting. In sworn video testimony Herschmann described the discussion, "What they were proposing I thought was nuts."[58] Lyons told the committee in videotaped testimony, "At times there were people shouting at each other, hurling insults at each other."[59]

At the meeting, the outside group proposed that Trump sign an executive order "effective immediately" that directed the Secretary of Defense to "seize, collect, retain, and analyze all machines, equipment, electronically stored information, and material records" concerning the 2020 election.[60] In another proposal, they asked that Powell be appointed special counsel and empowered to charge people with crimes concerning the election.

When the White House officials pointed out that Powell had lost dozens of lawsuits challenging the 2020 election, she allegedly replied, "Well, the judges are corrupt." When reminded that some of the judges were Trump appointees, she added the White House advisors "showed nothing but contempt and disdain of the president."[61] Cipollone testified,

> There was a real question in my mind … you know, particularly after the Attorney General had reached a conclusion that there wasn't sufficient election fraud to change the outcome of the election when other people kept suggesting that there was. The answer is, what is it? At some point, you have to put up or shut up.[62]

Trump did not accept either proposal, but at 1:42 a.m. on December 19, he posted a tweet on Twitter urging his supporters to arrive at the Capitol on January 6, "Statistically impossible to have lost the 2020 Election. Big protest in DC on January 6. Be there, will be wild!"[63] On December 21, 2020, Trump met with several Republican representatives at the White House to discuss Eastman's discredited theories and the plan to pressure Pence.

Evidence showed the march on the Capitol was not spontaneous as later claimed, but had been planned days before.[64] Trump's supporters quickly responded to his tweet of December 19.[65] Women for America First organizers (see Chapter 4 endnote 7) moved a rally planned for after Biden's inauguration to January 6.[66] Ali Alexander registered the website WildProtest.com as a clearinghouse for January 6 protest information, including event times, places, speakers, and details on transportation. Kylie Jane Kremer, an organizer of the Save America rally held on January 6, 2021, texted on January 4, 2021, "POTUS is going to have us march there/the Capitol.… It can also not get out about the march, … But POTUS is going to just call for it 'unexpectedly.'"[67]

Stephen Ayres, of Ohio, who pled guilty to disorderly conduct charges related to the attack on the Capitol, testified at the hearing, "the President got everybody riled up and told everybody to head on down. We basically was just following what he said." Had he known Trump's election fraud claims were false, Ayres also testified he would never have participated in the riot.[68]

Eighth Hearing—July 21, 2022

On July 21, 2022, as the Select Committee wrapped up its summer public hearings, Committee member Adam Kinzinger (R-Illinois) stated, "Donald Trump's conduct on Jan. 6 was a supreme violation of his oath of office and a complete dereliction of his duty to our nation." He intentionally sought to delay the electoral vote, notwithstanding the risk it posed to human life, and to force Congress either to send the election back to the states or to certify him as president.

As Hutchinson's testimony revealed, for over three hours during the afternoon of January 6, 2021, Trump refused to follow the advice of administration officials, congressmen, senators, and even his own staff and family members that he contact the rioters and order them to go home. He also ignored a plea for assistance from Kevin McCarthy (R-California), Minority Leader of the US House, who called from his offices in the Capitol. According to US Rep. Jaime Herrera Beutler's (R-Washington) testimony, Trump responded,

> He said, well, Kevin, these aren't my people.… these are Antifa. And Kevin responded and said no, they're your people. They literally just came through my office windows and my staff are running for cover. I mean, they're running for their lives. You need to call them off. And the president's response to Kevin, to me, was chilling.… He said, well, Kevin, I guess they're just more upset about the election, you know, theft than you are.… because the president was basically saying, nah, I — I'm okay with this."[69]

Instead, Trump watched Fox News coverage of the riot in his private dining room. General Mark A. Milley, Chairman of the Joint Chiefs of Staff, testified, "Commander in Chief, you got an assault going on on [*sic*] the Capitol of the United States of America. And there's nothing? No call? Nothing? Zero?"[70]

It is not clear under the Insurrection Act of 1807[71] that the president has power to command the military, National Guard, or police units to quell an insurrection in the District of Columbia. But it has been done.[72] Whether or not Trump had authority, the Select Committee found no evidence he attempted to do so. Guard units did arrive at the Capitol late in the afternoon, but apparently in response to a request Vice President Pence sent to the Secretary of Defense.[73]

When Trump asked his followers to leave late that afternoon, he posted a video on Twitter, since removed, "This was a fraudulent election, but we can't play into the hands of these people. We have to have peace. So go home, we love you, you're very special."[74]

The rioters only dispersed after additional police arrived and some riot leaders announced Trump wanted them to go home. As they left the Capitol, he stated, "Mike Pence let me down."[75] According to Hutchinson's testimony during the sixth hearing, Trump finally agreed to record a message to the nation out of concerns that he might be removed from office under the Twenty-Fifth Amendment or by impeachment.[76] In an outtake from the address Trump delivered on January 7, 2021, he stated, "I don't want to say the election's over. I just want to say Congress has certified the results without saying the election's over, OK?"[77]

Ninth Hearing—October 13, 2022

During the ninth hearing,[78] the Select Committee presented evidence that as early as July 2020, Trump insisted he would claim victory no matter the results of the 2020 election and no matter what it would take to accomplish. In a videotape recorded before the 2020 election, Steve Bannon said,

He's (Trump) gonna declare victory, but that doesn't mean he's the winner, he's just gonna say he's a winner … if Trump is losing by 10:00 or 11:00 at night,… he's gonna sit right there and say they stole it.… If Biden is winning, Trump is going to do some crazy shit.[79]

Other evidence revealed that contrary to Trump's ongoing public refusals to concede and claims of election fraud, he often admitted he lost in private conversations, for example with General Milley, "We lost."[80] Hutchinson (see also her testimony during the sixth hearing) confirmed that he admitted losing, "does the President really think he lost? And (Mark Meadows) said, you know, a lot of times he'll tell me that he lost, but he wants to keep fighting it … he pretty much has acknowledged that he — that he's lost."[81]

Other reports aired by the Committee showed it was known January 6 would be violent. On December 26, 2020, the Secret Service relayed a tip they had received from the FBI. According to the FBI's source, the Proud Boys would "outnumber the police so they can't be stopped … their plan is to literally kill people. Please, please take this tip seriously and investigate further."[82] On December 31, 2020, Secret Service agents sent out reports Trump's supporters planned to occupy the Capitol.

The committee aired a text from Jason Miller, a communications adviser to Mark Meadows, that read, "I Got the Base Fired Up," and sent a link to a webpage on TheDonald.win that posted violent threats, such as "Our lawmakers in Congress can leave one of two ways; one, in a body bag, two, after rightfully certifying Trump the winner."[83]

The committee ran new footage of representatives, senators, and their staffs fleeing the rioters, hunkering down within the Capitol, and being taken to secure locations. It also showed House Speaker Pelosi and Senate Majority Leader Schumer phoning Governor Ralph Northam of Virginia and Acting US Attorney General Jeff Rosen pleading for police or military reinforcements. The videos showed not only the savagery, but also the concern of the leaders of both chambers that the Joint Session reconvene and fulfill its duty to certify the election.[84]

As in the sixth and eighth hearings, the Select Committee presented evidence Trump ignored pleas that he issue a statement to his followers to end the violence at the Capitol. Newly received documents from the Secret Service contained warnings that "POTUS just tweeted about Pence; probably not going to be good for Pence." Anika Navaroli, a former Twitter employee, testified that the rioters were posting on Twitter, "literally calling for his execution."[85]

More evidence was aired concerning Republican Leader McCarthy's phone call to Trump during the riot (see also Beutler testimony during the eighth hearing above). Video testimony from Mick Mulvaney, a former chief of staff to Trump, confirmed the McCarthy phone call.[86]

The committee presented video clips of Vice President Pence sheltering with Secret Service agents in the Capitol basement and seeking to call out the National Guard and of him later informing the other leaders that the rioters had been cleared from the Capitol and that it was safe to resume the Joint Session to certify the results of the 2020 presidential election.

Cochairman Bennie Thompson summed up the testimony and evidence gathered during the Committee's investigation:

> we have left no doubt, none, that Donald Trump led an effort to up end American democracy that directly resulted in the violence of January 6. He tried to take away the voice of the American people in choosing their president and replace the will of the voters with his will to remain in power.
>
> He is the one person at the center of the story of what happened on January 6, so we want to hear from him.[87]

The Committee unanimously adopted a resolution to subpoena Trump to appear before the Committee and testify.

Conclusion

After the Democrats lost control of the House of Representatives in the 2022 midterm elections, the Select Committee was dissolved. After speaking to over 1,000 witnesses and reviewing the evidence, the Committee completed its investigation.[88] It published its final report and issued four criminal referrals to the DOJ that accused Trump of obstruction of an official proceeding (18 U.S.C. § 1512 (c) (2)); conspiracy to defraud the United States (18 U.S.C. § 371); conspiracy to make a false statement (18 U.S.C. §§ 371, 1001) and "inciting," "assisting," or "aiding or comforting" an insurrection (18 U.S.C. § 2383).[89]

Laurence Tribe, professor emeritus at Harvard Law School, stated in a *New York Times* guest essay, "But only by holding the leaders of the Jan. 6 insurrection– all of them – to account can (Merrick Garland) secure the future and teach the next generation that no one is above the law."[90]

After impeachment failed and the Select Committee dissolved, uncertainty set in. Attorney General Garland and Special Counsel Smith continued their investigations (see Chapter 4 Major Investigations and Indictments) while op ed pieces speculated a civil war might soon erupt in the United States.[91] Bolstered by opinion polls showing support from many Republican Party members, Trump continued to assert the 2020 election had been stolen, campaigned for and sometimes against primary candidates of his own party in the 2022 midterm elections, and announced he would seek the presidency again in 2024. In the midst of all of that, Trump posted a response on his Truth Social platform to reports that Twitter had blocked links to a *New York Post* article discussing emails found on Hunter Biden's laptop:

> So, with the revelation of MASSIVE & WIDESPREAD FRAUD & DECEPTION in working closely with Big Tech Companies, the DNC, & the Democrat Party, do you throw the Presidential Election Results of 2020 OUT and declare the RIGHTFUL WINNER, or do

you have a NEW ELECTION? … A Massive Fraud of this type and magnitude allows for the termination of all rules, regulations, and articles, even those found in the Constitution.[92]

Think about that post and the Select Committee's revelations. "Alarming" doesn't *begin* to describe it.

CHAPTER 6

The One Man, One Vote Principle and the Voting Rights Act—Efforts to Protect Voting Rights During the 1960s

Over our 237-year history the right to vote for federal and state executives and legislators has been influenced by competing trends. As voting was expanded to cover more citizens it came to be seen as a cornerstone of our Republic. But it is critical that all Americans understand the vital role that elections play in guarding the health of our Republic and how the right to vote continues to face partisan restrictions. Four challenges threaten the legal underpinnings of the one man, one vote principle, and also threaten the safety, sanctity, and validity of our elections:

1. congressional and state legislative voting districts have been grotesquely gerrymandered to favor the votes of some citizens over that of others;
2. filibusters and cloture rules frustrate majority rule by artificially bottling up legislation in the US Senate;
3. recent more stringent voting requirements and restrictions have been imposed at the state level that unreasonably burden the right; and
4. since the "Big Lie" and the events of January 6, 2021, media reports exposed physical threats against members of Congress based on how they vote and against local and state election officials and their families.

This chapter will discuss background constitutional issues, Chapter 7 will discuss the impact of gerrymandering, Chapter 8 will discuss efforts to correct gerrymandering and the independent state legislature doctrine, and Chapter 9 will examine other restrictions on the right to vote.

As political parties formed shortly after the birth of our nation, it became clear the original Constitution was inadequate to meet the needs and stresses partisan politics imposed on the developing nation. The Constitution provided for the selection of presidents, vice presidents, and representatives by the people and guaranteed a republican form of government to the states without addressing specific forms of discrimination that could, and later did, abridge or deny the right to vote. For example, Article I Section 2 provided only that the House of Representatives was to be composed of members *chosen* every second year by the people of the several states. With respect to the Senate, Article I Section 3 provided that the Senate would consist of two senators from each state "chosen by the *Legislature* thereof." (emphasis added).

When hotly contested claims of discrimination later arose, amendments to the Constitution were ratified to protect the right to vote from racial and other forms of discrimination. Among them the Fourteenth Amendment, ratified in 1868, is critical. Amendment XIV Section 1 provides that, *"All persons* born or naturalized in the United States, and subject to the jurisdiction thereof, are citizens of the United States and of the State wherein they reside." (emphasis added). The amendment bluntly and clearly provides that, "No state shall make or enforce any law … (that denies) *to any person* within its jurisdiction *the equal protection of the laws."* (emphasis added).

Later Amendments established that the right to vote could not be denied or abridged on account of race, color, or previous condition of servitude (Amendment XV, ratified in 1870), sex (Amendment XIX, ratified in 1920), or to those eighteen years of age or older (Amendment XXVI, ratified in 1971). Amendment XVII, ratified in 1913, amended Article I Section 3 to provide that the US Senate would be composed of two senators from each state "elected by the people thereof." Amendment XXIV Section 1 challenged the partisans in 1964, by providing

The right of citizens of the United States to vote in
any primary or other election for President or Vice
President, for electors for President or Vice President,
or for Senator or Representative in Congress, shall not
be denied or abridged by the United States or any State
by reason of failure to pay any poll tax or other tax.

These amendments emphatically established voting as a key right
entitled to the same vigorous protection that is accorded to freedom of
speech and the right to bear arms. The Constitution no longer provides
for classes of citizens—the right to vote belongs to *all* citizens who are
of age. Yet, it has never received the vigorous enforcement needed to
protect all citizens' voting rights. Throughout our history, partisans
focused on acquiring political power have relentlessly assaulted the
right. The Trump presidency that culminated in the attack that blared
from our televisions on January 6, 2021, drove that concern home.
(See Chapter 5.) Continued assaults on the right to vote carried over
to the 2022 midterm primary elections, and expanded into the 2024
presidential election. So yes, the threats to our right to vote are very real,
and it is time for the nation to see it as a key right, and to realize that
we could lose it or see it rendered meaningless.

Over our history the right to vote has been curtailed in many ways
– by property ownership requirements, racial and sex requirements, poll
taxes, literacy tests, gerrymandering, and voter ID requirements. The
Twenty-Fourth Amendment bans poll taxes and other taxes on the right
to vote, but efforts to deter voting by imposing monetary impediments
arose in other ways. Even worse, when you consider the effect poll taxes
had, the new laws made the violations punishable by stiff fines and
imprisonment.[1]

The case of Crystal Mason in Texas demonstrates that fines and
imprisonment for voting violations can restrict the right to vote. While
serving a supervised prison release from her conviction for federal
tax fraud, Mason voted a *provisional ballot* in a 2016 Texas election.
Her ballot was never counted, but language on the side of the ballot
application she signed stated it was unlawful for a convicted felon to

vote if the disqualification had not been lifted—which it was not. Her probation officer testified that he never warned her that she could not vote under federal supervised release.[2] Mason was fined and sentenced in 2018 to five years. In May of 2022, the Texas Court of Criminal Appeals sent the case back to the Tarrant County Second Court of Appeals to reexamine the intent issue.[3] On March 24, 2024, The *Texas Tribune* reported the latter court overturned her conviction.

Mason's case does not denigrate the fact that voter fraud is a serious matter. Her case tells us that draconian fining and jailing voter fraud for minor errors will keep many voters away from the polls just as poll taxes did. The principal victims will be minorities and the poor who cannot absorb oppressive fines or imprisonment that takes them from their families and jobs. Whether intended or not, threats of fining and imprisoning for voter fraud will have a racial discriminatory effect.

As an example of new voting restrictions, Republicans have pushed for federal legislation to require stringent proof of citizenship to vote in federal elections. A study by the Center for Democracy and Civic Engagement found that almost 10 percent of eligible voters lack access to documents proving citizenship, such as passports, birth certificates, or naturalization papers. Twenty-one million Americans do not have a valid driver's license for photo identification.[4] According to Lauren Kunis, director of Vote Riders, "Getting an ID can mean needing to track down underlying proof-of-citizenship documents like a birth certificate, navigating bureaucracy and paperwork, or spending hours at an ID-issuing office that is hard to reach ... voter ID laws make it more complicated, costly, and confusing to cast a ballot in America today."[5]

Estimates range from 700 to 1,200 rioters who broke into the Capitol on January 6 to halt the election results certification process and attack those performing it.[6] Most who pled guilty or were convicted of crimes related to the Capitol attack received lighter sentences than Mason's. For example, that guy with the horns drew a prison sentence of forty-one months (just under three and a half years) after pleading guilty to a felony charge of obstructing an official proceeding.[7]

Ever broader and more organized challenges, including threats of physical violence against local election officials and their families, have created a chilling effect on the right to vote. (See Chapter 9 Section C.) We are at an inflection point. Political partisanship continues to bottle up legislation designed to protect the right in our state legislatures and in Congress. And, as shown below, the US Supreme Court has imposed proof of specific discriminatory intent and other onerous restrictions on those who seek to enforce the right.

For a while it seemed the right would receive robust protection. Legislation and case law developed during the 1960s promised greater protection—but that promise has not been fulfilled. In 1962 the US Supreme Court established in *Baker v. Carr* that cases involving the boundaries of state election districts presented justiciable issues that federal courts could entertain and decide.[8] That step opened the doors of the federal courts to voting rights cases. Shortly after, during the civil rights battles of the 1960s, the Warren Court recognized the one man, one vote principle in *Reynolds v. Sims* to protect the right of all citizens to equal representation in voting.[9] Later, in *Wesberry v. Sanders*[10] the Court defined the one man, one vote rule to mean that "as nearly as is practicable, one man's vote in a congressional election is to be worth as much as another's" and it held that the states must draw congressional districts that contain roughly equal represented populations. The one man, one vote principle the Court established fortified the Equal Protection Clause of the Fourteenth Amendment, but over time it weakened.

While these decisions were coming down, the VRA[11] was enacted by Congress and signed by President Lyndon B. Johnson on August 6, 1965, to enforce the Fifteenth Amendment's proscription against racial discrimination. That act is discussed below. Then, in 1968, the Supreme Court applied the one man, one vote principle to state and local districts (*Avery v. Midland County*).[12] The latter case is significant to voting rights because it held the Equal Protection Clause of the Fourteenth Amendment reached the exercise of state power, whether exercised by the state or by a political subdivision.[13] But these events moved at glacial speed, all the while partisan challenges to the right continued apace out on the hustings.

A large area of concern arose from the need to apportion members of the House of Representative among the several states. Because the population of the nation continues to grow and move from state to state, and even from place to place within the states, the reapportionment of voting districts becomes acute every ten years. Pursuant to Article I Section 2 of the Constitution, the US House of Representatives "shall be composed of Members chosen every second Year by the People of the several States" and "apportioned among the several States … *according to their respective Numbers.*" (emphasis added) The allocation of representatives to each state was originally set up to start "within three years after the first Meeting of the Congress of the United States," and to change with population changes "within every subsequent Term of ten Years, in such Manner as (Congress) shall by Law direct" (Article I Section 2). A decennial census is taken nationally to allocate the number of US Representatives among the states based on their population. The last decennial census was taken in 2020. The current number of representatives has been set at 435 by Congress.

Apportionment requires that the states apportion the representatives authorized by Congress to legislative districts within each state. The districts must contain an approximately equal number of residents. Given the level of partisanship now dividing our nation, redistricting places a heavy cost burden and extensive litigation on state legislators and officials charged with redistricting election districts under Article I Section 2 of the Constitution. Chapter 7 will examine how gerrymandering corrupted House redistricting.

Even though the one man, one vote principle established in 1964 does apply to the House of Representatives, and that it and the Equal Protection Clause of the Fourteenth Amendment apply to our state legislatures and local governments, the vigor that created the rule has floundered—further eroded by partisan pressures. This will be explored further in Chapters 7, 8, and 9.

The US Senate is structurally different from the House, but voting rights are also watered down there. Perhaps even more so. The one man, one vote rule announced by the Supreme Court cannot be invoked with respect to the Senate because the problem there, though great, is constitutional. The Founding Fathers gave each state two senators irrespective of the number of persons they represented. It was an unavoidable political compromise to get the small states to agree to the new Constitution.[14]

The 2020 US Census, using April 1, 2020, as a reference point, found that the total apportionment population* of the fifty states equaled 331,108,434.[15] But even though our population greatly expanded (from 3.9 million in the 1790 census), states with low populations like Alaska (733,391) and Vermont (643,077) continue to have the same representation in the US Senate as do states with very high populations like California (39.54 million) and Texas (29.15 million).[16] Thus, a California senator represents 38,895,146 more persons than does a Vermont senator. A Texas senator represents 28,412,114 more persons than does an Alaska senator. And the number of voters needed *to elect* a California or Texas senator greatly exceeds the number needed to elect a Vermont or Alaska senator.

Census data for 2020 indicates that twenty-six states having approximately 20 percent of the total US population can theoretically elect fifty-two Senators (i.e., 52 percent of all US Senators) and control the Senate. Thirty states with approximately 27 percent of the total US population can theoretically elect sixty senators (i.e., enough to prevent cloture[†] now set at 60 percent of all US Senators.) This didn't result from partisan gerrymandering. The Constitution created a "gerrymandered" Senate.

The 2020 senatorial election demonstrated that Article I Section 3, by giving each state two senators regardless of their population, watered down voting rights the same as gerrymandered House districts do. That

---

* The 2020 apportionment population includes the resident and overseas populations of the fifty states but excludes the District of Columbia and inhabited US territories (Puerto Rico, Guam, Northern Mariana Islands, the US Virgin Islands, and American Samoa). The District of Columbia and the territories each have one nonvoting delegate to the House of Representatives and no representation in the Senate.

† Cloture (n.): procedure to limit further consideration of a proposal by calling for a vote to end a filibuster. See Chapter 9 section B for a fuller discussion.

may not have concerned the Founders as much as replacing the failed Articles of Confederation in 1787, but today, magnified by population growth, it cripples the ability of Congress to enact essential legislation or to confirm judges and justices. The 2020 election created a US Senate consisting of fifty senators from twenty-five red states representing approximately 41 percent of total US population, and fifty from blue states representing approximately 59 percent. That diluted the votes of millions of voters in states with large populations and stalemated legislation such as restrictions on semiautomatic firearms and protection of reproductive rights and voting rights.

However, members of Congress can work together if they choose to put aside partisan differences. On July 28, 2022, using budget reconciliation, the Democrats were able to avoid a cloture motion on a package of proposals without bipartisan support. They enacted the Inflation Reduction Act of 2022 to address several urgent problems.[17] Unfortunately for the Republic, this very rarely occurs.

The Senate's failure to control debate on the floor of the Senate through limits on filibusters and restructuring cloture[18] exacerbates the inequality in voting power in the Senate and is discussed below in Chapter 9 section B. The ongoing stalemate in the US Senate has created a "tyranny of the minority."[19]

Whether or not the method for selecting the nation's senators set out in the Constitution violates the one man, one vote principle, it can only be changed by Constitutional amendment. Under Article V of the Constitution, an amendment requires a two-thirds vote by both houses of Congress and ratification by the legislatures of three quarters of the states. Currently, amendment is not possible, and the only available means to address problems created by our stalemated Senate is through the ballot box.

CHAPTER 7

Gerrymandered Voting Districts—Violations of the One Man, One Vote Principle Over the Years

Lines have been drawn between white and black populations within our nation since its beginning:

> Ever since the Federal Convention of 1787 there had been a tacit political balance between these two sections, along the old Mason Dixon line and the Ohio River. This boundary divided slave-holding states and territories from those in which slavery had been abolished or was in process of extinction.[1]

> When Congress took up the question in January 1820, fear of a Federalist renaissance caused enough Northern Republicans to defect from antislavery to pass a compromise measure. Missouri was admitted as a slaveholding state, but slavery was prohibited in the territory of the United States north of Missouri's southern boundary, latitude 36° 30'.[2]

Within one month of Lincoln's inauguration, Fort Sumter was bombarded, and the Civil War erupted. After four brutal years, the Civil War ended at Appomattox with General Lee's surrender. As the end was being celebrated in 1865, Lincoln's assassination at Ford's Theatre deprived him of the opportunity to commence the reconstruction of the nation, and "to do all which may achieve and cherish a just and lasting peace among ourselves and with all nations." [3]

Three amendments to the Constitution were adopted soon after the Civil War. The Thirteenth Amendment, adopted in April of

1865, abolished slavery. The Fourteenth Amendment, ratified in July of 1868, defined citizenship to mean birth on United States soil or naturalization. It forbade state laws that abridged the privileges and immunities of citizenship, denied due process of law, or denied equal protection of the law. The Fourteenth Amendment also provided for the apportionment of US Representatives among the states, "according to their respective numbers." The Fifteenth Amendment, ratified in February of 1870, provided that the right to vote shall not be denied or abridged by the United States or any state on account of race, color, or previous condition of servitude.

These blockbuster Amendments are viewed as Lincoln's legacy to the nation. A recent opinion piece in the *New York Times* discussed Lincoln's contribution and described them as transforming

> the Constitution from a political compromise into a platform for defending moral principles by invoking its authority to end slavery ... The fact that the Constitution of 1787 was not so much modified as broken and remade during and after the Civil War should be a starting point for nuanced conversations about the true meaning of the Constitution today.[4]

Yet notwithstanding the magnitude of these three amendments, Southern states proceeded to disenfranchise racial minorities through Jim Crow* laws and an array of voting restrictions—literacy tests, poll taxes, requirements that voter registration applicants provide proof their grandfathers had voted†, and requirements that applicants be able to interpret particular documents (*United States v. Louisiana*).[5]

---

* Named after a black minstrel show character, Jim Crow laws existed from Reconstruction until 1968 and denied blacks the right to vote, hold jobs, and get an education or other opportunities.

† Grandfather Clause: a provision of several Southern states' constitutions in the late 1800s designed to deny suffrage to people who were illiterate or did not own property, unless they or their ancestors had voted before 1867.

From 1868 to 1908, the US Supreme Court generally shied away from efforts to control discrimination against racial minorities. This is seen in *Giles v. Harris* where the court failed to broadly interpret the three new amendments, holding instead that it would not decide political issues.

> the court has as little practical power to deal with the people of the state in a body ... Apart from damages to the individual, relief from a great political wrong, if done, as alleged, by the people of a state and the state itself, must be given by them or by the legislative and political department of the government of the United States.[6]

That holding turned the fox loose among the chickens, considering that many of the states' partisans were intent on restricting the right to vote. But it is equally clear that the Constitution also granted Congress power to override state election laws except with respect to US Senators. Article I Section 4 provides

> The Times, Places and Manner of holding Elections for Senators and Representatives, shall be prescribed in each State by the Legislature thereof; *but the Congress may at any time by Law make or alter such Regulations, except as to the Places of chusing* Senators.* (emphasis added).

While Article I Section 4 expressly provides Congress with power to "alter" discriminatory regulations adopted by the states that dilute voting power, Congress has bottled up legislation (See discussion of three recent bills later in this chapter.) in the Senate. So far as known

---

* Alternate spelling for "choosing" in use at the time of original writing. Both "chuse" and "chusing" appear in the original text. Modern transcriptions sometimes change occurrences to the current form. For a fuller discussion, see https://www.usconstitution.net/constmiss.html.

Amendment XIV Section 2's provisions for reducing representation in Congress to protect voting rights have never been used:

> But when ... the choice of electors for President and Vice-President of the United States, Representatives in Congress, the Executive and Judicial officers of a State, or the members the Legislature thereof, is denied to any of the male inhabitants of such State,... *or in any way abridged,...* the basis of representation therein shall be reduced in the proportion which the number of such male citizens shall bear to the whole number of male citizens twenty-one years of age in such State (emphasis added).

Congress's failure to act to protect voting rights became acute during the history of gerrymandering. The term came about when the governor of Massachusetts, Elbridge Gerry, redrew the state election maps in a way that one district resembled a salamander.[7] Gerry's concerns were political. Later, ethnic and racial classes of voters had their voting rights diluted through gerrymandered election districts. Whether viewed in the courts as "politically" or as "racially" motivated, the result has been the same. Both major parties acquired control of state legislatures and the US House of Representatives by gerrymandering. The practice took off as the states used demographic data and known voting patterns to maximize the number of districts favoring the party-in-power.

It has been said of gerrymandering that it allows politicians to select their voters instead of voters selecting their politicians.[8] An article posted on the internet by Kaz Welda of Rantt Media explains the pernicious results:

> Congress enjoys one of the worst approval ratings in America, hovering between 10–15% in any given year. Yet, again and again, incumbents sail through reelection with huge margins of victory. In 2016, only eight incumbents out of the 435 up for reelection lost

their seats. And many won with enormous margins that captured 60–70% of the vote in seemingly lopsided campaign races. It's a clear sign that democracy isn't working across large sections of the country.

America's electoral system has been rigged. Not by the Russians, but by good ole fashioned gerrymandering.[9]

The Welda article included the districting maps of ten states with the highest rates of gerrymandered Congressional districts: North Carolina, Maryland, Pennsylvania, West Virginia, Kentucky, Louisiana, Utah, Texas, Arkansas, and Ohio. A Statista Chart available on the web* shows maps of (1) Maryland's Third District, (2) Texas's Thirty-third District, (3) Illinois's Fourth District, (4) Texas's Thirty-Fifth District, and (5) Louisiana's Second District as "America's Most Gerrymandered Congressional Districts."[10]

Keep in mind when examining the Statista chart that counties within our states are fundamentally compact, contiguous areas bordered by straight lines except where waterways or mountainous terrain require an irregular line. Counties are not required to have roughly equal populations nor are their borders redrawn after each census. But by law the number of residents in a state's congressional districts must be roughly equal. Population densities are only one of several factors determining their borders. Also, gerrymandered voting districts, unlike counties, have lines that, "zig and zag east and west, north, and south and across city, township, and county lines as if for no reason at all. But the political impact is much more significant. Gerrymandering reduces the number of competitive congressional races."[11]

The literature describes the two types of gerrymandering: political or partisan gerrymandering where voting district lines are drawn to give one political party an unfair advantage over its rivals, and racial gerrymandering where the voting district lines are drawn to dilute the voting power of ethnic or linguistic minority groups.[12] Gerrymandering

---

* https://www.statista.com/chart/21313/most-gerrymandered-districts-us/

can occur either where voters of a particular political party preference, ethnic group, or color are "packed" into a single district or where they are broken up, "cracked," across several districts to dilute their voting power.[13]

The Supreme Court has declined to regulate gerrymandering for political purposes (*Rucho v. Common Cause*[14]). However, voting patterns show that black and other minority voters are grouped in or near metropolitan areas and vote predominately for Democratic candidates.* Black voters made up about 11–12%of the population in 2020. In the 2020 presidential election approximately 87–90 percent of black voters voted for Biden, the Democratic candidate.[15] Asian Americans voted for Biden approximately 63 percent of the time.[16] Latino voters in thirteen states supported Biden over Trump by a margin of at least 2 to 1.[17] In urban areas, even if voting districts are gerrymandered to benefit a particular political party, they cover substantially the same geographic areas as would districts gerrymandered for racial discrimination purposes. Amendments to the VRA may require the Court to deal with political gerrymanders that result in racial discrimination. (See below.)

The Supreme Court has considered the validity or invalidity of gerrymandered voting districts under both the Equal Protection Clause of the Fourteenth Amendment and the VRA. Section 2 of the VRA prohibited state governments from adopting voting laws that discriminated against racial or linguistic minorities.[18] Section 5 of the VRA created a "preclearance requirement" which prohibited certain states and other jurisdictions (those with a history of pronounced racial discrimination) from implementing any change affecting voting rights without receiving a "preapproval certification" from either the US Attorney General or the DC District Court that determined the proposed change would not discriminate against protected minorities. Section 4(b) of the VRA set forth a coverage formula to identify those states which had historically engaged in egregious voting discrimination

---

* Voting preferences can shift over time. Hispanic and other minority voters are showing growing support for the Republican Party. Scott Simon interview with Ruy Teixeira, NPR Weekend Edition, July 23, 2022, https://www.npr.org/2022/07/23/1113166779/hispanic-and-minority-voters-are-increasingly-shifting-to-the-republican-party.

against protected minorities and who were required to comply with the preapproval standard. Over the succeeding years, Congress revised the coverage formula in Section 4(b) several times.

Consider again, that in *Wesberry*[19] the Supreme Court defined the one man, one vote rule to mean that one man's vote in a congressional election will be worth as much as another's, and it held that the states must draw congressional districts that contain roughly equal represented populations. Yet Texas sought to maintain gerrymandered voting districts. One national commentator described the result, "the (Texas) congressional districts look more like Rorschach inkblots than representative swaths of real estate, the state's legislative makeup has been impacted by gerrymandering more than any other state, according to a study by the Associated Press."[20]

Texas became the poster child for federal inaction on gerrymandering, involving not only black but also Hispanic and Latino[21] communities, and generated a great deal of litigation in state and federal courts. The 2020 US decennial census reports 29,145,505 total population for Texas with racial and ethnicity as

Black/African American.........................(11.8%)
Hispanic/Latino......................................(39.3%)
Asian...(5.4%)
First Nations...(0.3%)
White..(39.7%)[22]

The thirty-six members of the Texas delegation to the US House of Representatives 117th Congress second session[23] consist of

Black/African American..........5.....(13.9%)
Hispanic/Latino.......................7......(19.4%)
White.....................................24.....(66.7%)
(no First Nations or Asian)
Total.......................................36.....representing 36 Districts[24]

The *Texas Tribune* demographic analysis shows the 2021 Texas Legislature composition as[25]

Race/Ethnicity	2021 Actual	Projected
Black	19......(10.6%)	22......(12.4%)
Hispanic/Latino	46......(25.7%)	72......(40.7%)
Asian	4.........(2.2%)	9..........(5.1%)
White	110......(61.4%)	74........(41.8%)
(no First Nations in analysis)		
Totals	179	177*

These numbers strongly support the claims of Hispanics and Latinos that their votes carry less weight than those of others when Texas chooses representatives. But the VRA, and Supreme Court opinions construing that statute, discarded statewide "proportionality" as controlling in cases where gerrymandered voting districts allegedly discriminated based on race or ethnicity.

The US Supreme Court in *Mobile v. Bolden*,[26] held that Section 2 of the VRA paralleled the language of the Fifteenth Amendment, and that an action by a state that is racially neutral on its face violates the Fifteenth Amendment *only if motivated by a discriminatory purpose*. It also held that the Equal Protection Clause of the Fourteenth Amendment does not require proportional representation.

On June 29, 1982, Congress amended the VRA to overturn *Bolden* and insert a "results test" in Section 2 (b) of the VRA that banned any practice that had `a discriminatory effect* (emphasis added):

> A violation of subsection (a) is established if, based on the totality of circumstances, it is shown that the political processes leading to nomination or election

---

* The Texas Legislature has 181 seats. One seat was vacant at the time of the *Texas Tribune* publication. The reporters could not verify the racial identity of one legislator, and so they used 179 for their 2021 analysis. For their projected scenario based on race and ethnicity proportions, Census data indicated three "other." The projected scenario column thus equals 177 seats.

in the State or political subdivision *are not equally open* (emphasis added) to participation by members of a class of citizens protected by subsection (a) in that its members have less opportunity than other members of the electorate to participate in the political process and to elect representatives of their choice. The extent to which members of a protected class have been elected to office in the State or political subdivision is one circumstance which may be considered: *Provided,* (emphasis in original) That [*sic*] nothing in this section establishes a right to have members of a protected class elected in numbers equal to their proportion in the population.[27]

Four years later, in *Thornburg v. Gingles,*[28] the US Supreme Court held that a claimant making a discriminatory claim based on the "results" test of Section 2 of the VRA must satisfy three preconditions:

1. A geographically compact minority population sufficient to constitute a majority in a single-member district,
2. political cohesion among the members of the minority group, and
3. bloc voting by the majority to defeat the minority's preferred candidate.

In addition to the three preconditions, it held that a Section 2 claimant must also prove that "under the totality of the circumstances," the district lines dilute the votes of the members of the minority group.

For years, Texas was subject to the VRA's Section 5 preclearance requirements. When the US 2010 Census revealed its population increased by four million new residents—many of them of Latino or African American heritage—Texas was granted four additional seats in the US House of Representatives, which required Texas to redraw its congressional districts. It prepared maps to comply with the preclearance requirements and submitted them to the DC District Court as required by the VRA. While preauthorization was pending before the DC District Court, *Perez v. Abbott*,[29] was filed in the US District Court for the Western District of Texas (herein Western District Court) by Texas citizens who asserted the 2011 redistricting maps diluted minority votes in violation of Section 2 of the VRA and the Equal Protection Clause of the Fourteenth Amendment.

Because the DC District Court had not issued preclearance and the 2012 elections were pending, a three-judge panel of the Western District Court approved interim districting plans for that election after extensive hearings. Texas then asked the US Supreme Court to stay the Western District Court's interim plans. The Supreme Court granted the stay in a *per curiam** opinion and noted probable jurisdiction.[30] *Perez* proceeded through the federal courts for the next seven years.

Meanwhile other redistricting decisions were gathering speed in states across the nation. In *Shelby County v. Holder*,[31] the Supreme Court had before it another case involving redistricting maps that followed the 2010 Census, this time from Alabama. That case concerned whether Congress's 2006 reauthorization of Section 5 of the VRA, while the pre-existing coverage formula of Section 4(b) of the VRA remained in effect, exceeded its authority under the Fourteenth and Fifteenth Amendments and thus violated the Tenth Amendment of the US Constitution. *Shelby County* (decided in 2013) struck down the coverage formula in Section 4(b) of the VRA on grounds it relied on old data and was no longer responsive to current conditions. By striking the coverage formula, the Supreme Court effectively disabled Section 5's preclearance requirement. Congress never subsequently amended the VRA's provisions to satisfy the concerns raised by the Supreme Court in *Shelby County*. Accordingly, the refusal of the DC District Court to preauthorize Texas's 2011 districting plans became moot.

Free of the preclearance requirement following *Shelby County*, the Texas Legislature repealed its 2011 maps and enacted new districting maps in 2013 with just a few minor changes. But *Perez v. Abbott*

---

* *per curiam*: adj. opinion by the court as a whole rather than by a single justice and usually without extended discussion.

continued to wend its way through the courts. In 2018, the US Supreme Court's opinion in *Abbott v. Perez*[32] (renamed on appeal to the Supreme Court) by Justice Alito upheld Texas's 2013 redistricting maps except for District 90 near Fort Worth, which Texas conceded constituted an impermissible gerrymander. The court ruled that a presumption of legislative good faith applies in redistricting cases, and held that a discriminatory claim made under Section 2 of the VRA *must satisfy the three preconditions* it had set forth in *Gingles*[33] (above), and also prove that "*under the totality of the circumstances*, the district lines dilute the votes of the members of the minority group."[34] In her dissent, Justice Sotomayor criticized the majority opinion, stating that "years of litigation" and "undeniable proof of intentional discrimination" was shown by the record.[35]

When the dust cleared, the 2011 districting maps for the Texas Legislature and the US House of Representatives remained essentially unchanged. Back at square one.[36]

Following the 2020 Census, Texas adopted new redistricting maps for its state legislature and Congressional districts in the early hours of October 12, 2021. Because of the *Shelby County* and *Abbot* decisions, Texas was no longer required to submit its new redistricting maps for preauthorization approval. Afterward, Ari Berman of *Mother Jones* tweeted, "Democracy (is) quite literally dying in (the) dark."[37]

The governor of Texas, Greg Abbott, signed the new redistricting maps on October 25, 2021, making them available for the 2022 midterm elections.[38] Texas voters and Voto Latino, a grassroots political organization, filed a new lawsuit in the Western District Court on October 25, 2021, alleging violations of Section 2 of the VRA. The complaint asserted that minority districts were reduced from eight to seven and that the voting power of minority communities was diluted

> because it strategically cracks and packs Texas communities of color. Senate Bill 6 particularly dilutes the voting power of Texas's Latino and Black communities to ensure that white Texans, who now make up less than 40 percent of Texas's population,

nevertheless form a majority of eligible voters in more than 60 percent of Texas's congressional districts.[39]

Texas asserted its new plans are blind to race.[40] The Western District Court consolidated multiple redistricting cases (including *Voto Latino*) into *League of United Latin Am. Citizens v. Abbott.*[41] On May 23, 2022, the Western District Court dismissed several of the plaintiffs' claims for lack of standing and held that the plaintiffs lacked organizational, associational, and individual standing to pursue their claims against several congressional districts.[42]

The Fourteenth Amendment states in Section 1, "No State shall make or enforce *any law* (that denies) … to any person within its jurisdiction the equal protection of the laws." (emphasis added) Section 1 of the Fifteenth Amendment is somewhat different. It provides that "The right of citizens of the United States to vote shall not be denied or abridged by the United States or by any State *on account of* race, color, or previous condition of servitude." (emphasis added)

It is significant that both the Fourteenth Amendment and the Fifteenth Amendment provided Congress with the power to enforce those articles by appropriate legislation. Congress attempted to do that in the VRA. Section 2 of the VRA originally covered only intentional discrimination:

> No voting qualification or prerequisite to voting, or standard, practice, or procedure shall be imposed or applied by any State or political subdivision to deny or abridge the right of any citizen of the United States to vote *on account of* race or color[43] (emphasis added).

As shown above, Congress retained intentional discrimination for one group of cases covered by Section 2 of the VRA when it adopted the 1982 amendment, but it also established a "results" test to determine if a given districting map discriminated on the basis of race. The Supreme Court's unwillingness to address so-called political gerrymandering provided state legislatures or districting panels inclined to do so with an easy path to skirt the racial discrimination issue. But the Fourteenth Amendment's Equal Protection Clause doesn't distinguish between political or racial gerrymandering. It states, "any law." Further, the results test adopted by Congress in 1982 destroyed the basis for keeping a judicially created exception for political gerrymandering if it resulted in racial discrimination. The question ought to be whether a gerrymandered voting district (whether politically, intentionally, happenstance, or negligently designed) discriminates against some voters based on race as a matter of fact and denies equal protection of the law.

Common sense dictates that a political party in control of a state's legislature will not incur the expense and work of gerrymandering voting districts unless the result increases the number of its candidates who get elected. By definition, "to gerrymander is to draw the boundaries of electoral districts in an irregular way so as to create an unfair advantage for a particular political party or faction."[44] By gerrymandering their state legislative districts, a political party can use the legislative power gained at the state level to also control the shape and area of US House of Representatives voting districts they redistrict pursuant to Article I Section 2 of the US Constitution. Gerrymandered state legislative districts are not only the highway to political power at the local level; they deliver the votes that place representatives in Congress.

CHAPTER 8

US Supreme Court Decisions on State Racial Gerrymandering—Complex Requirements of Proof and Inconsistent Results

Recent Supreme Court decisions have sown confusion concerning gerrymandering. Wisconsin's experience demonstrates that confusion. In the 2020 presidential election Biden received 1,630,866 (49.4%) of the Wisconsin popular votes and Trump received 1,610,184 (48.8%), which provided a snapshot of the statewide division of the Wisconsin electorate on a political party basis. Yet three Democrats (37.5%) and five Republicans (62.5%) won the state's eight Congressional seats in that same election.[1] Republicans also won a 61-38 majority in the Wisconsin Assembly and a 21-12 advantage in the Wisconsin Senate (a 63.6% majority in both chambers).[2]

The US Supreme Court had developed several tests for finding unlawful gerrymandering and applied them to Wisconsin. The 2020 decennial census revealed that Wisconsin's State Assembly and State Senate districts were no longer equally apportioned, and Wisconsin's legislature adopted new districting maps. Wisconsin's governor vetoed them, referred them to Wisconsin's Supreme Court, and the court invited the parties to submit new maps. The governor argued that the *intentional adoption* of a seventh majority black district was needed to comply with the VRA. In its March 3, 2022, opinion, the Wisconsin Supreme Court concluded "the governor's map complied with the Equal Protection Clause of the Fourteenth Amendment" because there were "good reasons" to think the VRA "may" require the additional majority-Black district. The court selected the Governor's districting maps *which intentionally created seven black state Senate districts*—one more than the previous maps.[3] On application by the Wisconsin State

Legislature, the US Supreme Court overruled the Wisconsin Supreme Court order and remanded for further proceedings in an unsigned *per curiam* opinion.[4] In reversing, the US Supreme Court set forth several rules for determining the validity of redistricting. It reasoned from its previous decisions that state districting maps that sort voters based on race "cannot be upheld *unless they are narrowly tailored to achieving a compelling state interest.*" (Emphasis added.) Compliance with the VRA would be a compelling state interest, but the court went on to say,

> If race is the predominant factor motivating the placement of voters in or out of a district *the State has the burden of showing that the design of the district withstands strict scrutiny* ... and that a state can meet that test by showing its race-based sorting of voters is *narrowly tailored to comply with the VRA*"[5] (emphasis added).

A state can show a violation of the VRA, the Court said,

> If, *based on the totality of circumstances*, it is shown that the political processes leading to nomination or election in the State or political subdivision are not equally open to participation by members of a [minority group] in that its members have less opportunity than other members of the electorate to participate in the political process and to elect representatives of their choice. 52 U.S.C. § 10301(b)[6] (emphasis added).

The Supreme Court recognized that Section 2 of the VRA prohibits the distribution of minority voters into districts in a way that dilutes their voting power citing *Gingles*,[7] and it again quoted the three preconditions for establishing the dilution of voting power set forth in *Gingles*. (See discussion above.)

The Supreme Court said the Wisconsin Court's analysis failed to show the *Gingles* preconditions had been met. Then the Court also said meeting the *Gingles* preconditions was not alone sufficient and that "courts must also examine other evidence in *the totality of circumstances*" (emphasis added) to show a VRA Section 2 violation. Significantly, an additional circumstance to consider the Court said was "whether the number of districts in which the minority group forms an effective majority *is roughly proportional to its share of the population in the relevant area.* (emphasis added)"[8]

The Supreme Court said the governor provided almost no other evidence or analysis for his map to support his claim that the VRA required seven majority-black districts. "Thus in *Cooper* we explained, for example, that "race-based districting is narrowly tailored … if a State had 'good reasons' for thinking that the Act *demanded* such steps.' … (emphasis added)" It cited *Shaw v. Hunt*[9] to say "the institution that makes the racial distinction must have had a strong basis in evidence to conclude that remedial action was necessary, *before it embarks on an affirmative-action program.*"[10] (emphasis added).

The US Supreme Court criticized the Wisconsin Supreme Court for reducing the *Gingles* third precondition *to only a consideration of proportionality.* It cited *Johnson v. DeGrandy* for the proposition that "*lack of proportionality by itself can never prove dilution.*"[11] (emphasis added) The Court quoted: "No single statistic provides courts with a shortcut to determine whether a set of single-member districts unlawfully dilutes minority voting strength." The court also said, "The question that our VRA precedents ask and the (Wisconsin) court failed to answer is *whether a race-neutral* alternative that did not add a seventh majority-black district would deny Black voters equal political opportunity."[12] (emphasis added) The Court did not clarify what it meant by "relevant area", state what a "race-neutral" alternative might consist of, or whether the creation of new white districts must satisfy the same tests.

Justice Sotomayor, joined by Justice Kagan, dissented, stating the Court's order overturning the Wisconsin Supreme Court was based on only a preliminary analysis, and that it faulted the Wisconsin Supreme Court for failure to comply with existing precedent that is "hazy at best."[13]

The Wisconsin Supreme Court in 2023 held Wisconsin's maps unconstitutional and ordered new maps.[14] See discussion of *Moore v. Harper* and *Costello v. Carter* below.

Recently, minority groups asserted it is not enough for a state to claim it established its voting districts in a "race-neutral" manner. They argue that districts should be re-gerrymandered to *maximize* the number of majority-minority districts. On October 4, 2022, Justice Jackson addressed these concerns. She asked counsel for Alabama in two redistricting cases combined for oral arguments before the US Supreme Court to explain why a "race-conscious" effort in redistricting cases would violate the Fourteenth Amendment's Equal Protection Clause. Elaborating on her question, she pointed out that the VRA stated "(all) citizens would have the same civil rights as enjoyed by white citizens."[15]

Texas and Wisconsin are not the only states where redistricting is at issue. The Brennan Center for Justice has a chart with state-by-state profiles depicting litigation over maps drawn after the 2020 Census. "As of October 12, 2022, a total of seventy-two cases have been filed challenging congressional and legislative maps in twenty-six states as racially discriminatory and/or partisan gerrymanders."[16] The *New York Times* noted that Republicans had increased their advantages in state legislatures in swing states like Arizona, Georgia, Michigan, North Carolina, Pennsylvania, and Wisconsin through aggressive gerrymandering.[17] Both Democratic and Republican parties gerrymander their state voting districts, but Republicans have had greater success in gerrymandering Congressional districts than have the Democrats:

> Conditions are ripe when one party controls both of a state's legislative chambers and the governor's office. Republicans have complete control over redistricting process in 20 states, Democrats in 10 states. That gives Republicans unimpeded power to draw 187 House districts, and Democrats 75.[18]

Michigan's recent experience in establishing a nonpartisan commission offers a means to address some of the concerns expressed by the majority in *Wisconsin Legislature*. A Michigan constitutional amendment was adopted by a referendum in 2018 that created the Michigan Independent Citizens Redistricting Commission to overhaul Michigan's congressional and state legislative districts.[19] The amendment set a fairness standard and established seven criteria for drawing congressional and state legislative districts that gave each voter's ballot the same weight[20] It prioritized those criteria as follows:

- Districts shall have roughly equal population as mandated by federal laws including the VRA, and the U.S. Constitution.

- Each district must be geographically contiguous – i.e., one must be able to travel between two addresses in a district without straying outside of it.

- Districts shall reflect the diverse population and communities of interest – voters who share significant characteristics, including cultural histories and economic interests. Communities of interest do not include relationships with political parties, incumbents, or political candidates.

- Districts shall not give a disproportional advantage to any political party. A disproportionate advantage to a political party shall be determined using accepted measures of partisan fairness.

- Districts shall not favor or disfavor a particular incumbent official or candidate.

- Districts shall reflect the Commission's recognition of existing county, city, and township boundaries.

- Districts must be reasonably compact.[21]

When the new Michigan congressional, State House, and State Senate districting maps were approved on December 29, 2021, they were seen as fair, competitive, and a path to undoing gerrymandering.[22] Michigan's new maps have gone into effect despite litigation. On April 1, 2022, the US Court of Appeals for the Sixth Circuit approved Michigan's new congressional districting maps.[23]

Gerrymandering involves the places where citizens register their votes, so it falls within Congress's Article I Section 4 powers to "regulate" the "Places and Manner of holding Elections." Efforts to raise voting rights issues in Congress, confronted by arcane filibuster and cloture rules, have bogged down in the US Senate. On January 4, 2021, Representative John P. Sarbanes (D-Maryland) introduced H.R. 1—the For the People Act of 2021[24]—in the House of Representatives. H.R. 1 was intended to correct some of the flaws in the VRA found by the Supreme Court. If enacted it would have provided

- voter registration, automatic and same day registration, vote by mail and early voting should be expanded;

- the removal of voters from voter rolls should be limited;

- the states should establish independent redistricting commissions to provide for congressional redistricting;

- election security should be improved;

- campaign finance should be regulated;

- ethics rules for all three branches of the federal government should be established, including a code of conduct for Supreme Court Justices, a prohibition on members of the House of Representatives from serving on the boards of for-profit entities, and that conflict of interest and ethics provisions for employees of the White House be established; and

- presidents, vice presidents, and candidates for those offices would be required to disclose ten years of their tax returns.

H.R. 1 was passed by the House of Representatives and sent to the US Senate for approval, but it was never called up for argument or passage by the Senate. Under the Senate's cloture* rules it would take sixty senators to pass it. After the 2020 election (117th Congress), the US Senate was divided 50/50 and H.R. 1 had no Republican support in the Senate.

H.R. 4, the John R. Lewis Voting Rights Advancement Act of 2021,[25] was passed in the House of Representatives on August 24, 2021. That bill sought to reinstate preclearance criteria for states with a history of racially discriminatory voting laws. Senator Amy Klobuchar (D-Minnesota) introduced the Freedom to Vote Act[26] in the US Senate on September 14, 2021. It set forth a list of specific changes to the criteria states use for congressional redistricting to prevent favoring or disfavoring of political parties. The act would also establish standards for federal courts to use in deciding redistricting litigation.[27] Regrettably, H.R. 1, H.R. 4, and S. 2747 did not move forward in the Senate. When brought up for a vote, the Democrats sought to amend the Senate's cloture rules to require a *speaking* filibuster and thus a simple majority vote. The motion failed. (See discussion in Chapter 9 section B.) The bills died after the 2022 midterm elections resulted in the 118th Congress. Representatives Rick Larsen (D-Washington) and Marc Veasey (D-Texas) reintroduced the America Votes Act of 2023 (H.R. 861).[28] It would permit voters to present a sworn statement to meet ID requirements in order to vote. They had originally included it in the For the People Act of 2021. So far, no action has been taken. No other means of controlling gerrymandering or other state restrictions

---

* Prior to 1917, the Senate rules had no way to end debate and force a vote on a measure. In 1917, the Senate adopted a rule to allow a two-thirds majority vote to end a filibuster, known as cloture. See the next chapter section B for a fuller discussion of cloture and filibuster.

on voting rights is now being pursued on the federal level. The 2022 midterm became the "Wounded Knee"* of voting rights for minorities.

Moore v. Harper,[29] a North Carolina redistricting case, and *Costello v. Carter*[30] (congressional redistricting in Pennsylvania) raised an issue known as the "independent state legislature doctrine." They asked the US Supreme Court to decide whether a state's judicial branch may nullify regulations and redistricting maps governing the "Manner of holding Elections for Senators and Representatives … prescribed … by the (state) Legislature thereof" as set forth in Article I Section 4 clause 1 of the US Constitution (here the Elections Clause), and replace them with regulations or districting maps created by the state courts or by appointed commissions. If the court adopted this interpretation of the Election Clause, it would have potentially curtailed plans for court redistricting as employed in Wisconsin, independent redistricting commissions as prescribed in Michigan, as well as the independent commissions proposed in federal statutes like the Sarbanes For the People Act (H.R. 1). As a practical matter, the adoption of the independent state legislature doctrine would further cripple efforts to rein in gerrymandering, undercut the one man, one vote doctrine the court approved in *Reynolds*[31] and *Wesberry,*[32] and impede efforts to reinstate the VRA.

In 2023, in *Moore,*[33] the Supreme Court reaffirmed the power of our courts to rein in a state legislature's power to create racially inspired gerrymandered legislative districts. Noting jurisdiction under Article III, Chief Justice Roberts wrote for the majority, "We hold only that state courts may not transgress the ordinary bounds of judicial review such that they arrogate to themselves the power vested in state legislatures to regulate federal elections."[34] The opinion authorized state courts to control racial gerrymandering if state law permitted it. While legal scholars said *Moore* prevented a future state legislature

---

* Wounded Knee: The site of two conflicts between First Peoples and representatives of the US government. An 1890 massacre left 150 Sioux dead in a clash with federal troops. In 1973, members of the American Indian Movement (AIM) occupied Wounded Knee for seventy-one days to protest conditions on the Pine Ridge Indian Reservation (South Dakota).

from overriding Article II, Section 1 of the Constitution, concerning presidential electors, that issue was not decided.

Principles from the 1960s concerning equal protection and "one man one vote" are still with us, but are subject to extensive judicial review. There are encouraging signs as well as discouraging developments. Gerrymandered redistricting maps have been set aside in some states, such as Alabama's in *Allen v. Milligan*, where the US Supreme Court held that Alabama's new districts "likely" violated the VRA, maintained an injunction requiring a new majority-minority district, and found Section 2 of the VRA to be constitutional.[35] Yet after litigation in the federal courts, other states such as South Carolina may keep their gerrymandered maps.[36] A liberal justice elected to Wisconsin's Supreme Court was threatened with impeachment by Republicans fearful their maps were at risk.[37]

The Supreme Court's redistricting jurisprudence did not separate racial from political gerrymandering nor are its stringent proof requirements applied consistently. But it did stir up partisanship. How heavily may the states rely on racial metrics? How can they apply them equally to *all* proposed districts? Notwithstanding *Allen v. Milligan* above, the Federal Court of Appeals for the Eighth Circuit ruled that only the federal government can sue under the VRA's Section 2.[38] What does that ruling mean for cases brought by private litigants already on the books and those to come? It's time for Congress to use its Article I, Section 4 powers, clear up the confusion, and legislate standards.

CHAPTER 9

Nationwide Threats to the Right to Vote After January 6—a Threat to Government of, by and for the People

For want of a Nail the Shoe was lost; for want of a Shoe the Horse was lost; and for want of a horse the Rider was lost, being overtaken and slain by the Enemy, all for want of Care about a Horse-shoe Nail.
—Benjamin Franklin (as Richard Saunders)

The one man, one vote principle confirmed that the right to vote for our elected officials on an equal basis is fundamental to the survival of our republic. But the principle has fallen by the wayside—eroded by political forces such as gerrymandering (discussed in Chapters 7 and 8). This chapter will discuss three other grave challenges.

A. Voting restrictions enacted at the state level will suppress the right to vote.

Following the dissension leading to the insurrection of January 6, 2021, the Republican Party, frustrated in its efforts to retain Donald Trump as president, instituted a nationwide program to change state election laws. These new laws go beyond gerrymandering and regulate not only voting itself but also voter registration and voter rolls, methods, times, and locations of voting, and the manner of counting votes. The Brennan Center for Justice has been tracking state voting-related legislation across the country and publishing their findings in a series of reports. Their "Voting Laws Roundup: June 2023" report states

> The total of 13 restrictive laws enacted so far this year surpasses the total number of restrictive laws enacted in any year in the last decade except 2021.

> Overall, at least 322 restrictive bills were introduced in 45 states. Of these, 35 bills are still moving through 10 state legislatures.[1]

The Brennan Center published an article on January 31, 2022, that described new voter suppression laws in five states (Florida, Georgia, Iowa, Texas, Montana, and Texas) as "death by a thousand cuts."[2] These new laws imposed regulations concerning voter ID, voting by mail, resource allocation at polling places, voter roll maintenance, and other election practices.

For example, Governor Brian Kemp of Georgia signed the Election Integrity Act of 2021,[3] originally known as Georgia Senate Bill 202, on March 25, 2021. It contained a wish list of voting restrictions that

- prohibit mailing unsolicited ballot applications;

- reduce time to request absentee ballots and return them by half;

- reduce time for mailing out absentee ballots to four weeks prior to elections;

- prohibit mobile voting buses (purchased in Fulton County to help with long lines);

- impose strict voter identification requirements;

- place new caps on the number of authorized drop boxes;

- prohibit anyone other than a poll worker to offer food or water to voters standing in line to vote;

- prohibit elections offices from receiving direct grants or donations;

- prohibit the count of out-of-precinct ballots ("wrong polling place") cast unless they meet strict criteria;

- impose a reported daily count (but not tabulation of votes) of absentee ballots issued, received, accepted, or rejected, including a count of in-person early voters;

- impose a reported count of all ballots cast (early, absentee, provisional, and in-person) by 10:00 p.m. on election night; and

- impose a tabulation deadline of all votes by 5:00 p.m. the following day along with changes to local elections offices, procedures for resolving long lines and wait times to vote, voting equipment, and training and placement of poll watchers.[4]

The *New York Times* published an analysis of Georgia's new voting law, which, in addition to the changes noted above, expanded early voting in many small counties but probably not in populous counties, made it more difficult to extend voting hours if problems arose, and added a mix of additional changes to vote-counting procedures.[5]

That act also provided for the removal of Georgia's Secretary of State from the State Election Board and the replacement of him or her with a new nonpartisan member selected by a majority of Georgia's Republican-controlled legislature. It also permitted the removal of "underperforming" county election officials and their replacement with a single individual.[6] Recall that Trump had asked Georgia's Secretary of State, Brad Raffensperger, to "find" him enough votes to put him ahead of Biden and that Raffensperger refused.[7] It is not unreasonable to conclude that next time the losing candidate will have his man in Raffensperger's chair.

In early February 2021, a Brennan Center for Justice Voting Laws Roundup Report stated

In a backlash to historic voter turnout in the 2020 general election and grounded in a rash of baseless and racist allegations of voter fraud and election irregularities, legislators have introduced well over four times the number of bills to restrict voting access as compared to roughly this time last year.

Thus far this year, thirty-three states have introduced, prefiled or carried over 165 bills to restrict voting access. These proposals primarily seek to: (1) limit mail voting access; (2) impose stricter voter ID requirements; (3) slash voter registration opportunities; and (4) enable more aggressive voter roll purges. These bills are an unmistakable response to the unfounded and dangerous lies about fraud that followed the 2020 election.[8]

On December 21, 2021, the Brennan Center for Justice issued an updated report:

Between January 1 and December 7, at least 19 states passed 34 laws restricting access to voting. More than 440 bills with provisions that restrict voting access have been introduced in 49 states in the 2021 legislative sessions... state legislatures enacted far more restrictive voting laws in 2021 than in any year since the Brennan Center began tracking voting legislation in 2011...at least 13 bills restricting access to voting have been pre-filed for the 2022 legislative session in four states. In addition, at least 152 restrictive voting bills in 18 states will carry over from 2021.[9]

Charles M. Blow, an Opinion columnist for the *New York Times*, stated in an editorial published in the *New York Times* on March 1, 2021, "This is an electoral fleecing in plain sight, one targeting people of color."[10]

Amid the many state laws to restrict voting rights introduced, the US Supreme Court released its opinion in *Brnovich v. Democratic National Committee* on July 1, 2021.[11] Arizona had been one of the states subject to the VRA's preclearance requirements. *Brnovich* involved two Arizona statutes. One enacted in 1970 required the disposal of ballots cast in the wrong precinct.[12] The other statute made it a felony for anyone other than a postal worker, an election official or a voter's caregiver, family member, or household member to knowingly collect an early ballot.[13] The Democratic National Committee filed suit (*Brnovich*) alleging that the two statutes had an adverse and disparate effect on Arizona's First Nations, Hispanic, and African American citizens in violation of Section 2 of the VRA and the First and Fifteenth Amendments. Plaintiffs asserted that the legislation purposely discriminated against minority voters by making it "particularly burdensome" for voters in counties with large minority populations to vote since they had fewer voting locations.[14]

The US District Court for the District of Arizona (herein Arizona District Court) rejected the plaintiff's claims, but the Ninth Circuit sitting *en banc** held that both the out-of-precinct policy and the ballot collection restriction of Arizona's statutes violated the "results test" of Section 2 of the VRA and imposed a disparate burden on ethnic minority voters. The *en banc* court, citing *Gingles*,[15] also held that the Arizona District Court had committed reversible error in finding that the ballot collection statute was not enacted with discriminatory intent. It found that in the 2016 election, minority groups were more than twice as likely to vote out of precinct as did white voters, and that white voters were four times more likely to have home mail delivery and pickup compared to minority groups.

The Supreme Court held in *Brnovich* that neither of the two Arizona statutes violated Section 2 of the VRA, and that the ballot collection

---

* *En banc*: French for "on the bench." All judges in an appellate court jurisdiction sit to review a case, as opposed to sitting in three-judge panels, where the case is significant or parties in the case have requested it.

restriction was not enacted with a racially discriminatory intent. The court explained that Section 2 is violated only

> where "the political processes leading to nomination or election" are not "*equally open* to participation" by members of the relevant protected group "*in that its members have less opportunity* than other members of the electorate to participate in the political process and to elect representatives of their choice."[16] (emphasis in original).

The Court said, "Mere inconvenience is insufficient." It also said, "In light of the modest burdens allegedly imposed by Arizona's out-of-precinct voting policy, the small size of its disparate impact, and the State's justifications, we conclude that the rule does not violate Section 2 of the VRA."[17]

Justice Kagan, in a forty-one-page dissent, joined by Justices Breyer and Sotomayor, wrote, "What is tragic is that the court has damaged a statute designed to bring about 'the end of discrimination in voting.'"[18]

President Biden commented, "In a span of just eight years, the court has now done severe damage to two of the most important provisions of the Voting Rights Act of 1965."[19]

An article in the *Detroit Free Press* on October 19, 2021, had this alarming paragraph: "The appointment of new canvassers across Michigan comes at a time of growing concern that partisans at the local level could derail the election certification process."[20]

B. US Senate filibuster and cloture rules prevent the voices of the people from being heard equally.

Recall again that Article I, Section 4 of the Constitution gave Congress the power to override discriminatory state election laws. Also recall that under current practices and rules in the US Senate, forty-one senators can block legislation.

The Constitution requires a two-thirds vote on some issues: impeachment, expelling a member, overriding a presidential veto, ratifying treaties, and for constitutional amendments. Aside from those provisions: "Each House may determine the Rules of its Proceedings, punish its Members for disorderly Behavior*, and, with the concurrence of two thirds, expel a Member."[21]

Both the House and Senate rulebooks originally provided for a motion known as the previous question motion. The House retained that motion and allows its use today, but the Senate removed it from its books in 1806. When the previous question is moved in the House, it cuts off debate on the bill then before the House and brings it up before the entire House for an up or down vote. That is not allowed in the Senate.[22]

The tactic of using long speeches to delay action on legislation started in the first session of the Senate. On September 22, 1789, Pennsylvania Senator William Maclay wrote in his diary that the "design of the Virginians ... was to talk away the time so that we could not get the bill passed."[23] "Talking a bill to death" became common enough to get its own term "filibuster" by the 1850s. The term is coined from a Dutch word for "freebooter" and the Spanish "filibusteros" (to describe the pirates then raiding Caribbean islands). One of the first filibusters took place in the Senate in 1837. President Andrew Jackson had been censured by the Senate and sought to remove the resolution censuring him. The Whigs filibustered to prevent the expungement of the censure.[24]

Later, in response to growing frustration, the Senate passed Rule 22 to allow cloture motions to kill off a filibuster and end debate.[25] That started accidentally in 1917 when one was used to defeat a bill to allow the arming of merchant ships† during World War I.[26] Originally,

---

* Spelling per the National Archives transcription of the US Constitution: https://www.archives.gov/founding-docs/constitution-transcript. Other transcriptions often modernize the archaic spellings originally used.

† Merchant ship, merchant vessel, trading vessel, or merchantman: a watercraft that transports cargo or carries passengers for hire. Contrast with pleasure craft used for personal recreation and naval ships used for military purposes.

Senate cloture rules required a vote by two thirds *of the senators voting* to end debate. When the Treaty of Versailles (to create the League of Nations) came before the Senate in 1919, it was rejected due to a failed cloture vote.[27]

Huey Long and other Southern Democrats employed the filibuster tactic on numerous occasions. As originally practiced, the Senators engaged in a filibuster would read whatever was handy to hold the floor of the Senate. While they read Shakespeare, telephone directories, and even recipes into the record, absent a successful cloture motion, no other business could come before the Senate. A bill before the Senate in 1946 to prevent discrimination in the workplace by creating a permanent Fair Employment Practice Committee died when a cloture vote to end a filibuster failed and the bill was removed.[28]

In 1949 the Senate amended its rules to say that a vote to invoke cloture required two thirds *of the entire Senate*, not just of those voting. That meant sixty-four senators were required to close debate and bring a bill up for a vote since Alaska and Hawaii had not yet attained statehood. Strom Thurmond set a record while objecting to the adoption of the Civil Rights Act of 1957.[29] Thurmond filibustered for twenty-four hours and eighteen minutes.[30] Although the act passed, its impact was limited due to compromises needed for passage.

In 1959 Majority Leader Lyndon Johnson restored the cloture rule that required only two thirds *of those voting* to end debate. A seventy-five-hour filibuster by Southern Senators against the Civil rights Act of 1964 failed when the Senate invoked cloture. A "Two Track" system adopted in the 1960s allowed the Senate to have more than one item of business on the floor at the same time as another means of preventing a filibuster from shutting down other business.

In 1975 the Senate changed the cloture rule again so that three fifths of "sworn senators" (sixty votes out of a hundred) could limit debate. The latter became known as the sixty-vote supermajority requirement.[31]

There are exceptions. The nuclear option involves "changing the Senate rules to lower the threshold needed for judicial nominees to a simple majority. It is viewed as such a dramatic step in the procedural arms race that it's been likened to nuclear warfare."[32] To invoke the nuclear option, the majority leader raises a point of order, the presiding officer denies the point of order, and the ruling of the chair is appealed and overruled by a simple majority vote. Other exceptions to filibuster rules include budget reconciliation, "Fast Track" authority to negotiate trade agreements, congressional review of executive position appointments, national emergencies, and War Powers Resolutions to authorize or withdraw troops from overseas.[33]

Under its current filibuster/cloture rules it takes 60 percent of all the senators' votes to pass most legislation that comes before the Senate. Thus, forty-one (out of one hundred) senators can block most legislation without appearing on the floor of the Senate or giving one word of debate. As discussed in Chapter 8, three voting rights bills introduced in 2021 (two in the House and one in the Senate) died when they failed to pass before the 117th Congress ended. None of these bills could muster the sixty votes needed to get past a filibuster or cloture vote to advance.[34]

On January 19, 2022, the Democrats brought a bill to the Senate floor that combined H.R. 4 and S 2747 for an up or down vote. To avoid the imposition of the Senate's filibuster/cloture rules the Democrats used the nuclear option described above for the combined bill. The motion to amend asked that the combined bill be debated on the floor for not more than two hours by each senator who chose to do so, after which the combined bill would become law if a simple majority of all senators voted in favor of it. The motion to amend failed 52-48 when two Democratic senators voted no. Senate Democrats also failed to break the filibuster on the combined bill by a vote of 49-51. Senate Majority Leader Chuck Schumer changed his vote to no before the vote was gaveled so that he could offer a motion to reconsider the vote.[35]

Critically, the Klobuchar Bill would have addressed the Supreme Court's refusal to regulate political gerrymanders on the grounds there were no legislated standards, by establishing guidelines for the federal courts to follow where a state has gerrymandered its voting districts. But the Klobuchar Bill, like the others, never made it to committee let alone the floor of the Senate.

Bottom line with respect to voting rights:

- Notwithstanding express powers granted to Congress to do so by Article I, Section 4, and Amendments XIII, XIV, and XV, the VRA of 1965, watered down by Supreme Court decisions, has not been amended or reenacted.

- The Senate's filibuster/cloture rules theoretically grant sixty senators representing only 27 percent of the US population power to block voting rights legislation that comes before the Senate.[36]

- The de facto fifty-fifty party affiliation split in the Senate also prevents consideration of proposals like Senator Klobuchar's, let alone passage, of voting rights and election procedure legislation.

- Gerrymandered state legislative and congressional voting districts and state voter suppression laws remain in place, and in many locations grow worse.

- The will of most Americans who support voting rights protection has been frustrated because the stalemate in the US Congress thwarts needed legislation.

C. Death and physical threats made against members of Congress based on how they vote on legislation and against local and state election officials and their families challenge the right to freely vote.

Trump supporters and far-right groups have forced representatives and their families to relocate and take precautions for their safety. They must remain accessible to their constituents while dealing with death threats and physical intimidation for doing their jobs. For example, Representative Norma Torres (D-California) received an anonymous video of someone following her car. It featured a nine-millimeter handgun on the seat as a male voice says: "I see you. I got something for you." After the January 6 insurrection, Capitol Police recorded over 4,135 threats against members of Congress in 2021.[37]

The nation over the years has relied on the staffs of state and local election officials to conduct our elections and accurately report the results in a professional manner. Until "The Big Lie," there has never been any significant claim that our elections were permeated with fraud or corruption. But reports of death threats and threats of personal injury to state election officials are increasing. Reuters has identified "more than one hundred threats of death or violence made to US election workers and officials, part of an unprecedented campaign of intimidation inspired by Trump's false claims that the 2020 election was stolen. The response so far: only four known arrests and no convictions."[38] Recall the Select Committee hearing testimony of Ms. Moss and her mother Ms. Freeman in Chapter 5 (Fourth Hearing). For example, workers in the Nevada Secretary of State's office received phone calls that that they were "going to f—— die." One worker documented the threats and alerted police, who identified and interviewed the caller. But detectives said there was nothing they could do—the man had committed no crime.[39]

The Detroit Department of Elections ballot counting staff had to deal with obstreperous protesters interfering with counting procedures at the TCF Convention Center. One observer noted "things came to a fever pitch when challengers chanted stop the vote, and at some points on Wednesday, people challenged every single vote at some election workers' tables."[40] The workers taped cardboard onto windows to stop illegal videotaping of the counting.[41]

The Republican National Committee (RNC) planned to have election integrity directors in 15 battleground states to recruit thousands of poll workers and watchers for the 2024 election. The RNC's army of workers were there to monitor voting, vote counting and certification.[42] Unscrupulous, unsubstantiated claims of election fraud or irregularities must be prosecuted just as proven election interference and fraud must be. This is not something to sweep under the rug. Stressed out election workers are resigning in droves from intimidation and harassment when we need their experience and expertise more than ever. It's time we protect our election officials and thoroughly investigate threats to their lives, families, and careers. Our right to vote in fair and open elections depends on it. The time for Congress "to make or alter" state voting regulations under Article I, Section 4 is now.

Not next year. *Now.*

CHAPTER 10

Oaths by Our Leaders to Defend the Constitution and Faithfully Perform their Duties—an Essential Pillar of Our Republic

Before a president begins execution of the office, he or she swears or affirms "that I will faithfully execute the Office of President of the United States, and will to the best of my Ability, preserve, protect and defend the Constitution of the United States."[1]

The oath our presidents take with their hand on a Bible held by their spouse is not a photo op formality. It is a contract with the American people made in response to words recited by the chief justice of the United States that are spelled out in the Constitution. It is a pledge given in exchange that if entrusted with the powers of the presidency, the president-elect will defend and protect the Constitution and faithfully perform the duties of the office. It is the moment when the power to execute the laws of the United States passes from one president to the next. When a president goes rogue, they break their oath and contract with the American people.

President Trump took that oath on January 20, 2017. News articles and pundits asserted that if not by his actions prior to January 6, 2021, Trump's militant speech that day inciting a rally of supporters to march to the Capitol and "fight like hell,"[2] broke his oath of office. With a Constitutional procedure under way at the Capitol before a joint session of Congress, he didn't safeguard that procedure, the government officers following that procedure, or defend the Constitution.

According to testimony taken by the Select Committee, after inciting the mob to march on the Capitol, he watched the ensuing riot unfold on television back at the White House. (See Chapter 5 Eighth Hearing.)

He ignored all recommendations from his staff and others to take action to stop the riot at the Capitol. (See Chapter 5 Sixth and Eighth Hearings.)

As the violence at the Capitol grew worse and a mock gallows was raised to hang the vice president, he did and said *nothing* to aid the officials and staff assembled there or the law enforcement personnel tasked with defending them. (See Chapter 5 First and Eighth Hearings.)

He didn't explore whether any powers (military or otherwise) vested in him as chief executive gave him the means to quell the riot and ensure that the laws of the United States were faithfully executed under Article II, Section 3.

When he finally did ask his followers to leave the Capitol very late that afternoon, they left, demonstrating he could have tried to stop the riot earlier.

Except for Richard Nixon's actions during the Watergate scandal, no comparable breach of the presidential oath has ever occurred.

Former Vice President Mike Pence, on the other hand, did honor his oath to protect the Constitution that night by certifying the election results and refusing to interfere. He called for military assistance to quell the riot, secure the Capitol, and protect the certification process.

> On Jan. 6, I said that I believe there were irregularities about which I was concerned, and I wanted them to have a fair hearing before the Congress, but from the founding of this nation forward, it's been well established that elections are to be governed at the state level and that the only role that Congress has is to open and count the electoral votes that are submitted by states across the country, no more, no less than that,[3]

Oaths are fundamental. The enormous powers entrusted to the president when he or she takes the oath are set forth in Article II of the Constitution. The president then becomes the commander in chief of the military, the official who signs into law or vetoes legislation enacted by Congress, the treaty negotiator with foreign nations, and the grantor of pardons and reprieves. Federal officials in all three branches and state officials down to local officials* "shall be bound by Oath or Affirmation to support the United States Constitution."[4]

When the US Senate sits to try impeachment cases, "they shall be on Oath or Affirmation."[5] The oath the President Pro Tempore Patrick J. Leahy took and then administered to all one hundred senators in the 2021 impeachment trial of former President Donald Trump read,

> Do you solemnly swear that in all things appertaining to the trial of the impeachment of Donald John Trump, former president of the United States, now pending, you will do impartial justice according to the Constitution and laws, so help you God?[6]

All the senators attending recited the oath and signed the log attesting to their oath on national television.

At the first impeachment trial of President Trump in January 2020, Senator Mitt Romney (R-Utah) publicly announced that his religion defined who he was, that he took his oath seriously, and that upon considering the evidence and law presented, he found the president to be guilty of the charges contained in the first Article of Impeachment (abuse of power), which meant he would vote to find him ineligible to hold or seek federal office. Senator Romney (who was nominated as the presidential candidate by his party in 2012) was quickly castigated by fellow Republicans and threatened with expulsion.[7] Later, after President Trump was acquitted, witnesses who testified under oath during the investigations that led to the Articles of Impeachment, resigned under duress, were removed from office, or were demoted by the President.

---

* This text is commonly used: I, _____, do solemnly swear [or affirm] that I will support the Constitution of the United States and the Constitution and laws of the State of Washington, and all local ordinances, and that I will faithfully and impartially perform and discharge the duties of the office of _____, according to the law and the best of my ability.
https://mrsc.org/stay-informed/mrsc-insight/december-2019-1/ the-oath-of-office-for-local-elected-officials.

One, a decorated military combat veteran and the top Ukraine policy officer on the National Security Council, was marched out of the White House by armed guards.[8]

Oaths are fundamental to the administration of justice. Not only are justices and judges required to take an oath to support the Constitution, but oaths are administered to jurors called to service in our courts. Witnesses signing affidavits of fact are required to swear or affirm before a notary public that the facts stated in their affidavit are true to the best of their knowledge and belief. A court will not accept an affidavit not so signed—it is a nullity.* One signing a false affidavit is subject to the contempt power of the court, which can mean fines or jail time. Witnesses called to testify in our courts are sworn in open court by the clerk of the court to tell the truth, the whole truth, and nothing but the truth.

We assume that when one gives or signs an oath, he or she intends to act pursuant to the oath—that they will keep and defend it, no matter whether their hand rests on a Bible, Qur'an (Keith Ellison, D-Minnesota), Bhagavad-Gita (Tulsi Gabbard, D-Hawaii), or an official copy of the Constitution.[9] Their oaths are the *only* assurance voters receive that their elected officials will faithfully execute the trust placed in them pursuant to the Constitution. Our right to rely on the oaths of our public officials includes a right to insist that their word is their bond, and that they will conduct the affairs of government with decency, civility, honesty, and trust. If we can't rely on their oaths, what can we rely on? If our elected and appointed officials are not held to their oaths, we lose the entire ethical foundation on which our Constitution and our Republic rests, and government of, by and for the people collapses.

Our courts hold jurors and witnesses in contempt for violating their oaths, and attorneys may be disbarred for violating theirs, but *the Constitution* does not provide a remedy for the violation of an oath taken by a public official. Except for impeachment for the commission

---

* nullity (n. pl.): -ties (1) the quality or state of being null or (2) an act, proceeding, or contract void of legal effect.

of high crimes and misdemeanors (Article II Section 4) or removal from office for engagement in "insurrection or rebellion against (the United States)" (Amendment XIV Section 3), the Constitution does not set forth specific remedies to cure violations of an office holder's oath.

Section 3 of the Fourteenth Amendment, which provides remedies for the violation of oaths of office by federal and state legislators and officeholders, has been rarely used. As pertinent here, Section 3 provides as follows:

> No person shall be a Senator or Representative in Congress, or elector of President and Vice-President, or hold any office, civil or military, under the United States, or under any State, who, having previously taken an oath, as a member of Congress, or as an officer of the United States, or as a member of any State legislature, or as an executive or judicial officer of any State, to support the Constitution of the United States, *shall have engaged in insurrection or rebellion against the same, or given aid or comfort to the enemies thereof.* But Congress may by a vote of two-thirds of each House, remove such disability (emphasis added).

Many issues have emerged concerning Section 3's enforceability. Who gets to decide and what constitutes engagement in insurrection or rebellion are among them.[10] During Reconstruction after the Civil War, Section 3 was intended to remove officials linked to the Confederacy. But enforcement has been plagued by political concerns. Jefferson Davis, the president of the Confederacy, was unsuccessfully pursued for years under Section 3.[11]

In August 2023, Professor Tribe and Judge Luttig wrote that Trump's efforts to set aside the 2020 election disqualify him from seeking the presidency. They stated that Amendment XIV, Section 3

> automatically excludes from future office and position of power in the United States government—and also

> from any equivalent office and position of power in
> the sovereign states and their subdivisions—any person
> who has taken an oath to support and defend our
> Constitution and thereafter rebels against that sacred
> charter, either through overt insurrection or by giving
> aid or comfort to the Constitution's enemies.[12]

But does Section 3 apply. It doesn't list presidents. It does bar, among others, "officers of the United States" who, having taken an oath to support the constitution, "engaged in insurrection or rebellion against the same or given aid or comfort to the enemies thereof." But even if January 6 and surrounding events are held to constitute insurrection or rebellion, is the president an "officer?"[13] Several states are reviewing Trump's ballot eligibility. The US Supreme Court has not ruled on the issue.[14] But it should be noted that Section 3 specifies senators, representatives, and presidential electors—none of whom are considered executive officers of the United States. They are legislative or limited to elections. By including civil and military office holders, Section 3 expands the list of disqualified persons to a large number of "officers." Section 3 does not exempt the president, and the president is both chief executive officer of the United States and commander in chief of its military forces. Those holding command positions in the military are commonly understood to be officers.

Recently, a New Mexico District Court judge used Section 3 to remove Couy Griffin, a cofounder of Cowboys for Trump,[15] from his post and barred him *for life* from public office for participating in an insurrection after taking his oath as commissioner of New Mexico's Otero County.[16] Griffin, having taken an oath to support the Constitution, was earlier convicted in the DC District Court of breaching the grounds of the US Capitol during the January 6 attack. He was the second defendant to stand trial for participation in that attack.[17] No similar ruling barring a public official from office had been made for over a hundred years.[18]

Efforts to disqualify several members of Congress based on allegations they participated in the January 6 attack have failed.[19] As discussed in Chapter 4, the special counsel's August 1, 2023, indictment charged Trump and others with conspiracy but not with insurrection. Legislation introduced in Congress to declare the January 6 attack an insurrection and to facilitate civil suits to enforce oaths of office, died when the 117th Congress ended.[20] Moreover, not all acts or omissions that breach an officeholder's oath of office involve insurrection or rebellion. Breach of the duty to faithfully perform is among them. Given the nation's spotty history with enforcing Section 3, legislation is needed to broaden its coverage and provide effective enforcement, although that is unlikely in the current Congress.

The U.S.C. does provide specific remedies for the violation of an oath of office given by defined officers and employees in certain cases. U.S.C. Title 5 (Government Organization and Employees) provides that "an individual, *except* the president" (emphasis added) who has been elected or appointed to an office of honor or profit in the civil service or uniformed services of the United States shall take an oath to support the Constitution, "against all enemies foreign and domestic" and to "faithfully discharge the duties" of their office.[21] In a separate section (5 U.S.C. § 3333), Title 5 also provides that an individual who accepts an office *or employment* in the US government or the District of Columbia shall execute an affidavit that their acceptance or holding of the office or employment will not violate 5 U.S.C. § 7311. That section prohibits an individual from accepting or holding a position in the US Government if they advocate "the overthrow of our constitutional form of government … or are a member of an organization that he knows advocates its overthrow."[22] 18 U.S.C. § 1918, a criminal provision, provides that one who violates Section 7311 "shall be fined under this title or imprisoned for not more than one year and a day, or both."[23]

No provisions found in the U.S.C. provide a specific remedy for violations of the presidential oath unless the word *individual* in 5 U.S.C. §§ 3333 and 7311 is somehow construed to include the president. But the language of 5 U.S.C. § 3331 expressly excepts the president from the definition of "An individual" required to take the following oath or affirmation:

I, AB, do solemnly swear (or affirm) *that I will support and defend the Constitution of the United States* against all enemies, foreign and domestic; that I will bear true faith and allegiance to the same; that I take this obligation freely, without any mental reservation or purpose of evasion; and that I will well and faithfully discharge the duties of the office on which I am about to enter. So help me God[24] (emphasis added).

Some ambiguity may arise from 5 U.S.C. § 3333, which though headed "employee affidavit" requires that *an individual* (emphasis added) who accepts an office or employment must submit an affidavit that their acceptance or their holding of an office or employment will not violate 5 U.S.C. § 7311. While Sections 3333 and 7311 do not expressly except the president from submitting such an affidavit, 5 U.S.C. § 2104 defines the word *officer* as one required to be appointed into the civil service by the president or other specifically described officials and who is subject to their authority. 5 U.S.C. § 2105 defines an *employee* as one similarly appointed and supervised. Under these two definitions the president is neither an "officer" nor an "employee" for purposes of Title 5 and at least facially would not be subject to the remedies in Sections 3333 or 7311. Thus, Title 5 does not supply additional remedies for violations of the presidential oath.

As pointed out in Chapter 5 above, the Select Committee found President Trump broke his oath to faithfully execute the laws of the United States when he sat watching televised accounts of the riot of January 6, 2021, and took no action to call in military or police forces to quell the riot or even tweet or otherwise notify his supporters to stop the violence until late in the afternoon. A president can be impeached for the commission of high crimes and misdemeanors and, if Section 3 of the Fourteenth Amendment applies, removed from office for engaging in insurrection or rebellion. There is no comparable remedy for a violation of his or her oath to faithfully perform the duties of their office other than the ballot box.

There ought to be one.

CHAPTER 11

A Cornucopia of Cherished Freedoms—Basic Inalienable Rights that Could Be Lost

Our Declaration of Independence declared that governments are "instituted among men" to "secure" our inalienable rights. There are two concepts imbedded in that statement: the existence of inalienable rights, and the need for a government that will enforce them. The Constitution was ratified to secure both. It established the many rights and liberties described below that our citizens now enjoy. The first inalienable right listed in the Declaration of Independence is the right to life. As shown by the following, our Constitution protects that right in numerous ways.

Authoritarian regimes remove dissidents or those they deem undesirable by execution or brutal imprisonment. For example, upon assuming power in Germany, Hitler's Nazis embarked on a crusade to eliminate the Jewish population from Germany and occupied territory—"the final solution to the Jewish problem." During Kristallnacht,* approximately 7,500 Jewish-owned businesses, homes, and schools were plundered, and ninety-one Jews were murdered. 30,000 Jewish men were arrested and sent to concentration camps.[1]

The Nazis confiscated art works, investments, and other property belonging to Jewish citizens without notice or compensation. Jewish citizens were barred from positions in the arts, professions, and academia. The Roma and Sinti peoples† suffered similar fates as the other main

---

* "Crystal Night," or "The Night of Broken Glass," refers to the thousands of shattered windows that littered the streets afterward.

† Often called Gypsies, the Roma and Sinti have advocated the term *genocide* for their experience during WW2 under the Nazis. For further information, see "Genocide, Holocaust, Porajmos, Samudaripen," https://www.romarchive.eu/en/voices-of-the-victims/genocide-holocaust-porajmos-samudaripen/.

group singled out for extermination."[2] Trains transported the victims in cattle cars to concentration camps where on arrival, identifying numbers were tattooed onto their arms, and they were assessed for survival or execution. The survivors were used as slave labor and in medical experiments. When General Dwight D. Eisenhower discovered the concentration camps during WW2 and saw the piled, emaciated bodies, crematoriums, and horrific camp conditions, he ordered his troops to visit them to witness the monstrous policies of the Nazi regime that they were fighting.

Estimates differ due to circumstances of war and statistical source reliability, but generally range from 35 to 60 million civilian and military deaths in WW2.[3] Some estimates go up to 75 million.[4] (For comparison, France's population was estimated at 62.8 million in 2022)[5] Over 20 million Russians lost their lives during the Stalinist Terror, counting those sent to the Gulag system of labor camps, forced collectivization, famine, and executions.[6] More than 47 million died during Mao Zedong's Long March, Great Leap Forward, and Cultural Revolution.[7] Other governmental genocides include the Khmer Rouge killing fields and the Ottoman Turkish campaign against Armenians.[8]

Authoritarian governments continue to get rid of their dissidents. During their 1970s Dirty War, the Argentine military junta caused 30,000 people to "disappear." The mothers and grandmothers of the victims still demand justice every Thursday in the Plaza de Mayo.[9] More recent reports indicate that on October 2, 2018, Jamal Khashoggi, a Saudi Arabian dissident journalist on the staff of the *Washington Post*, was imprisoned in a Saudi Consulate in Turkey, killed there by a squad of Saudi assassins and dismembered. Khashoggi was enticed to go to the Saudi Consulate to obtain papers for his upcoming wedding.[10]

Liberty is the second inalienable right described in the Declaration of Independence. After the delegates convened in Philadelphia in 1787 to draft the replacement for the failed Articles of Confederation, the absence of a declaration of individual rights delayed the states' ratification of their new Constitution. The original document spelled out what the new government could do but not what it couldn't do regarding individual rights. Americans demanded guaranteed protections for their newly won freedoms. After four years of intense debate, James Madison's draft of a Bill of Rights led to ratification in 1791.[11] This chapter discusses civil rights derived from the Constitution and its amendments; Chapter 12 discusses rights provided in the Constitution that apply to our judicial system; and Chapter 13 reviews economic rights that arise from the Constitution.

Citizenship. Section 1 of the Fourteenth Amendment states that all persons (not just white males owning property) become citizens of the United States if they are "born or naturalized in the United States and subject to the jurisdiction thereof." That provision reversed the decision of the US Supreme Court in *Dred Scott* (see Chapter 2). But the right has broader ramifications than ending a vestige of slavery. Immigrants may become US citizens through naturalization, and all their children born on our soil are citizens. The path to citizenship is complex and subject to extensive regulation, however. For example, visa issuance, the first step, requires applicants to meet country of origin or job skills quotas or to meet asylum requirements, if applicable.

But as citizens they enjoy the privileges and rights of citizenship written into the US Constitution. Only citizens can vote, but the right can have restrictions such as a felony conviction or lack of documented proof of citizenship (see Chapter 6). Other democracies, however, do not always recognize the right of a person to be a citizen. For example, in 2022[12] the British Parliament passed a new clause into the Nationality and Borders Bill that exempts the government from giving notice of a decision to strip a person of British citizenship if authorities do not have the subject's contact information or if it is not "reasonably practical" to give notice.[13]

Religious freedom. The First Amendment provides that "Congress shall make no law respecting an establishment of religion, or prohibiting the free exercise thereof." This provision, known as the Establishment Clause, created a wall of separation between government and religion. In effect, it rendered unto Caesar that which is Caesar's, and unto God that which belonged to God. There are exceptions to this right. In *Town of Greece v. Galloway,* the US Supreme Court ruled that town hall meetings that began with prayers used by *different denominations* did not violate the Establishment Clause.[14] Permitting the prayers of *only one* religion would have violated the Establishment Clause.

Thorny issues arising out of religious displays on public property have come before the Supreme Court. In one such case, *McCreary County v. American Civil Liberties Union of Kentucky*[15] three Kentucky counties had posted large readily visible copies of the Ten Commandments in their courthouses. Two counties adopted similar resolutions in an effort to demonstrate that the display was to show that the Commandments are Kentucky's "precedent legal code."[16] The US District Court for the Eastern District of Kentucky (herein Kentucky District Court) enjoined the displays as a violation of the Establishment Clause, and the Sixth Circuit Court of Appeals affirmed the Kentucky District Court relying on *Stone v. Graham*.[17] The US Supreme Court, in a 5-4 decision, affirmed and allowed the injunction that banned the displays to remain in place.

In her concurring opinion in *McCreary County*, Justice O'Connor wrote,

> There is no list of approved and disapproved beliefs appended to the First Amendment—and the Amendment's broad terms ("free exercise," "establishment," "religion") do not admit of such a cramped reading … The (Framers) did know that line-drawing between religions is an enterprise that, once begun, has no logical stopping point … The Religious Clauses, as a result, protect adherents of all religions, as well as those who believe in no religion at all.[18]

In 1940, the Supreme Court held that the Free Exercise Clause of the First Amendment applied to the states pursuant to the Due Process Clause of the Fourteenth Amendment.[19] The Religious Restoration Act of 1993 was enacted to protect religious freedom. The act prohibits any federal or any state government body or official from burdening the exercise of religion. The US Supreme Court has strongly supported the right. The right may be burdened only where the burden furthers "a compelling governmental interest" and is the "least restrictive means" available.[20] In *Burwell v. Hobby Lobby Stores,* the Supreme Court ruled that a contraceptive mandate adopted under the Patient Protection and Affordable Care Act violated a private for-profit corporation's right to religious freedom.[21]

A right to speak freely. Congress shall make no law "abridging the freedom of speech" (Amendment I). Alexei Navalny's story tells in stark terms why the First Amendment's protection of speech is critical.[22]

Navalny, a Russian dissident attorney, severely criticized the Russian political establishment, organized anti-corruption demonstrations, and attracted more than 2 million followers. He published material on corruption in which he criticized the Russian leadership as a "party of crooks and thieves." Twice convicted on spurious charges of embezzlement, he received a suspended sentence and probation. The European Court of Human Rights (ECHR) later ruled that Navalny's embezzlement conviction was unlawful.[23] When Navalny launched a presidential campaign, the Russian Federation's Central Electoral Commission barred him from registering as a candidate because of his criminal convictions. In August of 2020 Novichok, a nerve agent was placed in his underwear. Navalny fled to Berlin where he received life-saving medical care. When he returned to Russia, he accused Russia's leaders of poisoning him. At his well-publicized trial, he was sentenced to a prison labor camp in northern Russia where he died in 2024, branded as a terrorist.[24] In October of 2021, the European Parliament awarded the Sakharov Prize to Navalny for his work on human rights.[25]

Because our courts rigorously enforce the First Amendment's right of free speech, Americans never experience the silencing of speech that occurs in other nations. Human Rights Watch reported on November 12, 2021, that the Russian Supreme Court issued orders to shut down Memorial International, a respected organization that commemorated the terror under Stalin, investigated post-Soviet abuses, and promoted human rights with its platform for open debate, and resisted efforts to close Memorial's Human Rights Center.[26] Andrei D. Sakharov,[27] a Nobel Peace Prize laureate, had cofounded Memorial. In her article in the *Moscow Times*, Tanya Lokshina* said, "Russia's government cannot wipe out historic memory and people's aspirations for fundamental freedoms and the rule of law."[28]

Recent reports from China indicate that, like the Soviet Union, the Chinese government uses psychiatric confinement to stifle dissent. Li Tiantian, a rural teacher, told friends before she disappeared that police had forced their way into her home and were taking her to a psychiatric hospital. The authorities had targeted her for violating the bounds of officially acceptable comment on social media.[29]

Free speech can take many forms. For example, the First Nations' "Stand Up / Stand N Rock #NoDAPL (Official Video)"[30] was created to protest a proposed oil pipeline across the Standing Rock Sioux reservation. You will not find dissent allowed to remain online and publicly accessible for years in the Russian Federation or the People's Republic of China. "Stand Up" has been online since December 2016.

Freedom of the press. Congress shall make no law abridging "freedom of the press" (Amendment I). Issues arising out of the First Amendment's guarantee of freedom of the press have been litigated since the Colonies. In 1735 John Peter Zenger printed articles in his newspaper, the *New York Weekly Journal*, in which he criticized the Royal Governor of New York, William Cosby. Cosby issued a proclamation that condemned Zenger's newspaper as being seditious and later sued, claiming libel. The jury in the *Zenger* case accepted his claim of truth as a defense to libel and returned a verdict of not guilty. The *Zenger* case laid the groundwork for freedom of the press although it did not establish a legal precedent.[31] In 1804 Harry Croswell, a journalist, sought but failed to establish truth as a defense to libel. Croswell was convicted, and the New York appellate court ruled against him in *People v. Croswell*.[32] The New York Assembly later passed a law that allowed truth as a defense.

---

* Associate Director, Europe and Central Asia Division of Human Rights Watch, an international organization investigating and reporting on human rights issues since 1978.

New York Times v. Sullivan was decided in 1964. There the US Supreme Court ruled that where a publication involves a public figure the plaintiff must prove that the publisher acted with actual malice.[33] In *Gertz v. Robert Welch, Inc.* the Supreme Court held in 1974 that the First Amendment required only a "negligence standard" where a private party is sued for libel as distinguished from an institutional media defendant.[34]

Freedom of the Press applies not only to printed newspapers, however. Broadcast radio and television, internet news sites, and blogs have the right. In *Obsidian Finance Group, LLC, and Kevin Padrick v. Crystal Cox* the plaintiffs—Obsidian, a financial firm managing a bankruptcy and its cofounder Kevin Padrick—sued Crystal Cox for her blog posts that accused them of corrupt and fraudulent conduct. The jury ruled in favor of the plaintiffs and awarded damages of $2.5 million. The US Court of Appeals for the Ninth Circuit reversed. It held that the posts concerned a public issue, but that the jury could not find the blogger liable for defamation unless the blogger acted negligently. It said that individual bloggers and professional journalists are equally protected under the First Amendment because

> the protections of the First Amendment do not turn on whether the defendant was a trained journalist, formally affiliated with traditional news entities, engaged in conflict-of-interest disclosure, went beyond just assembling others' writings, or tried to get both sides of a story.[35]

The US Supreme Court did not rule on the specific issues decided in *Obsidian* so the issue is clouded.

The purpose here is not to lay out all the case law on freedom of the press. Rather, the objective is to demonstrate that loss of that freedom would strike a devastating blow to all our freedoms. Reporters, editors, and news analysts bring us knowledge of public affairs that we need to oversee governmental operations and vote competently for officials to lead us. Recent developments that challenge the press's ability to continue doing that are explored in Chapter 14.

A right to peaceably assemble. "Congress shall make no law respecting ... the right of the people peaceably to assemble" (Amendment I). Dr. Martin Luther King extensively exercised this right in his crusade for racial equality. King's efforts led to the Civil Rights Act of 1964.[36] Today, the right of assemblage is exercised in protest marches like Black Lives Matter (2013 forward)[37], the Women's March on Washington (2017),[38] and in the March for our Lives (2018)[39] on Washington by young people who organized to promote gun control following the Parkland school massacre in Florida. By contrast, the authorities arrested at least 15,000 Russians participating in anti-war protests over the invasion of Ukraine.[40] In June 1989, the Chinese government's crackdown on the Tiananmen Square student pro-democracy protesters ended in a massacre.[41]

Of course, this right does *not* apply to violent protesters such as the 2017 Unite the Right rally participants at Charlottesville, Virginia,[42] or to the guy with the horns and his associates rioting at the Capitol.

A right to petition for redress of grievances. "Congress shall make no law ... abridging ... the right of the people ... to petition the government for a redress of grievances" (Amendment I). The Navalny case in Russia, discussed above, demonstrates that autocrats do not countenance dissidents who petition for relief from tyranny. Here in America, we contact our elected representatives, circulate petitions for ballot proposals and recalls, write letters to the editor and editorials, post on social media, and present proposals and calls for action before legislative and municipal bodies. Without looking over our shoulders.

A right to bear arms. "A well-regulated Militia, being necessary to the security of a free State, the right of the people to keep and bear Arms, shall not be infringed"* (Amendment II). Described by dissenting Justice Stevens as a "dramatic upheaval of the law,"[43] the US Supreme Court ruled in *District of Columbia v. Heller* that the

---

* Capitalization and punctuation per the National Archives, "The Bill of Rights: A Transcription," https://www.archives.gov/founding-docs/bill-of-rights-transcript.

Second Amendment created a right for "law-abiding" Americans living in the District of Columbia, a federal enclave, to keep handguns in their home for self-defense.[44] Then in *McDonald v. City of Chicago*, it held that the right to bear arms it declared in *Heller* applied to the states under the Due Process Clause of the Fourteenth Amendment.[45] While the two decisions resulted in dissension over the validity of the court's rulings and the extent of the Second Amendment's *private right* to bear arms, extensive discussion of these decisions and their societal and constitutional ramifications extends far beyond the scope of this text. But an authoritarian regime would quickly abrogate this right regardless.

A right to jury trial in civil cases. "In Suits at common law, where the value in controversy shall exceed twenty dollars, the right of trial by jury shall be preserved" (Amendment VII). Today, citizens who wish to litigate private claims (e.g., negligence, fraud, breach of contract, etc.) have a right to jury trial in our federal and state courts (this right excludes special courts such as Small Claims and contract agreements for arbitration to settle disputes).

A right to refuse to quarter soldiers. "No Soldier shall, in time of peace be quartered in any house, without the consent of the Owner, nor in time of war, but in a manner to be prescribed by law" (Amendment III). Due to conflict with the French and First Nations, the Founders and their fellow citizens had firsthand experience with the king's soldiers quartered in their homes without their consent. Although no litigation has occurred over this right, it implies civilian control of the armed forces and protection from governmental intrusion into one's home. It might also apply to issues of eminent domain and militarization of the police.[46]

A right to due process of law. The Fifth Amendment to the Constitution provides among other things, "nor shall any person … be deprived of life, liberty, or property, without due process of law." This provision was originally held to bind only the federal government. Later, the Fourteenth Amendment made it binding on the states, "nor shall any State deprive any person of life, liberty, or property without due process of law." The government cannot act by decree or fiat against its citizens—as long as we keep our Constitution.

The Due Process Clause is not limited to the procedures in criminal cases that are discussed in Chapter 12. The US Supreme Court has enforced civil rights against the states, such as the right of privacy (discussed below). That type of incorporation became known as *substantive due process*. Justice Alito extensively reviewed that history in his opinion in *McDonald v. The City of Chicago*.[47]

A right to equal protection of the law. "No State shall … deny to any person within its jurisdiction the equal protection of the laws" (Amendment XIV Section 1). The foremost expression of this right is the decision of the Supreme Court in *Brown v. Board of Education of Topeka* where the Court declared that "separate but equal schools" violate the right to equal protection.[48] It has also scrutinized other civil rights areas such as interracial marriage.[49] Currently, this right is being vigorously employed to promote racial equality and to secure our voting rights. See discussion for its application in criminal cases in Chapter 12.

Freedom from involuntary servitude. "Neither slavery nor involuntary servitude, except as a punishment for crime whereof the party shall have been duly convicted, shall exist within the United States, or any place subject to their jurisdiction" (Amendment XIII Section 1). This right emanated from the Civil War. Dr. Martin Luther King continued the quest for equal justice under the law, and it is pursued today by those involved in Black Lives Matter. Equal Protection of the law, guaranteed by Amendment XIV extended this right. "No State shall … deny to any person within its jurisdiction the equal protection of the laws." We still have a way to go to reach that goal.

Implied personal rights. Some rights not expressly set forth in the Constitution have been implied from rights that are. For example, the right of privacy is no less a right than the others discussed here. The US Supreme Court in *Griswold v. Connecticut*[50] found that the right emanated from other rights that are expressly stated, such as the Due Process Clause of the Fourteenth Amendment, the First Amendment's protection of the right of association, the Third Amendment's prohibition on the quartering soldiers, the Fourth Amendment's protection of a person's houses, papers, and effects, and the Fifth Amendment's protection against self-incrimination. In *Griswold,* the court struck down a Connecticut statute that penalized the possession of birth control devices by a husband and wife in their home on the grounds the statute violated their right of privacy.

The right of privacy with regard to reproductive choices, however, has come under a cloud after the Supreme Court overturned the settled law of *Roe v. Wade.*[51] The court's 2022 decision in *Dobbs v. Jackson*[52] stated that the Constitution does not confer a right of abortion and gave individual states full power to regulate abortion access. Some experts have expressed concern that other rights, such as access to contraception and transgender treatments may be also affected.

A new area of litigation and legislation concerns data privacy or personal information protection on the internet and in digital devices.[53] Supreme Court Chief Justice Roberts wrote in *Riley v. California,* "The fact that technology now allows an individual to carry such information in his hand does not make the information any less worthy of the protection for which the Founders fought."[54]

Express personal rights also give rise to aspirational rights. "The pursuit of Happiness" is the third inalienable right described in the Declaration of Independence. It flows from the more specific rights that President James Madison wrote into the Bill of Rights (Amendments I–X). It is a concept that led President Reagan to proclaim our nation to be a "shining city on a hill,"[55] and that is embodied in the term "American exceptionalism"*—where individual initiative, self-development, and the exploration of the world we live in is encouraged.

Personal associations. Under the shield of the Constitution, state laws protect our right to form associations—Americans are joiners. Now we flock to social media sites. Associations have broader aspects than leisure and entertainment, however. People rally to movements bringing pressure for social, environmental, and political change. For example,

---

* American Exceptionalism: the belief that the United States differs qualitatively from other developed nations because of its national credo, historical evolution, or distinctive political and religious institutions.

a new election procedures proposal on the November 2022 ballot was approved after Voters Not Politicians[56] attracted wide support and petition signatures for it (see Chapter 8). The business and economic aspects of the right to associate are discussed in Chapter 13.

The Constitution preserves one's personal freedom to create and pursue happiness, and to aspire to live in peace, dignity, and tranquility in a clean environment. The personal freedoms described in this chapter, the protections granted from arbitrary, unjust incarceration under the judicial system described in Chapter 12, and the economic freedoms outlined in Chapter 13 flesh out the means through which Americans can energetically pursue happiness in our republic.

If we can keep it.

CHAPTER 12

The Rule of Law and Our Independent Judiciary—Our Protection from Arbitrary Incarceration

The rule of law put in place another pillar for our republic. It created a right in every citizen to believe that our Constitution, the laws of the United States, and all treaties made under the authority of the United States are the supreme law of our land as opposed to decrees issued by monarchs, oligarchs, or dictators. Article VI clause 2 of the Constitution (the Supremacy Clause) clearly states this principle:

> This Constitution, and the Laws of the United States which shall be made in Pursuance thereof; and all Treaties made, or which shall be made, under the Authority of the United States, shall be the supreme Law of the Land; and the Judges in every State shall be bound thereby, any Thing in the Constitution or Laws of any State to the Contrary notwithstanding.

Our criminal laws operate under a dual federal/state system. As a group, they embody fundamental principles that came into being early in the Civil Law and in the English Courts. They embody rights as well as sanctions that have been expounded and fortified by the decisions of our courts over our 237-year history. In addition, Congress's Article I delegated powers, and especially the Necessary and Proper Clause, granted it power to enact federal criminal statutes. The Supremacy Clause requires federal courts to enforce laws enacted by Congress, and it bound the states by them. The Tenth Amendment reserved to the states all powers not delegated to the United States, which permitted them to enact state criminal statutes that are enforced in our state courts. Under these provisions, a US citizen accused of committing a crime on American soil possesses a well-reasoned bundle of rights that are protected by the Constitution and available in both federal and state courts. But if we lose our Constitution, we lose not only the Supremacy Clause; the entire legal structure of statutes and case law that support these fundamental principles would disappear with it.

Consider that the right to be tried in a court of law before an independent judiciary embodies the framework expressed in the Constitution. It's where the rubber meets the road. Our first chief justice of the Supreme Court laid down a marker in *Marbury v. Madison*: "The Government of the United States has been emphatically termed a government of laws, and not of men."[1] Then Chief Justice Marshall announced that our nation does not countenance autocrats and tyrants decreeing our laws when he said in *Marbury*, "It is emphatically the province and duty of the Judicial Department to say what the law is."[2] *Marbury* lies at the center of our judicial system. It has survived over the life of our nation.

Article III produced an independent judiciary that tells us what the law is. The Due Process Clause of the Fourteenth Amendment binds our state courts to the rule of law. They must follow the rulings of the US Supreme Court concerning the meaning of the Constitution. The decisions of our judiciary aren't perfect. But they would never have acquired the force they now have but for the Constitution.

Currently the independence and non-partisanship of our Supreme Court has been questioned concerning the right to bear arms, reproductive rights, voting rights, and campaign finance. But the role of the court and the federal judiciary is still firmly entrenched in our Constitution and the long history of the court. Compare that with the havoc weakening judicial independence would cause. Prime Minister Benjamin Netanyahu's overhaul of the Israeli judicial system to allow the government to overrule Supreme Court decisions and have direct say in choosing judges sparked massive protests and widened the rift between ultra-nationalist/orthodox religious and secular Israelis. Although a democracy, Israel lacks a constitution and bill of rights. The Israeli courts decide controversial issues such as women's rights, occupation and settlement of Palestinian territories, and LGBTQ* rights. Weakening their authority will have international as well as domestic consequences for Israeli citizens, military personnel, and Palestinians.[3]

It bears forceful repeating that the rule of law, our independent judiciary, and the rights belonging to criminal defendants will be forfeit if we should ever lose our Constitution.

Unreasonable searches and seizures. "The right of the people to be secure in their persons, houses, papers, and effects, against unreasonable searches and seizures, shall not be violated" (Amendment IV). In a landmark decision, *Mapp v. Ohio*,[4] the US Supreme Court established an exclusionary rule that precludes prosecutors from introducing evidence obtained in violation of Amendment IV. This exclusionary rule applies to both federal and state police forces and prosecutors. The Court extended the exclusionary rule in *Silverthorne Lumber Co. v. United States* to hold that evidence derived from illegally obtained evidence is also inadmissible unless it can be obtained independently through legal means, else it "reduces the Fourth Amendment to a form of words."[5]

Arrest and search warrants. "and no Warrants shall issue, but upon probable cause, supported by Oath or affirmation, and particularly describing the place to be searched, and the persons or things to be seized." Per Amendment IV, law enforcement cannot summarily arrest someone without cause. Police must convince a judge that a crime has probably been committed and that the subject of the requested arrest warrant was involved. An arrest warrant identifies the crime, names the person to be arrested, and may restrict the way an arrest may be made.[6] The Supreme Court has ruled that even historical mobile phone location data collection by police requires a search warrant.[7]

Habeas corpus. "The Privilege of the Writ of Habeas Corpus shall not be suspended, unless when in Cases of Rebellion or Invasion the public safety may require it" (Article I Section 9). The purpose of a writ†￼of *habeas corpus* is to bring a party before a court or judge to determine

---

* LGBTQ: acronym for lesbian, gay, bisexual, transgender, queer or questioning sexual identity.

† Writ (n.): a form of written command issued by a court or other legal authority to act or abstain from acting.

if the state has detained or imprisoned that party without due process of law.[8] In certain instances, even noncitizens have the right. In 2008, the Supreme Court decided in *Boumediene v. Bush* that Guantánamo detainees could challenge the lawfulness of their detention in federal court by filing writs of habeas corpus.[9]

Bills of attainder and ex post facto laws. "No Bill of Attainder*[10] or ex post facto Law†[11] shall be passed" (Article I Section 9). For example, The Congressional Research Service (CRS) published a report on ways congressional legislative responses to the January 6, 2021, insurrection could avoid bills of attainder issues (i.e., riot participation by members of Congress).[12] The rule of law also depends on the prohibition against bills of attainder to counteract vigilante and mob mentality. See discussion of "Lock her up" chants in Chapter 3.

Grand jury indictments. "No person shall be held to answer for a capital, or otherwise infamous crime, unless on a presentment or indictment of a Grand Jury, except in cases arising in the land or naval forces, or in the Militia, when in actual service in time of War or public danger" (Amendment V). A grand jury does not find guilt or determine punishment of a defendant. It decides only whether to indict (formally charge with a serious crime). Unlike public preliminary hearings, grand jury proceedings are usually secret to encourage witnesses to speak freely and to protect the defendant's reputation if the grand jury decides not to indict.[13]

A right to be informed of criminal charges. "In all criminal prosecutions, the accused shall enjoy the right … to be informed of the nature and cause of the accusation" (Amendment VI). Knowing exactly what he or she is being charged with—the facts of the crime, applicable statutory language, etc.—enables a defendant to mount a defense and prevent later double jeopardy.[14]

Trial by jury. "In all criminal prosecutions, the accused shall enjoy the right to a speedy and public trial, by an impartial jury of

---

* Bill of attainder (n.): a legislative act that singles out an individual or group for punishment without a trial.

† Ex post facto law (n.): a law enacted to criminalize retroactively behavior that was legal when committed.

the State and district wherein the crime shall have been committed" (Amendment VI). See *Duncan v. Louisiana*.[15] While the defendant is not entitled to a jury composed of his or her own race, the state may not use its peremptory challenges* to exclude potential jurors based on race. See *Batson v. Kentucky*.[16]

Pretrial publicity in criminal cases can conflict with the right to a fair trial by interfering with the ability to select impartial jurors. In certain cases, it can also intimidate potential jurors. To mitigate the effect, trial courts may impose gag orders to restrict media reporting and counsel statements, keep the jury panel names anonymous, or close courtrooms entirely.[17]

To preserve impartiality, judges admonish jurors to avoid use of the internet for either research or outside discussion of the case during a trial with varying success. But smartphones and the internet pervade life to such an extent that preventing jurors from using social media and internet web sites is a growing problem.[18] The *Federal District Court Trial Handbook for Jurors* forbids independent research by jurors in very specific terms.[19]

Bail, fines, and cruel and unusual punishments. "Excessive bail shall not be required, nor excessive fines imposed, nor cruel and unusual punishments inflicted" (Amendment VIII). The definition of what constitutes "cruel and unusual" has changed since 1791. The Supreme Court has developed, with varying success, an evolving standards of decency test.[20] The court has held that a death sentence is not inherently cruel and unusual (*Gregg v. Georgia*).[21] However, laws making the death penalty mandatory, leaving no discretion to consider the individual defendant and their crime, have been ruled cruel and unusual. The court has also identified certain types of cases, severe mental impairment (*Atkins v. Virginia*)[22] and minor age (*Roper v. Simmons*)[23] for example, where the death penalty rises to the level of cruel and unusual punishment. Full discussion of developing views and

---

* Peremptory challenge (n.): A challenge resulting in the exclusion of a potential juror without giving any reason or explanation—unless the opposing party presents a prima facie argument that this challenge was used to discriminate based on race, ethnicity, or sex.

the application of capital punishment extend beyond the scope of this book, however.

Bail and fines are also receiving attention for the disparate impact they have on lower income persons. A class action lawsuit recently settled in Detroit requires the court to reform bail practices, including limiting its ability to impose unaffordable bail on defendants.[24]

Due process of law. "No person shall be held to answer for a capital, or otherwise infamous crime … without due process of law" (Amendment V); "nor shall any State deprive any person of life, liberty, or property, without due process of law" (Amendment XIV Section 1). Amendment V applies only to the federal government. Amendment XIV extended due process protection to the actions of the states.[25] Procedural due process addresses which legal procedures are required, such as notice, opportunity for hearing, confrontation and cross-examination of witnesses, discovery, and availability of counsel.[26]

Double jeopardy. "nor shall any person be subject for the same offence to be twice put in jeopardy of life or limb" (Amendment V). The Double Jeopardy Clause prohibits charging someone twice for essentially the same crime.[27] This right also applies to juvenile offenders later charged as adults for the same crime (*Breed v. Jones*).[28]

Self-incrimination. "No person … shall be compelled in any criminal case to be a witness against himself" (Amendment V). In *Miranda v. Arizona* the US Supreme Court held that during a police interrogation the accused must be warned that his statements and admissions may be used against him and if he is not so warned his statements may not be used as evidence.[29]

A new development on digital privacy concerns law enforcement trying to force someone to unlock their mobile phone or other digital device (compelled decryption) for a search. Does surrendering a biometric (fingerprint or facial recognition) or passcode to unlock a device mean that law enforcement is compelling someone to "testify against himself" and is therefore impermissible? The courts have reached different conclusions. The determination whether the right applies currently depends on the jurisdiction where the case is.[30]

Eminent domain. "No person shall be … deprived of life, liberty, or property, without due process of law; nor shall private property be taken for public use, without just compensation" (Amendment V). Recent issues concern civil asset forfeiture and compensation or return of confiscated property have arisen in criminal cases.[31] Some state laws permit asset forfeiture even if no conviction results from the charges. Unfortunately, the US Supreme Court did not settle all questions regarding civil asset forfeiture in their *Timbs v. Indiana* decision.[32] For discussion of civil private property and easements, see Chapter 13.

Equal protection of the law. "nor shall any State … deny to any person within its jurisdiction the equal protection of the laws" (Amendment XIV Section 1). However, Section 2 allows states to disenfranchise citizens convicted of certain crimes: "But when the right to vote at any election … is denied … or in any way abridged, *except for participation in rebellion, or other crime*, the basis of representation therein shall be reduced."[33] (emphasis added). Many states have laws making convicted felons ineligible to vote, in some cases permanently after sentence completion. (See discussion of the Crystal Mason case in Chapter 6.) Over the last few decades, the states have tended to reinstate the right to vote although this is a state-by-state policy choice.[34]

Presumption of innocence. There is no specific Constitutional provision that protects the presumption of innocence. It is, however, covered and protected by the due process provisions of Amendments V and XIV and routinely stated in jury instructions that judges read to juries in criminal cases. It is "a cardinal principle of our system of justice that every person accused of a crime is presumed to be innocent unless and until his or her guilt is established beyond a reasonable doubt."[35] Though it may vary in detail, the instruction read to juries on the presumption of innocence is essentially the same across all federal and state trial courts. For example, the Michigan Model Criminal Jury Instruction on presumption of innocence reads in part as follows:

(1) A person accused of a crime is presumed to be innocent. This means that you must start with the presumption that the defendant is innocent. This presumption continues throughout

the trial and entitles the defendant to a verdict of not guilty unless you are satisfied beyond a reasonable doubt that [he/she] is guilty.

(2) Every crime is made up of parts called elements. The prosecutor must prove each element of the crime beyond a reasonable doubt. The defendant is not required to prove [his/her] innocence or to do anything. If you find that the prosecutor has not proven every element beyond a reasonable doubt, then you must find the defendant not guilty.

(3) A reasonable doubt is a fair, honest doubt growing out of the evidence or lack of evidence. It is not merely an imaginary or possible doubt, but a doubt based on reason and common sense.[36]

Right to confront witnesses against you. "In all criminal prosecutions, the accused shall enjoy the right … to be confronted with the witnesses against him" (Amendment VI). The right includes the right to cross-examine the witnesses called against the accused. The courts have issued many decisions concerning whether the Confrontation Clause applies to hearsay. Generally, the only acknowledged exceptions are the two existing from the time of the founding: dying declarations by a speaker who was aware that he was dying, and statements of a witness who was detained or otherwise unavailable to testify.[37] Crime victims and witnesses also have rights that must be coordinated with those of the defendant, including the right to protection from the accused and to stay informed about and attend court proceedings.[38]

Compulsory process. "In all criminal prosecutions, the accused shall enjoy the right … to have compulsory process (subpoenas) for obtaining witnesses in his favor" (Amendment VI). This provision gives the defendant the right to present a defense with his or her version of the facts.[39]

Assistance of counsel. "In all criminal prosecutions the accused shall enjoy the right … to have the Assistance of Counsel for his defence"

(Amendment VI). In *Gideon v. Wainwright,* the Supreme Court held that if the accused lacks the funds to hire an attorney to represent him the state must provide one for him.[40] In *Escobedo v. Illinois,* the Court held that an accused has a right to counsel during a police interrogation.[41] If defense counsel is later shown to be inadequate, the courts may order a new trial.

Right to an interpreter. The right to a court-appointed interpreter is implied in the Fifth, Sixth, and Fourteenth Amendments. Understanding the charges against him or her, confronting witnesses, and having effective counsel is meaningless if a defendant has limited or no English proficiency.[42] However, the Supreme Court ruled that whether an interpreter is required for a particular defendant is at the court's discretion (*Perovich v. United States*).[43] In order to address the growing need for providing interpreters to parties in court proceedings, Congress enacted the Court Interpreters Act of 1978.[44] But this act only provides statutory guidance for using interpreters and translators.

Right to appeal. The right to appeal to a higher court is also included in the right to due process established by Amendments V and XIV and is set forth in detailed federal and state statutes and court rules. The courts may not penalize a defendant for exercising the right to appeal. Note that the government does not have the right of appeal in criminal cases.[45] With regard to terrorism, the federal government still grapples with the question of whether detainees held in the Guantanamo, Cuba, facility have rights of due process and appeal to US courts.[46]

Our states have enacted statutes to provide state and local law enforcement protection. However, police overreach that created Black Lives Matter and aggressive traffic stops, mobile phone tracking and forced unlocking (see self-incrimination above), and the over-militarization of our police forces have raised concerns about law enforcement conduct. While those issues must be addressed, our police forces must be supervised and supported, not defunded.

The foregoing rights are far more detailed in their application than is attempted here. They are rights that a defendant and their attorney can use to defend against an accusation that the defendant committed a crime. Judges use them to instruct our juries and conduct proceedings. Appellate courts rely on them to determine whether the evidence introduced in the case supports the verdict and whether the defendant received a fair trial. In autocracies and dictatorships, if they exist at all, they lack the force and vigor that our Constitution supplies.

We must *never* give them up.

CHAPTER 13

Economic Freedoms—a Basket of Opportunities an Autocrat Would Sweep Aside

Our Constitution established a free-market system that too many of us take for granted. It provides our citizens with the opportunity to pursue their dreams free from government interference whether in the arts, professions, trades, business, science, or politics. And it equips citizens with the power to build their lives, achieve their goals, and to acquire wealth. The following economic freedoms and rights are expressly stated in the Constitution; they arise from powers given to Congress in clauses like the Interstate Commerce Clause, or they derive from federal statutes enacted pursuant to the Constitution. It hasn't always been a smooth road—the Depression, wars, and pervasive discrimination have raised obstacles. But without the Constitution, all rights described below cease to exist.

Private contracts. The Constitution established a right to enter enforceable contracts with other persons or entities. "No State shall ... pass any ... Law impairing the Obligation of Contracts" (Article 1 Section 10). The US Supreme Court held in *Trustees of Dartmouth College v. Woodward* that the charter of Dartmouth College was a contract that New Hampshire could not impair.[1] *Dartmouth College* has been heralded as one of the cases that gave rise to the American business corporation and to free enterprise. Private citizens have used contracts to guarantee services and goods are as promised, and to obtain redress when they are not. (That new car *will* have the features promised in the dealership lease contract, and its replacement parts *will* be genuine when installed, for example.)

Copyrights and patent rights. "The Congress shall have Power ... To promote the Progress of Science and useful Arts, by securing for limited Times to Authors and Inventors the exclusive Right to their respective Writings and Discoveries" (Article I Section 8).

Congress enacted the first federal patent law, effective April 10, 1790. It granted patent owners "the sole and exclusive right and liberty" to make and sell their inventions for a term of fourteen years, after which the invention would fall into the public domain. Later, the term was extended to twenty years. The federal copyright statute was signed into law on May 31, 1790.[2] It "secured" the right of authors to publish their works for fourteen years which could be extended by fourteen more years. Today, for works created after January 1978, a copyright term can extend for the life of the creator plus seventy years. Copyright protection covers creative works in print, audio, and digital formats.

Hundreds of thousands of American patents[3] and copyrights[4] have generated great wealth for their creators. A few of the patents listed by the Constitutional Rights Foundation[5] include Eli Whitney's cotton gin (1794), Alexander Graham Bell's telephone (1876), Thomas Edison's incandescent light bulb (1880), and Enrico Fermi and Leo Szilard's atomic reactor (1955). Bill Gates and his companies have accumulated thousands of patents for the Microsoft Windows operating systems, personal computers, and other devices.[6] Amazon holds over 24,300 patents globally.[7] Monsanto has aggressively litigated several patents for its genetically modified seeds.[8] CRISPR-Cas9* has presented many legal and ethical issues stemming from its gene editing technology.[9]

The Library of Congress is filled with the writings and creations of those who have benefited from our copyright laws. Harper Lee's *To Kill a Mockingbird* and Rachel Carson's *Silent Spring* come to mind, and the screens full of motion pictures and TV series do as well. When creations such as Leonard Bernstein and Stephen Sondheim's *West Side Story* exploded onto the scene with that of other musicals like Motown's

---

* CRISPR (pronounced *crisper*, full name "CRISPR-Cas9."). The protein Cas9 (Cas stands for "CRISPR-associated") enzyme acts as molecular scissors for cutting strands of DNA and for editing genomes. CRISPR allows researchers to easily alter DNA sequences and modify gene function.

"My Girl," they demonstrated not only the great swath of creativity* protected by US copyrights but also the freedom to create it.

Current intellectual property controversies include e-licenses more commonly known as shrink wrap, click wrap, and browse wrap licenses.[10] Click wrap and browse wrap license agreements are often called sneak wrap or stealth due to the provider's ability to change terms after user consent and without notification.[11]

Ask yourself, would an autocrat allow and protect the creative genius that produced this huge and often controversial body of work? Aleksandr Solzhenitsyn might have something to tell us on that subject. Mr. Solzhenitsyn spent eight years in Soviet labor camps for writing a letter criticizing Stalin. After his release, he published *One Day in the Life of Ivan Denisovich*, and other works. In 1970 he won the Nobel Prize for literature. His publication of volume one of the *Gulag Archipelago* led to his arrest for treason and exile from the Soviet Union in 1974. Mr. Solzhenitsyn's Russian citizenship was restored in 1990.[12]

Eminent domain. Citizens have a right to not have private property taken for public use without just compensation (Amendment V). The concept that individual citizens can own private property may seem obvious, but when the government wants a utility line easement or a new street it may not simply usurp the land of its citizens. It must file eminent domain or condemnation proceedings to establish a public need for the land and then call appraisers to establish the value of land to be taken. The landowner can call his or her own experts to establish that the intended use is not a public use and that the value of land is higher than that proposed by the government's witnesses. The power of eminent domain may be exercised only through legislation or legislative delegation. Although such delegation is usually to another governmental body, it may also be to private corporations and public utilities when they are promoting a valid public purpose.[13] The General Motors Poletown plant offers an example. In 1980, the cities of Detroit

* For an idea of how much popular music exists, see "The 500 Greatest Songs of All Time" list by *Rolling Stone*, September 15, 2021, https://www.rollingstone.com/music/music-lists/best-songs-of-all-time-1224767/.

and Hamtramck condemned an entire working-class neighborhood to clear ground for a new automotive assembly plant and boost the economy with over 6,000 jobs. While most residents and businesses accepted the buyout offers, litigation ensued.[14] The Michigan Supreme Court first denied the challengers (*Poletown Neighborhood Council v. Detroit*[15]) but later reversed in 2004 (*County of Wayne v. Hathcock*[16]). Contrast with British citizens' experience during WW2. Their homes and property (farms for example) could be requisitioned for government or military use, usually on very short notice.*[17]

Eminent domain has been interpreted also to include personal property. See Chapter 12 for the discussion of eminent domain as applied to asset forfeiture. Eminent domain may also apply to intellectual property like patents or copyrights.[18] Although intellectual property seizure has remained hypothetical, the COVID-19 pandemic has raised the possibility that the federal government may seize vaccine and pharmaceutical patents by right of eminent domain.[19]

Private property. State laws that protect the right to own and deal in private property are much broader than the eminent domain rights discussed above. They protect our right to own real property, tangible personal assets, business property, and investments. Our courts and state laws provide not only the means of acquiring and owning private property, but they also protect our right to transfer or sell that property, and a right to inherit property. These rights are protected by Article I Section 10's provision that the states may not impair the obligation of contracts but also by a long legal history of state laws that protect the right to own and deal in private property. Consider again that during Kristallnacht and afterward the Nazis looted and destroyed the private

---

* Less well-known than the rationing that continued into the mid-1950s, during WW2, British landowners had to vacate property if the government or military requisitioned it. Bletchley Park (Enigma code breaking and other cryptography projects) is an example. https://www.historyhit.com/locations/bletchley-park/

property of Jewish and other citizens of Germany. Anti-discrimination laws have been enacted to counter redlining*.

Interstate commerce. The Constitution provided Congress with power "To regulate Commerce with foreign Nations, and among the several States, and with the Indian Tribes" (Article I Section 8). Several substantial federal programs have been enacted under the Commerce Clause that greatly enlarged the ability to engage in commerce. Appendix A's extensive list of statutes sets forth a broad legal and economic foundation starting in 1887. They protect employers and employees, retirees, the financial system, and our health care delivery system.

One major set of programs operated during the Great Depression of the 1930s. Franklin Delano Roosevelt implemented New Deal programs[20] by executive orders pursuant to various statutes to revive the economy and restore citizens' livelihoods. The WPA was a federal infrastructure program set up to build projects such as the Tennessee Valley Authority (TVA) and Hoover Dam. It also provided jobs and employed approximately 8.5 million Americans until it was dissolved in 1943. It was a forerunner of the current infrastructure project initiated by President Biden.[21] It wasn't the only one. Social Security and various regulatory bodies got their start during the New Deal.

Later in response to the Great Recession,[†] Congress enacted the American Recovery and Reinvestment Act of 2009.[22] This act aimed to counter further economic deterioration; provide economic stimulus via spending on infrastructure, health care, and education; and make tax cuts. Unemployment insurance and Medicaid also provided stabilizers.[23]

---

* redlining: denial of loans, insurance, or other financial services to residents of certain areas deemed a poor risk due to ethnicity or low-income levels. Sociologist John McKnight coined the term in the 1960s from how the federal government and lenders drew a red line on a map around the neighborhoods they would not invest in. https://www.investopedia.com/terms/r/redlining.asp.

† The Great Recession (2007 through 2009) impacted the global economy as the longest economic downturn since WW2 and the most severe since the Great Depression. Major triggers included the collapse of the US subprime mortgage bubble and drastic shrinkage of banks' resources to provide loans and credit to businesses and consumers.

The Federal Reserve System drastically cut interest rates and instituted a purchase program for mortgage-backed securities.[24]

Federal laws are starting to regulate virtual assets, such as cryptocurrencies* (Bitcoin for example) verified by blockchain† that exist only as digital algorithms. Unlike traditional currencies such as the dollar, no government issues them or sets their value. Their usage continues to grow, as do digital payment systems like PayPal‡ and Venmo§. Regulation of financial instruments and payment systems (tangible or virtual) and currency substitutes helps to ensure the safety of users, maintain trust and security of commerce, and prevent criminal activity such as money laundering and fraud.[25]

Losing the Constitution and its Commerce Clause would mean losing the entire foundation of our economic system along with essential tools to stabilize our economy and provide financial security.

State laws protected by the Constitution. But there is another aspect to the economic rights we could lose. Article 4 of the Constitution guarantees to every state a republican form of government. The Ninth Amendment provides that the enumeration of rights in the Constitution shall not be construed to deny or disparage others retained by the people. The Tenth Amendment provides that powers not delegated to the United States by the Constitution nor prohibited by it to the states are reserved to the states or to the people. From the Common Law in Mediaeval England, through the Constitution, and embellished by thousands of court opinions, we have well-reasoned protections against negligent conduct, fraud, and other torts. The different forms of owning real estate (a few examples: fee simple, life tenancy, and partnerships)

---

* cryptocurrency (n.): a digital currency in which transactions are verified and records maintained by a decentralized system using cryptography, rather than by a centralized authority such as a government Treasury.

† blockchain (n.): a public digital ledger record of transactions made in cryptocurrencies, encrypted, and stored across multiple computers linked in a network.

‡ PayPal is an online payment system to send and receive money. Users can link their bank account, credit card, or debit card.

§ Venmo allows friends to pay and request money from each other or pay authorized merchants by using a smartphone instead of cash.

are creatures of the common law. State laws also provide a framework of professional licenses and business operations oversight. Think about that the next time you eat at a restaurant or remodel your house. It's worth repeating that without the Constitution, our states are not required to have a republican form of government, and with it protect our rights.

Implied, Aspirational Economic Rights Derived from Express Rights

Some economic rights flow from rights like free speech, contract rights, and property rights that are expressly stated in the Constitution and amendments.

Education. If you give someone a fish, you feed them for a day. If you teach someone to fish, you feed them for a lifetime. The right to seek an education at schools and institutions of higher learning is protected by our Constitution and laws created under it. The Northwest Ordinance provided that in the Northwest Territories, "Schools and the means of education will forever be encouraged."[26] Those words were later etched into the façade of Angell Hall on the University of Michigan's campus. While a rigorous educational system is essential to our way of life, we haven't done justice to the promise of education as an aspirational right for all Americans. Yet there are bright spots and advances we could build on. We will always need an educated citizenry to choose our leaders wisely, recognize misinformation, and oversee our government.

The military offered a path to qualified veterans via GI Bill[27] benefits after honorable discharge. After WW2, most returning soldiers received generous education and home mortgage-backed benefits to enable them to better their lives and that of their families. Unfortunately, that promise was denied to 1.2 million returning black veterans.[28] Women veterans also encountered systemic discrimination trying to receive GI benefits.*[29] Many First Nations veterans took advantage of education benefits, but they could not use the bill's housing provisions because the Bureau of Indian Affairs would not sign a waiver to the title to the land. Reservations are lands held in trust by the federal government. Without the waiver, they could not secure a loan, even under the GI Bill.[30] Later versions of the GI Bill have sought to redress the earlier denials of benefits.

The Supreme Court decision in *Brown v. Board of Education of Topeka*[31] sought to address institutional educational inequalities dating back to the Jim Crow era. Over sixty years later we are still struggling with the repercussions of segregation and discrimination, although one can say that recognizing that a problem exists is the first step toward finding solutions. All Americans have a stake in combating inadequate education and resulting economic insecurity and inequality. Else, Mr. Lewis's dystopian novel may be the future of our nation.

Many young people lack access to good schools, their families may not live in safe and healthy neighborhoods, and their communities lack enough economic opportunities. Head Start,[32] one of President Lyndon B. Johnson's War on Poverty initiatives, has incurred funding and other setbacks over the years, but research has shown that properly implemented and made available, it continues to help prepare disadvantaged children for school.

Congress enacted Title IX of the Education Amendments Act of 1972[33] to protect people from discrimination based on sex in education programs or institutions that receive federal financial assistance. These recipients include thousands of educational institutions, libraries, and museums. Also included are vocational rehabilitation agencies and education agencies of 50 states, the District of Columbia, and US territories.[34]

The No Child Left Behind Act of 2001 (NCLB)[35] also attempted to address educational inequalities. Over concerns that the US education

---

* Like their sisters, civilian wartime workers (the "Rosies") encountered major obstacles trying to stay in the post-war workforce. They never received any educational or economic assistance benefits like the GI Bill for their service.

system was no longer internationally competitive, the NCLB aimed to boost performance of students whose academic progress trailed that of their peers. The requirements to measure progress created an uproar over which standardized tests to use, how to restructure curricula and evaluate teachers, what to do about under-performing schools, and allocating resources to pay for it.[36]

Nontraditional education, including online certificate courses, has evolved to supplement lifelong learning for better job opportunities. Unfortunately, many for-profit colleges have low graduation and job placement rates, especially for minority students. The government has recently begun implementing regulations to address the problem of predatory for-profit colleges.

Although they can be burdensome to repay due to high tuition costs and low initial wages, student loans offered by the federal government provide one path to help our young people earn post-secondary degrees. However, students received a major setback when the US Supreme Court ruled that the Biden administration overstepped its authority in cancelling $400 billion in student loan debt.[37] Then on June 29, 2023, the Court held that race based affirmative action programs violated the Fourteenth Amendment.[38]

Private enterprise. Derived from the doctrine of sanctity of contracts it is a right to own and operate a service firm (accounting or law for example), invest in business ventures, and vigorously engage in private enterprises like Mom-and-Pop stores and startups.* The economy has a long history of startups becoming Ford Motor Company, Walmart, and Apple Computers. Alphabet (f.k.a. Google), Amazon, Meta (f.k.a. Facebook), and Tesla have become "unicorns" (startup companies now valued at more than $1 billion). A couple of those startups† will likely colonize the moon, Mars, and the rest of the solar system, just as the East India and West India Companies launched into the New World.

---

* Startup (n.): a company in the first stage of its operations, often financed by its entrepreneurial founders during the initial starting period.

† SpaceX founded by Elon Musk, and Blue Origin founded by Jeff Bezos.

Business associations. Economic growth and employment opportunities increase through personal contacts made in professional organizations, social media, and formal events. Now it's called networking and linking. The right to economic association also includes the formation of limited liability companies (LLCs), partnerships, and cooperatives along with other business formats that offer economic opportunities. The US Constitution protects our right to do that, but our state laws also provide protection for these rights.

Sometimes a delicate balance occurs between freedom of association and discrimination, especially for private organizations and political parties.[39] Employment discrimination regarding private organizations' staffing continues to generate litigation. Certainly, problems arise from these associations and must be addressed. Private membership clubs do not meet the test of public accommodation if they are not open to and serve the public, and their membership policies provide clear notice of specific criteria for membership. But the criteria must be relevant to the club's purpose.[40] Yet even with regulation that arose out of these issues, the perception of "old boy" business dealing and legacy advantages for their children lingers on. Other litigation arose over mandatory fees charged to union members for ideological and political activities not part of the union's collective bargaining mission.[41] Yet the balance has started to shift in retail operations and services as more minority groups gain legal recognition. Informal grassroots movements can also become a means to compete for resources and advocate for economic and other needed changes. Just ask the baristas of Starbucks Workers United.[42]

Any discussion of the many economic freedoms and rights that Americans enjoy must begin with the protections accorded those rights by the US Constitution printed in coauthor Nelson's little brown book. Should the dissolution of our Constitution ever occur, our rights and prosperity could be replaced by collective farms and factories, assigned careers, restricted higher education, and draconian economic plans.

CHAPTER 14

Newspaper Closures, Social Media, and "Fake News"—the Erosion of Our Ability to Oversee Our Leaders and Vote Wisely

The investigative reporting of Carl Bernstein and Bob Woodward that exposed the Watergate Scandal demonstrates the critical role of the press as it used to be. Their carefully researched news reports on the Watergate burglary and its two-year aftermath ended Richard Nixon's fight to keep his presidency. Their book *All the President's Men*[1] documenting their investigation later became a blockbuster movie. But for the work that they and others like them performed, the full story of the Watergate burglary and its consequences may never have made its way into the history books. That is legitimate and responsible journalism at its best. The exposure of Nixon and his allies' crimes came about because members of the press had cover under the Constitution to pursue the story wherever it led. The national nightmare[2] of Watergate alone tells us that we cannot tolerate the loss of our free press.

The Supreme Court has ruled against governmental censorship of the press; prior restraints may not be imposed on the press except in cases where the nation is at war or when the speech being restrained would incite violence.[3] In the weeks prior to *New York Times v. United States,* President Nixon tried to use executive authority to restrain the *New York Times* from publishing classified government documents (the *Pentagon Papers**). The question before the Court: did freedom of the press guaranteed under the First Amendment override the government's need to maintain secrecy of sensitive information? The Court ruled that

---

* Full title: *Report of the Office of the Secretary of Defense Vietnam Task Force, 6/1967– 1/1969* (National Archives Identifier: 5889786), a Department of Defense history of US political and military involvement in Vietnam from 1945 to 1967.

publication could proceed. The government had not met the burden of proving that publication would cause inevitable, direct, and immediate danger to the United States.[4]

There is a stark difference between the freedoms the press enjoys under the First Amendment with the treatment accorded them in many other nations. Compare the Woodward-Bernstein experience with that of their colleagues from Belarus. In February of 2021, two young journalists reported on a demonstration against the rule of President Aleksandr G. Lukashenko. After their arrest, the court convicted them to two years in prison for inciting unrest.[5] Lukashenko even ordered a MIG-29 to intercept a commercial flight with dissident journalist Roman Protasevich onboard and escort it to Minsk where the authorities arrested him as a terrorist. The Ryanair jet from Athens to Vilnius was in international airspace when the MIG-29 diverted it.[6]

But that is not to say that our system has remained a journalistic ideal. Today, the role of the press is changing; we hear disquieting reports emanating from the activities of some members of the press. Where does good journalism end? Where does politics begin?

The *New York Times*, which some on the right describe as far too liberal, stands as an example of what the press used to be. Founded in 1851, the "Gray Lady"* prints up in the left corner on page A1 of every single copy, "All the news that's fit to print." Inside you will find news stories scrupulously printed apart from editorials and news analysis pieces. You will also find published in the *Times* corrections of errors found in prior editions. Online versions of the stories include updates and corrections as needed. It is undoubtedly true that *Times* reporters who investigate and write the news articles have their own political biases as do their editors. Still, newspapers like the *Times* and the *Washington Post* are modern examples of news outlets striving to achieve the ideals of classic journalism.

---

* The nickname "Gray Lady" refers to the *Times's* careful deliberative journalism as well as its refusal to use color until well after most other newspapers added color photographs and illustrations.

Many others disagree. For example, Sharyl Attkisson plots the left-right bias of many current news outlets in her "Media Bias Chart: Analysis."[7] The Attkisson chart places the *New York Times* far to the left. AllSides Media also ranks the *Times* as "Left."[8] The "Media Bias Chart" by Ad Fontes Media, Inc., places the *Times* "Skews Left" just outside of "Middle" (neutral). Ad Fontes Media also plots it high on an axis of "Fact Reporting" vs. "Inaccurate/Fabricated Info."[9] These three charts rank hundreds of news outlets for bias but don't agree on the rankings. Perhaps bias is in the eye of the beholder.

Over history extreme media bias has occurred in other nations. Look at three Russian news organizations that date from the Bolshevik revolution in 1917 and still publish today. *Izvestiya* (Russian: Известия "News" or "Tidings") was published in Moscow as the official Soviet government newspaper from 1917 until 1991.* As an instrument of the Soviet state, it covered international relations and acted as the official voice of government policy. It became an independent publication frequently at odds with communists and nationalists although not independent as we define the term.[10] *Pravda*, (Russian: Правда "Truth") was the official organ of the Communist Party of the Soviet Union from 1918 to 1991. The newspaper was distributed nationwide, promoted the party line, and carried no Western-style news. It now publishes Russian nationalist commentary.[11] TASS (Russian: Информацио́нное аге́нтство ТАСС) the leading Russian news agency, began as a telegraph wire service in 1904 under Tsar Nicholas II. It merged with the Soviet government press bureau in 1918. The news agency had one of the biggest networks of correspondents in the world, competing with the Associated Press and Reuters services. It publishes news and public policy information online and as a wire service reflecting government positions.[12] None of these organizations operate as independent news providers protected from government shutdown and criminal charges. In fact, eighty-three reporters in the Russian Federation have been

---

* After governmental disintegration, including an attempted coup in the preceding months, the Soviet Union (USSR) officially dissolved on December 31, 1991, resulting in fifteen independent countries. The Russian Federation is one of them.

murdered since 1992 for doing their work.[13] Since Russia's attack on Ukraine began in February of 2022, the press in Russia was essentially closed down.

Article I of the Constitution called for a free press without attempting to divide the Pulitzers from the "yellow"* or to differentiate between classic journalism and social media newsfeeds. Perhaps Ben Franklin, who had published *Poor Richard's Almanack*,[14] convinced the Founding Fathers that all members of the press were righteous. But over time the press, like our nation, became widely divided over a spectrum of political views. We see that division during presidential State of the Union addresses. Viewed from the rear of the chamber, as the president speaks before Congress and members of his Cabinet, with Supreme Court Justices seated uncomfortably upfront, one sees to the right the full contingent of Republican Representatives and Senators and to the left the full contingent of Democratic Representatives and Senators separated by the middle aisle. As a Democratic president works his way through his speech and reaches passages that the Democrats like, they jump up in unison and boisterously applaud and cheer, while their Republican counterparts across the aisle sit silent with disinterested expressions. When a Republican president makes a remark in his State of the Union address that pleases the Republicans, they pop up and cheer as a body with equal vigor while the Democrats remain unsmiling in their seats. There is little or no camaraderie shown between the two sides.

Republicans and Democrats commonly refer to each other as being from across the aisle. But why should there be an aisle that separates our leaders? We are after all one nation. Perhaps we should make them pass a rule† to seat our representatives and senators alphabetically in their

---

* yellow journalism (n.): journalism based upon sensationalism and crude exaggeration to attract readers and increase circulation. The term was coined in the late 1800s to describe the extreme competition between two New York newspapers.
† For an explainer on seat assignments, see Rachel Roubein and *National Journal*, "How Senators Pick Their Seats: Power, Friends, and Proximity to Chocolate," *The Atlantic*, June 1, 2015, https://www.theatlantic.com/politics/archive/2015/06/how-senators-pick-their-seats-power-friends-and-proximity-to-chocolate/456015/.

chambers or randomly as in law school classes. Then they could rub elbows, talk to each other, hear views they don't like to hear, maybe even like each other, find common ground, and compromise. Congress needs to find a way to heal the chronic political impasse that has rendered it impotent. The press should help us find it.

The division we see in Congress and the press reflects the same division that exists in the electorate. Red states and blue states* reveal a right/left conservative/liberal nation; call it what you will. Tip O'Neal, a former Democratic speaker of the House of Representatives, once remarked that "all politics is local." The truth of that is demonstrated by the way our representatives and senators make frequent trips back home where they smile, fawn, and play to their base. While it is logical for them to do that if they expect their constituents to support them— climate change, international tensions and wars, global migration, emerging artificial intelligence, gun control, and a host of other grave issues surpass local prejudices and politics. That is what they are elected and paid to deal with, and that is precisely where the press comes in to play. Congress will remain divided unless a diligent and trustworthy press shines a light on their work and how well (or badly) they do it.

The press plays a vital role in educating the public on these issues; it helps to shape public opinion and motivate them to act. But today while each side strives to satisfy their own base, the press exacerbates the polarization that ties up Congress and the nation. Early on in his rallies during the 2016 campaign, Donald Trump pointed at the media in the back of the room and dubbed all of them the *fake news*. He repeated the line frequently, and his followers and the right-wing news media cheered him on as he did. As a result, the divisiveness in and distrust of the press greatly increased during Trump's campaigns and his presidency.

Trump and his followers were well within their rights if in fact they had discovered anything that materially distorted the results of the 2020 presidential election. But when declaring their claims of election

---

* For an explainer how "red" and "blue" came about, see Ron Elving, "The Color of Politics: How Did Red and Blue States Come to Be?" NPR, November 13, 2014, https://www.npr.org/2014/11/13/363762677/the-color-of-politics-how-did-red-and-blue-states-come-to-be.

fraud, they were obligated to produce objective supporting evidence. Recall that in the Nixon scandal, the Supreme Court ordered Nixon to hand over the doctored tapes that contained incriminating White House conversations. Florida had several documented snafus during the 2016 election. Broward County elections employees destroyed counted ballots, secretly opened mailed-in ballots, and some absentee voters received ballots missing a Florida constitutional amendment proposal.[15]

But no significant, verifiable evidence of irregularities was produced in the dozens of court proceedings (by some counts over 60[16]) that Trump and his followers filed contesting the 2020 presidential election. None of the objections they made to state election officials produced such evidence either. US Attorney General William Barr, in televised remarks on December 2, 2020, stated he saw no sign of major fraud in the 2020 presidential election. He repeated his assertion in his testimony during the second Select Committee hearing (see Chapter 5).

Nevertheless, the right-wing media relentlessly published unproven allegations following the 2020 election. They preferred to trumpet the party line. Images of "Trump Won" and "Stop the Steal" placards waved by Trump's supporters saturated the social media and right-wing news outlets.

As a result, too many Americans came to believe the election had in fact been stolen from Trump. As a matter of politics that was bad enough. But when right-wing writers, cable news commentators, and bloggers adopted Trump's claims, the deception took on a whole new dimension.

Certainly, the right-wing press had a responsibility to investigate and report provable fraud or irregularities. But they had no right under the First Amendment to dress up Trump's false claims as news, or as Franklin put it, "a vehicle of instruction." That's propaganda, not journalism. Now that threat has metastasized into a massive undermining of our elections and a threat to the Constitution itself.

We no longer have a robust, professionally trained, and experienced cadre of journalists and editors. We no longer read or watch news reports from universally shared and trusted sources, such as Walter Cronkite,

Edward R. Morrow*, or Barton Gellman and Glenn Greenwald[17]. Now we listen to our newsfeeds and like-minded bloggers instead. Local news stations and newspapers face extinction. News broadcasts, assuming they still have an audience, favor visual sensationalism with soundbites.[†] Social media is accelerating this decline by flooding our screens with dodgy accounts and misinformation. It doesn't matter whether we see it on a broadcast news show, hear it in a podcast, or read it in a newspaper—we need to recognize and support the solid information and analysis that good journalists provide.

Also fueling the erosion of investigative journalism, a very disturbing development worsened during Trump's first campaign and continued through his presidency. All content providers (including news organizations) need an audience for their advertisers and to pay for their staff and operations. They saw an opportunity to save their bottom lines and keep shareholders happy. It didn't hurt their owners' bank accounts either. The ones who didn't or weren't able to cash in, folded. Trump and his operation were irresistible clickbait.[‡] Sensationalism and breaking news alerts attract advertisers and users—they don't pause to let us ask questions like, "What are the true facts here? Who should I listen to? Have I been conned or lied to? Why do they keep saying our election system is riddled with fraud?" As one columnist put it, "It might drive many in the media and even more of their readers and viewers crazy to admit it, but two years of Donald Trump as president has been very good for their journalism, and even better for their company bottom lines, if not necessarily for the nation's future."[18]

---

* On March 9, 1954, Edward R. Morrow devoted an episode of his respected program "See It Now" to show his viewers, in Senator Joseph McCarthy's reckless words and deeds, that he had created deep fear and repression in America. For more information: https://www.huffpost.com/entry/edward-murrow-joseph-mccarthy-60-years-later_n_4936308.

† soundbite (n.): a short extract from a recorded interview, chosen for its pungency or appropriateness.

‡ clickbait (n.): the practice of writing sensationalized or misleading headlines in order to attract clicks on a piece of content. It often uses exaggerated claims or omits key information in order to encourage traffic. From https://coschedule.com/marketing-terms-definitions/what-is-clickbait.

Big business has taken over the news business through a process of mergers, consolidations, and buyouts. Media consolidation has reached the point where six corporations now own 90 percent of the media in America. For comparison, fifty companies owned American media in 1983.[19] The exact mix changes, but major players Comcast, Disney, AT&T, Viacom CBS, Sony, and Fox control almost everything Americans hear, watch, and read.[20] Since the start of the twenty-first century the number of print newspapers has shrunk. It has been reported that from 2005 to 2021 approximately 2,200 American local newspapers folded.[21] According to a recent analysis, in 2008, there were about 114,000 total newsroom employees—reporters, editors, photographers, and videographers—in five industries that produce news: newspaper, radio, broadcast television, cable, and other information services (digital news publishers). By 2020, that number had dropped to about 85,000, a loss of about 30,000 jobs.[22] We may never get them back.

As a result, the public is not receiving trustworthy information it needs, and students (and many older people) aren't mastering critical thinking skills they need to verify reports on scientific developments, foreign activities, and candidates' platforms. They confuse situation changes and new developments with useless information. Worse, too many citizens lack the focus to look for the difference.

Voters need to remember that a candidate running for public office is asking the voters to hire them. An ethical and professional press is indispensable if the voters are to have complete and accurate information before they go to the polls to hire their public officials. Today the nation badly needs journalistic ethics like that shown in the Morrow and Cronkite years. When Donald Trump denigrated other candidates, when he refused to supply his tax returns, and when he dubbed the press the fake news, the press had clear signs that he was not a suitable candidate for the presidency. When right-wing elements of the press and the Republican Party extoled him as the messiah who would "Make America Great Again," they failed all the voters. The whole nation paid the price for that on January 6, 2021.

We must never do that again.

CHAPTER 15

The Unfinished Work of Abraham Lincoln

When coauthor Nelson began the practice of law back in 1957, he found himself at a luncheon with his fellow lawyers where the conversation turned to Abraham Lincoln.

One of the new recruits asked, "What was Lincoln's contribution?"

Another answered, "He abolished slavery."

But an older lawyer broke in, "He saved the Union."

Reflecting on that conversation of so many years ago, and seeing again the faces around that table, it now comes through that Lincoln was credited with doing both. Except, we have not abolished the vestiges of slavery, and a partisan chasm again threatens the union. It has been suggested recently that most Americans believe our government does not work and that it is time to change it.[1] It has also been suggested that some of our states should secede from the union.[2] The words Lincoln spoke at Dickinson College in 1858 are as true today as they were then, "A house divided against itself cannot stand."[3]

Back in the grades during penmanship classes, Nelson never realized what a magnificent piece of literature Lincoln created when he penned the Gettysburg Address as he rode the train to Gettysburg. It is that. It also been said, "The power of words has rarely been given a more compelling demonstration than in the Gettysburg Address."[4] The words Lincoln spoke at Gettysburg followed the "most costly" battle in US history. When the three-day Battle of Gettysburg ended, 3,155 Union soldiers and 3,903 Confederate soldiers lay dead and were buried across that field.[5] Had the South prevailed, the Union Army would have been broken, and the way would have opened for Lee to march on Washington, DC. The survival of our republic was on the line at Gettysburg.

In the first sentence, he uttered at Gettysburg Lincoln spoke of a new nation the Founding Fathers had "brought forth on this continent" eighty-seven years before he spoke. Lincoln described it as being "conceived in liberty, and dedicated to the proposition that all men are created equal." He reminded the crowd that came to Gettysburg to consecrate the battlefield that "the great civil war" tested "whether that nation or any nation so conceived and dedicated might long endure." Then he cautioned them, "The brave men living and dead who struggled here have consecrated (the battlefield) far above our poor power to add or detract." Looking across that battlefield, he told the crowd, "It is for us the living rather to be dedicated here to the unfinished work which they who fought here have thus far so nobly advanced ... that we here highly resolve ... that this nation under God shall have a new birth of freedom."[6] It is critical as we read these words eight score years after Lincoln spoke at Gettysburg that we understand they are addressed to us. In his Gettysburg Address Lincoln told us, "It is rather for us to be here dedicated to the great task remaining before us." The "great task" Lincoln alluded to has not been finished.

Other nations have democracies that are based on democratic principles like ours. They believe, undoubtedly, that their systems are as good as ours and maybe even better. But we've had our representative republic for 237 years. We have built it into it a balanced government that is dedicated to the rule of law and to the freedom of its people. Why would we ever allow any person or group to replace it?

Our nation today faces mounting danger from hostile nations; we confront a peril from other nuclear nations along with the war in Ukraine; and we have barely begun climate change mitigation and regulation of scientific advances and technology that could change or destroy us. It is today more critical than ever that we take steps to resolve the issues that undermine our Constitution and world order. We will need our allies going forward and they will need us. Perhaps it's time we heed advice like that Polonius gave to Laertes, "Those friends thou hast, and their adoption tried, Grapple them unto thy soul with hoops of steel."[7]

Over history, the world experienced Pax Romana* and later Pax Britannica.† Those were periods of substantial peace and prosperity created by the Roman and British empires. Doris Kearns Goodwin explained in her Pulitzer Prize winning book, *Team of Rivals: The Political Genius of Abraham Lincoln*, that Lincoln handled the problems facing the republic by organizing a cabinet composed of his rivals.[8] Given the problems dividing us today, we need a new team of rivals to protect, defend, and preserve the pillars of our republic. The nations of the world need to see that America works, and that its people are committed to the bona fides of our Constitution and the power of democracy. If we can keep their trust and build on it, we can move forward, perhaps even to Pax Americana.

The guest essay by Laurence Tribe and others published in the *New York Times* (see Chapter 5 discussion), urged Attorney General Garland to investigate Giuliani, Meadows, Bannon, and even Trump and possibly indict them.[9] That essay, the investigations,‡ and resulting indictments, tell us that it is unknown what the fallout from the January 6 insurrection will ultimately be. Inexplicably, Trump became the nominee of the Republican Party—the party of Lincoln—and was again elected president on November 5, 2024. We are entering a period of great uncertainty.

But have no doubt, if a future vice president at a joint session of Congress obeyed a president's instructions to cast aside the votes of presidential electors, the nation would plunge into a constitutional crisis. The terms of the sitting president and vice president end on January 20, the President Pro Tempore and Speaker of the House's

---

* A 200-year period of Roman history from 27 BCE to 180 CE (the death of Marcus Aurelius) that has been described as the golden age of Roman Imperialism.

† A period of peace from 1815 to 1914 referred to as Britain's imperial century. In this period, Adam Smith wrote the *Wealth of Nations*, and free trade became a central principle of British policy.

‡ On January 12, 2022, a federal grand jury for the District of Columbia returned indictments against eleven leaders of the Oath Keepers. The indictments alleged a seditious conspiracy directed at the United States that led to and supported the January 6 attack.

terms end at expiration of the Congress, and Cabinet Secretaries and the Attorney General serve at the pleasure of the president who appointed them.[10] Recall too, that as stated in Chapter 4, eight Republican US Senators and 139 Republican US House of Representatives members voted to sustain objections to counting the votes of presidential electors at the Joint Session of January 6, 2021. Had they prevailed, the nation would not have had a legitimate, elected, and certified president and vice president to inaugurate on January 20. The offices of both the president and vice president would be vacant, and the nation would not have a command structure to react to domestic threats or those from foreign adversaries. The path would open for authoritarian government as Washington, Hamilton, and Lincoln warned. Our rights would be sliced off with little hope of getting them back.

When Nelson visited the Lincoln Memorial in Washington, DC, many years ago and stood beneath the mammoth sculpture of that humble man seated in his chair, he discerned the many tragedies that had marked his life etched into the eternity of his face. He slowly read the words Lincoln spoke at Gettysburg that are carved into one wall of his memorial and those he delivered at his second inaugural carved into the opposing wall. Over the years, the words Lincoln spoke kept coming back to him "let us strive on to finish the work we are in,"[11] "that this nation under God shall have a new birth of freedom—and that government of the people by the people for the people shall not perish from the earth."[12] Coauthor Serpento also visited the Lincoln Memorial but at night. Standing before Lincoln, she remembers the warm bright glow as balm against the darkness and troubles beyond.

Later, Nelson came across the news article[13] that explained how it was that the Thirteenth, Fourteenth, and Fifteenth Amendments to our Constitution, ratified after Lincoln died, had rewritten the moral foundation of our Republic. Then it struck him—those three amendments truly are Lincoln's legacy to the nation. They redefined and expanded the Constitution to cover all of us.

When the tragedy of January 6, 2021, and its aftermath unfolded, Nelson picked up his little brown book, looked out the window of his study, and asked himself: What do "we the people of the United States" now have that we might lose? Serpento asks, Do we have what it takes to keep it?

APPENDIX A

Major Federal Statutes

The statutes below do not constitute an exhaustive list of protections and freedoms enacted pursuant to the Constitution, but rather present an overview of legislation.

Civil Rights and Protections

Civil Rights Act of 1866. (14 Stat. 27–30, codified as amended at 42 U.S.C. §§ 1981-1986 (1982)) The first US legislation enacted to define citizenship and affirm equal protection for all citizens. It mainly applied to former slaves but not to First Nations peoples.

Indian Citizenship Act. (Pub. L. 68–175, 43 Stat. 253 (1924)) The act authorized the Secretary of the Interior to issue certificates of citizenship to First Nations people (American Indians) born in US territories. The act is silent re: Inuit people (Eskimos). Alaskan Inuits gained US citizenship with the Immigration and Nationality Act of 1952 (Pub. L 82-414, 66 Stat. 163 66 Stat. 163 (1952).[1]

Civil Rights Act of 1964. (Pub. L. 88–352, 78 Stat. 241 (1964)) The act prohibits discrimination based on race, color, religion, sex, national origin, and later amendments added sexual orientation and gender identity. It prohibits unequal application of voter registration requirements, racial segregation in schools and public accommodations, and employment discrimination.

Federal Housing Act (FHA). (Pub. L. 88–352, 78 Stat. 241 (1964)) Originally enacted as Title VIII of the Civil Rights Act of 1968, the act protects against discrimination based on race, color, religion, or national origin. Later amendments have extended protected classes.

Voting Rights Act of 1965. (Pub. L. 89–110, 79 Stat. 437 (1965), codified at 52 U.S.C. § 10101 et seq.) The act and its later amendments sought to protect voting rights of minorities through provisions regulating election procedures.

Education Amendments of 1972. (Pub. L. 92–318, 86, Stat. 235 (1972), codified at 20 U.S.C. ch. 38 § 1681 et seq.) Title IX in particular has advanced opportunities for women in education programs and activities such as athletics.

Americans with Disabilities Act of 1990 (ADA). (Pub. L. 101–336, 104 Stat. 327 (1990), codified at 42 U.S.C. ch. 126 § 12101 et seq.) The ADA prohibits discrimination based on disabilities. The ADA's definition of *disability* also includes people with mental illnesses who have a physical or mental impairment that greatly limits one or more major life activity.[2] Employers must provide reasonable accommodation. The act also imposes accessibility requirements on public facilities and transport.

National Voter Registration Act of 1993. (Pub. L. 103–31, 107 Stat. 77 (1993), codified at 42 U.S.C. ch. 20, et seq. transferred to 52 U.S.C. §§ 20501–20511) Also known as the Motor Voter Act, it requires state governments to simplify voter registration procedures and restricts voter name removals from voter rolls without meeting strict criteria.

Religious Restoration Act of 1993. (Pub. L. 103–1412, 107 Stat. 1488 (1993), codified at 42 U.S.C. ch. 21B § 2000bb et seq.) The act prohibits an agency, department, or official of the United States or any state government from burdening the exercise of religion.

* * *

Economic Rights and Freedoms

The Constitution provided Congress with power, "To regulate Commerce with foreign Nations, and among the several States, and with the Indian Tribes." (Article I Section 8) It also provided that "No Tax or Duty shall be laid on Articles exported from any State." (Article I Section 9) A number of substantial federal programs have been enacted under the Commerce Clause that greatly enlarged the ability to engage in commerce. They include the following:

Interstate Commerce Act of 1887. (Pub. L. 49–104, 24 Stat. 379 (1887)) This is the first act Congress enacted to regulate interstate commerce. It made interstate railroads the first public transportation industry to be regulated by the federal government with respect to rates and services.

Sherman Antitrust Act of 1890. (26 Stat. 209 (1890), codified as 15 U.S.C. §§ 1 -38) The first act to curtail monopolistic practices (trusts, monopolies, and cartels) that interfered with competition in interstate trade and commerce.

Federal Reserve Act of 1913. (Pub. L. 63–43, 38 Stat. 251 (1913)) A central banking system known as the Federal Reserve System (the Fed) came online on December 23, 1913, when President Woodrow Wilson signed the act. It consists of twelve regional Federal Reserve Banks and the Board of Governors. The Fed conducts monetary policy, regulates financial institutions and activities, and promotes consumer protection, community development, and financial system stability.[3]

Clayton Anti-Trust Act of 1914. (Pub. L. 63–212, 38 Stat. 730 (1914), codified at 15 U.S.C. §§ 12 – 27) This act defined unethical business practices, such as predatory price fixing, interlocking directorates, tying contracts, anticompetitive mergers, and other unethical corporate behavior. It upheld the rights of labor and established the FTC and the Antitrust Division of the DOJ as the enforcement agencies.

Norris-LaGuardia Act of 1932. (Pub. L. 72–65, 47 Stat. 70 (1932), codified at 29 U.S.C. ch. 61 et seq.) Banned Yellow Dog contracts (agreements not to join a union), banned federal courts from issuing injunctions against nonviolent labor disputes, and enjoined interference with labor unions.

Agricultural Adjustment Act of 1933 (AAA). (Pub. L. 73–10, 48 Stat. 31 (1933), codified at 7 U.S.C. ch. 26 § 601 et seq.) This act provided subsidies to farmers in exchange for their limiting production as a means of stabilizing prices for agricultural products. Along with other New Deal initiatives, the federal government began efforts to promote citizens' economic welfare. Agricultural Adjustment Act Amendment of 1935 (Pub. L. 74–320, 49 Stat. 750 (1935)) later gave the president power to impose quotas when imports interfered with commodity price stabilization programs.

Securities Act of 1933. (Pub. L. 73–22, 48 Stat. 74 (1933), codified at 15 U.S.C. § 77a et seq.) This act was enacted following the crash of the securities markets in 1929 to regulate the original sale of stock certificates and related securities.

Securities Exchange Act of 1934. (Pub. L. 73–291, 48 Stat. 881 (1934), codified at 15 U.S.C. § 78a et seq.) Also enacted following the crash of 1929 to regulate the secondary trading of stock and related securities in the stock and financial markets. It created the Securities and Exchange Commission to oversee securities exchanges, securities brokers and dealers, investment advisors, and mutual funds. The SEC's mission under the act is to promote fair dealing, disclosure of information, and the prevention of fraud in the securities markets.

National Labor Relations Act of 1935. (Pub. L. 74–198, 49 Stat. 449 (1935), codified at 29 U.S.C. §§ 151–169) Also known as the Wagner Act, this act regulated wages and working conditions in interstate commerce. It guaranteed the right of workers to organize and provided a framework for collective bargaining. It created the National Labor Relations Board.

Motor Carrier Act of 1935. (Pub. L. 74–255, 49 Stat. 543 (1935)) Enacted to amend the Interstate Commerce Act of 1887, this act gave the Interstate Commerce Commission the power to regulate the rates and services of interstate truck and bus transportation.

Social Security Act of 1935. (Pub. L. 74–271, 49 Stat. 620 (1935), codified at 42 U.S.C. §§ 1376 u-5 et seq.) This act created a system of payroll deductions and employer contributions to support the payment of retirement benefits to retirees over sixty-five. It also created Old Age and Survivors Insurance, Aid to Dependent Children, and Aid to the Permanently Disabled.

Rural Electrification Act of 1936. (Pub. L. 74–605, 49 Stat. 1363 (1936), codified at 7 U.S.C. ch. 31 § 901 et seq.) This act established programs for the installation of electric distributions systems in rural America.

Robinson Patman Act of 1936. (Pub. L. 74–692, 49 Stat. 1526 (1936), codified at 15 U.S.C. § 13) This act amended the Clayton Act to outlaw price fixing, bid rigging, and predatory pricing.

Servicemen's Readjustment Act of 1944. (Pub. L. 78–346, 58 Stat. 284 (1944)) Commonly known as the GI Bill, provided a range of educational and financial benefits for many of the returning WW2 veterans (commonly referred to as GIs). The original GI Bill expired in 1956, but the term "G.I. Bill" is still used to refer to programs created to assist qualified US military veterans.

Taft Hartley Act of 1947. (Pub. L. 80–101, 61 Stat. 136 (1947), codified at 29 U.S.C. Ch. 7 §§ 141-197) Also known as the Labor-Management Act, this act amended the Wagner Act. It followed a period of major strikes during 1945 and 1946. The act sought to curtail illegal practices by unions, forbid encouraging other industries to participate in a labor strike, and to allow free speech by employers. It tightened constraints on labor unions by banning most strikes, secondary boycotts, and mass picketing. It also sought to regulate threats to close down an employer location if its employees were not represented by a labor union.

Social Security Amendments of 1965. (Pub. L. 89–97, 79 Stat. 286 (1965), Title 11 (x1) of the Social Security Act, codified at 42 U.S.C. § 426a et seq.) This act amended the Social Security Act to provide medical insurance benefits and prescribed drug assistance to seniors (Medicare) and matching funds to states for citizens below specified income levels (Medicaid).

Higher Education Act of 1965. (Pub. L. 89–329, 79 Stat. 1219 [1965] codified at 20 USC § 1070a, as amended) was enacted as part of President Lyndon Johnson's Great Society program. It increased federal money given to universities, created scholarships, and gave low-interest loans for students. The Pell Grant program awards scholarships to undergraduate students and a few graduate program applicants (teacher certification) who can prove exceptional financial need.

Equal Employment Opportunity Act of 1972. (Pub. L. 92–261, 86 Stat. 103 (1972), codified at 42 U.S.C. §§ 2000e–2000e-8 and 5

U.S.C. § 5108) This act empowers the Equal Employment Opportunity Commission (EEOC) to take employment discrimination enforcement actions on behalf of minority employees and require employers to make reasonable religious accommodations.

Family and Medical Leave Act of 1993 (FMLA). (Pub. L. 103–3, 107 Stat. 6 (1993), codified at 29 U.S.C. § 2601) The FMLA requires covered employers to provide employees with up to twelve weeks of job-protected, unpaid leave for qualified medical and family reasons. The FMLA covers leave for the birth or adoption of a child, to care for the employee's spouse, child, or parent who has a serious health condition, or for a serious health condition that makes the employee unable to perform the essential functions of his or her job.

Health Insurance Portability and Accountability Act of 1996. (Pub. L. 104-191, 100 Stat. 2548) HIPAA required creation of national standards to protect sensitive patient health data from being disclosed without knowledge or consent, and to enable people to keep health insurance.

Sarbanes-Oxley Act of 2002. (Pub. L. 107–204, 116 Stat. 745 (2002)) Also known as the Corporate Responsibility Act, the act's provisions aimed at improving regulation of businesses' financial activities and financial reporting and providing more oversight of corporate and financial activity.

Patient Protection and Affordable Care Act of 2010. (Pub. L. 111–148, 124 Stat. 119 – 1025 (2010)) Also known as Obamacare, the act expanded healthcare insurance to cover all adults with incomes below 138 percent of the Federal Poverty Level (FPL). It also banned insurers refusing or surcharging patients for pre-existing conditions.

Infrastructure and Jobs Act of 2021. (Pub. L. 117–58, 135 Stat. 429 (2021)) This act funds rail transit, ports, airports, electric grids, water systems, broadband, and other physical infrastructure projects. It functions as a piece of the Build Back Better Act (H.R. 5376, 117 Congress) (BBB) plan proposed by President Biden to fund social support and education programs.

Inflation Reduction Act of 2022. (Pub. L 117-169 (2022). This act addressed programs to control greenhouse gases, sought to lower the national debt, lower prescription and health care costs, lower energy costs and established a minimum 15 percent tax rate for corporations.

* * *

Public Health and Safety Rights

Pure Food and Drug Act of 1906. (Pub. L. 59–384, 34 Stat. 768 (1906), codified at 21 U.S.C.) This was the first consumer protection act. It created the Pure Food and Drug Administration and regulated interstate traffic in adulterated food and drug products.

Federal Food, Drug, and Cosmetic (FDC) Act of 1938. (Pub. L. 75-717, 52 Stat. 1040 (1938), codified at 21 U.S.C.) It extended control to cosmetics and therapeutic devices, provided that safe tolerances be set for unavoidable poisonous substances, authorized factory inspections, and started a new system of drug regulation to require proof of safety before marketing and sale.

National Traffic and Motor Vehicle Safety Act of 1966. (Pub. L 89-563, 80 Stat. 718 (1966), codified at 49 U.S.C. ch. 301) This act was the first to require development of safety standards for motor vehicles and to address road traffic safety in response to rapidly increasing traffic fatalities. It eventually led to creation of the National Highway Safety Administration (NHTSA).

Occupational Safety and Health Act (OSHA). (Pub. L. 91–596, 84 Stat. 1590 (1970), codified at 29 U.S.C. ch. 15 § 651 et seq.) The act aims to ensure that employers protect their workers from recognized hazards and unsanitary conditions. Currently used to issue mandates for COVID-19 vaccinations for employers of one hundred employees or more.

Clean Air Act of 1970. (Pub. L. 91–604, 84 Stat. 1676 (1970), codified at 42 U.S.C. ch. 85) The Clean Air Act (CAA), the comprehensive federal law that regulates air emissions from stationary and mobile sources. The Environmental Protection Agency (EPA) is required to set pollutant levels standards to address public health risks.

Clean Water Act of 1972. (Pub. L. 92–500, 86 Stat. 816 (1972), codified at 33 U.S.C. § 1251 et seq.) The act establishes the basic structure for regulating discharges of pollutants into the waters of the United States and regulating quality standards for surface waters.

Consumer Product Safety Act. (Pub. L. 92–573, 86 Stat. 1207 (1972), codified at 15 U.S.C. ch. 47 § 2051 et seq.) The act established the Consumer Product Safety Commission to develop safety standards and require recalls of products with an unreasonable risk of injury or death. It excludes products regulated by other agencies such as the Food and Drug Administration.

Comprehensive Environmental Response, Compensation, and Liability Act (CERCLA Superfund). (Pub. L. 96–510 (1980), 94 Stat. 2767 codified at 42 U.S.C. § 9601 et seq.) The act established the cleanup program, administered by the EPA, to investigate and remediate contaminated sites.

APPENDIX B

Websites for Further Information

The websites below do not constitute an exhaustive list of available resources, but rather give the reader a place to begin research. Note: website links are subject to change. If a link no longer works, try navigating to the site's home page and use the search box to find the current link.

https://www.archives.gov/founding-docs/constitution-transcript

A transcription of the Constitution as it was inscribed by Jacob Shallus on parchment on display in the Rotunda at the National Archives Museum. The spelling and punctuation reflect the original. Quoted excerpts from this version are used in the text.

https://www.archives.gov/founding-docs/bill-of-rights-transcript

A transcription of the enrolled original of the Joint Resolution of Congress proposing the Bill of Rights on permanent display in the Rotunda at the National Archives Museum. The spelling and punctuation reflect the original. Quoted excerpts from this version are used in the text.

https://www.archives.gov/founding-docs/declaration-transcript

A transcription of the stone engraving of the parchment Declaration of Independence on display in the Rotunda at the National Archives Museum. The spelling and punctuation reflect the original. Quoted excerpts from this version are used in the text.

https://guides.loc.gov/federalist-papers/full-text

Federalist Papers: Primary Documents in American History. This site has all eighty-five essays in full text. Quoted excerpts from this version are used in the text.

https://avalon.law.yale.edu/subject_menus/major.asp

The Avalon Project of the Lillian Goldman Law Library, Yale Law School has digital documents in the fields of law, history, diplomacy, and government. To name a few: the Code of Hammurabi, Magna Carta, Charters for the Colonies, Articles of Confederation, Emancipation Proclamation, Nuremberg War Crimes Trial, and 9/11 Commission Report.

https://www.congress.gov/

Congress.gov is the official website for US federal legislative information for Members of Congress, legislative agencies, and the public. The Library of Congress (LOC) maintains it using data from the Office of the Clerk of the US House of Representatives, the Office of the Secretary of the Senate, the Government Publishing Office, Congressional Budget Office, and the LOC's Congressional Research Service (site below).

https://www.govinfo.gov/

GovInfo is a service of the US Government Publishing Office (GPO), a federal agency in the legislative branch. It provides free public access to official publications from all three branches of the federal government. For example: Code of Federal Regulations, Congressional bills and statutes, Congressional Record, the US Code, directories of organizations and officials, Independent Counsel publications, presidential documents, and much more.

https://www.supremecourt.gov/opinions/opinions.aspx

The opinions include case decisions written by the justices, per curium (author not identified) decisions, among others. Volume and page numbers are given for official texts of case decisions as published in *United States Reports*.

https://caselaw.findlaw.com/court/us-supreme-court

For opinions prior to 1991, Findlaw offers a free searchable database of opinions going back to 1791. Note: these are not official texts.

https://pacer.uscourts.gov/

PACER provides public access to electronic federal court case documents and dockets (case documents index and status of proceedings). Not free, but PACER waives charges for document pages retrieval under a $30 total per quarter.

https://www.law.cornell.edu/

LII publishes free online versions of core federal administrative, legislative, and case law, with legal commentary and explanations in their WEX legal dictionary and encyclopedia. The LII Supreme Court Bulletin has analysis of cases to be argued before the Supreme Court. LII recently added regulations for the fifty states.

https://crsreports.congress.gov/

The Congressional Research Service (CRS) is the public policy research service of the Library of Congress for members of Congress and committees. CRS staff members analyze current policies and present the impact of proposed policy alternatives. Note: selected reports are available to the public but those are free.

https://www.gao.gov/

Government Accountability Office (GAO) provides Congress, the heads of executive agencies, and the public with timely, fact-based, nonpartisan investigations on how the government spends taxpayers' dollars. For example: recent reports on information security, national defense, climate change costs, etc.

https://vault.fbi.gov/

The Vault is FBI's FOIA Library, containing 6,700 documents and other media that have been scanned from paper into digital copies available online. Find documents on homeland security, individuals involved with civil rights, etc.

https://www.ncsl.org/

The National Conference of State Legislatures (NCSL) includes information to assist voters on state election primaries.

https://www.nass.org/

The National Association of Secretaries of State has resources for election administration, cybersecurity, and related topics.

https://www.factcheck.org/

FactCheck.org is a nonpartisan, nonprofit project of the Annenberg Public Policy Center of the University of Pennsylvania. It aims to reduce the level of deception and confusion in US politics by monitoring the factual accuracy of what is said by major US political players in TV ads, debates, speeches, interviews, and news releases. They aim to apply the best practices of both journalism and scholarship, and to increase public knowledge and understanding.

https://adfontesmedia.com/interactive-media-bias-chart/

Ad Fontes Media is incorporated as a Public Benefit Corporation (PBC)[1] in Colorado. Ad Fontes Media's mission is to rate the news for reliability and bias to help people navigate the news landscape. Ad Fontes has created a system of news content ratings on two axes:

liberal-neutral-right and fact-reliability variation-selective fact report-inaccurate/fabricated reporting.

https://guides.library.cornell.edu/evaluating_Web_pages

The Cornell University library's "Evaluating Web Pages: Questions to Consider" site has tools for checking content accuracy, objectivity, and how recently the website published or updated.

https://library.georgetown.edu/tutorials/research-guides/evaluating-internet-content

Georgetown University has a set of questions for evaluating websites, including Wikipedia. "The responsibility is on the user to evaluate resources effectively."

https://www.brennancenter.org/

Named for Supreme Court Justice William J. Brennan, the Brennan Center for Justice is a nonpartisan institute supporting democracy, justice, and liberty and national security on national, state, and local government levels. Current project includes tracking state legislation on voting rights.

https://www.aclu.org/

The American Civil Liberties Union (ACLU) advocates in courts, legislatures, and communities for individual rights guaranteed under the Constitution and US laws.

https://www.splcenter.org/

The Southern Poverty Law Center (SPLC) specializes in legal advocacy for civil rights and public interest litigation. They track and profile hate groups and offer education resources.

https://www.eff.org/

Founded in 1990, the Electronic Frontier Foundation (EFF) is a nonprofit organization working to ensure that technology supports freedom of expression, user privacy, and innovation.

https://www.cia.gov/the-world-factbook/

The CIA's World Factbook has basic intelligence profiles on the history, people, government, economy, energy, geography, environment, communications, transportation, military, terrorism, and transnational issues for 266 world entities.

OTHER READING

Applebaum, Anne, *Twilight of Democracy, The Seductive Lure of Authoritarianism*, New York: Anchor Books, a division of Penguin Random House LLC, 2021.

Baker, Peter, and Susan Glasser, *The Divider: Trump in the White House, 2017–2021*, New York: Doubleday, 2022.

Beeman, Richard R., *Our Lives, our Fortunes and our Sacred Honor: The Forging of American Independence, 1774–1776*, New York: Basic Books, A Member of the Perseus Books Group, 2013.

Berman, Geoffrey, *Holding the Line: Inside the Nation's Preeminent US Attorney's Office and its Battle with the Trump Justice Department*, New York: Penguin Press, an imprint of Random House LLC, 2022.

Bernstein, Carl, and Bob Woodward, *All the President's Men*, New York: Simon & Schuster, 1974.

Bowden, Mark, and Mathew Teague, *The Steal: The Attempt to Overturn the 2020 Election and the People Who Stopped It*, New York: Atlantic Monthly Press, 2022.

Brown, Dee, *Bury my Heart at Wounded Knee: An Indian History of the American West*, New York: Ishi Press International, 2014.

Cheney, Elizabeth L. (Liz), *Oath and Honor: A Memoir and a Warning*, New York: Little, Brown and Company, 2023.

Findlay, Bruce Allyn and Esther Blair Findlay, *Your Rugged Constitution*, Stanford: Stanford University Press, reissue of 1969 Edition, 2014.

Flexner, Eleanor, and Ellen F. Fitzpatrick, *Century of Struggle: the Woman's Rights Movement in the United State*s, Cambridge: Belknap Press of Harvard University Press, 1996.

Gates Jr., Henry Louis, *Life upon These Shores: Looking at African American History*, 1513–2008, New York: Alfred A. Knopf, 2011.

Goodwin, Doris Kearns, *Team of Rivals: The Political Genius of Abraham Lincoln*, New York: Simon & Schuster, 2005.

Haberman, Maggie, *Confidence Man: The Making of Donald Trump and the Breaking of America*, New York: Penguin Press, an imprint of Random House LLC, 2022.

Hamilton, Alexander, et al, *The Federalist,* New York: Barnes & Noble Books, 2006.

Hett, Benjamin Carter, *Death of Democracy: Hitler's Rise to Power and the Downfall of the Weimar Republic*, New York: Henry Holt and Company, 2018.

Hutchinson, Cassidy, *Enough*, New York: Simon & Schuster, 2023.

Karl, Jonathan, *Betrayal: The Final Act of the Trump Show*, New York: Dutton, An Imprint of Penguin Random House LLC, 2021.

Leonnig, Carol, and Philip Rucker, *I Alone Can Fix It: Donald J. Trump's Catastrophic Final Year,* New York: Penguin Press, An Imprint of Random House LLC, 2021.

Lewis, Sinclair, *It Can't Happen Here*, New York: Signet Classics, 2014.

Meacham, Jon, *The Soul of America: The Battle for Our Better Angels*, New York: Random House, 2018.

McQuade, Barbara, *Attack from Within: How Disinformation Is Sabotaging America*, New York, Seven Stories Press, 2024.

Murray, Melissa and Weissmann, Andrew, *The Trump Indictments: The Historic Charging Documents with Commentary*, New York: W.W. Norton & Company, 2024.

Raskin, James B., *Unthinkable: Trauma, Truth, and the Trials of American Democracy,* New York: Harper, an imprint of HarperCollins, 2022.

Schiff, Adam B., *Midnight in Washington: How We Almost Lost Our Democracy and Still Could,* New York: Random House, 2021.

Shirer, William L., *The Rise and Fall of the Third Reich: A History of Nazi Germany*, New York: Simon & Schuster, 1988.

Snyder, Timothy, and Nora Krug, *On Tyranny: Twenty Lessons from the Twentieth Century*, New York: Tim Duggan Books, An Imprint of the Crown Publishing Group, a division of Penguin Random House LLC, 2017.

Van Tilburg Clark, Walter, *The Ox-Bow Incident*, New York: Modern Library, 2004.

Underhill, James (Ed.), *Charters of Freedom: Founding Documents of American Democracy*, Old Saybrook: Konecky & Konecky, 2012.

Underhill, James, Wasserman, Louis, *Modern Political Philosophies and What They Mean*, Garden City: Garden City Books, 1951.

Wills, Garry, *Lincoln at Gettysburg: The Words that Remade America*, New York: Simon & Schuster, 1992.

Wolff, Michael, *Landslide: The Final Days of the Trump Presidency*, New York: Henry Holt and Company, 2021.

Woodward, Bob, and Robert Costa, *Peril*, New York: Simon & Schuster, 2021.

Woodward, Bob, *Rage*, New York: Simon & Schuster, 2020.

ABOUT THE AUTHORS

David L. Nelson graduated from Northern Michigan University in 1954. He earned a juris doctor degree from the University of Michigan Law School in 1957. While at law school, he served as an associate and later assistant editor of the Michigan Law Review. He is a member of the Michigan Bar Association and authorized to practice in federal courts, including the US Supreme Court. He practiced law in Michigan for more than forty years, principally with the Sommers Schwartz firm in Southfield, Michigan where he is of counsel, specializing in commercial litigation. He retired in 2001. He is the author of three books: *Tool Marks Don't Lie*, *River of Iron*, and *Chasing Blood Money*. He also helped his family publish *Wandering Verse*, a book of his mother's poetry.

Mary Margaret Serpento graduated from Pennsylvania State University with a B.A. in 1976. She earned an A.M.L.S. from the University of Michigan in 1977. While at Penn State, she joined the Phi Beta Kappa Society in her junior year. She was a law librarian for forty years until her retirement in 2020. She is the editor of three of her coauthor's books. She is a lifelong historian and science fiction reader.

NOTES

Mission Statement

[1]   Tom LoBianco and Ashley Killough, "Trump pitches black voters: 'What the hell do you have to lose?'" CNN, updated 8:22 p.m. EDT, August 19, 2016, https://www.cnn.com/2016/08/19/politics/donald-trump-african-american-voters/index.html.

[2]   Charles M. Blow, "America's Thirst for Authoritarianism," *New York Times*, December 14, 2023, p. A25.

[3]   *Id.*

[4]   Anjali Huynh and Michael Gold, "Trump Says Some Migrants Are 'Not People' and Predicts a 'Blood Bath' if He Loses." *New York Times*, published March 16, 2024, updated March 18, 2024, https://www.nytimes.com/2024/03/16/us/politics/trump-speech-ohio.html.

Introduction

[1]   U.S. District Attorney's Office, District of Columbia, "35 Months Since the Jan. 6 Attack on the Capitol," updated December 6, 2023, https://www.justice.gov/usao-dc/33-months-jan-6-attack-capitol-0.

[2]   Declaration of Independence (U.S. 1776).

      According to the endnotes in *The Declaration of Independence: A Study in the History of Political Ideas* by Carl Lotus Becker, (New York: Harcourt, Brace, 1922): "The Rough Draft reads '[inherent &] inalienable.' There is no indication that Congress changed 'inalienable' to 'unalienable'; but the latter form appears in the text in the rough journal, in the corrected journal, and in the parchment copy. John Adams, in making his copy of the Rough Draft, wrote 'unalienable.' Adams was a member of the committee which supervised the printing of the text adopted by Congress, and it may have been at his suggestion that the change was made in printing. 'Unalienable' may have been the more customary form in the eighteenth century."

[3]   Alexander Hamilton and George Washington, "Farewell Address," *American Daily Advertiser*, September 19, 1796, at https://founders.archives.gov/documents/Washington/05-20-02-0440-0002.

[4]   Alexander Hamilton, *Federalist* No. 9, (1787, 1788), available at https://guides.loc.gov/federalist-papers/full-text.

5   "The Perpetuation of Our Political Institutions" Address by Abraham Lincoln before the Young Men's Lyceum of Springfield, January 27, 1838, *Journal of the Abraham Lincoln Association,* Volume 6, Issue 1, 1984, pp. 6–14, available at https://quod.lib.umich.edu/j/jala/2629860.0006.103/--perpetuation-of-our-political-institutions-address?rgn=main;view=fulltext.

6   *Eastman v. Thompson,* Cen. Dist. Calif., No. 8:22-cv-00099-DOC-DFM (Order Re Privilege of Documents Dated January 4–7, 2021), available at https://www.cacd.uscourts.gov/sites/default/files/documents/DOC%20Eastman%20Order_0.pdf.

7   Luke Broadwater, Alan Feuer, and Maggie Haberman, "Federal Judge Signals Trump Committed Crimes," *New York Times*, March 29, 2022, p. A1.

8   Annie Karni and Maggie Haberman, "Trump Pressured Pence and Incited a Mob Against Him," *New York Times*, June 17, 2022, p. A1.

9   "Remarks by President Biden in Statement to the American People." Address by Joseph R. Biden Jr. from the White House Oval Office July 24, 2024. Transcript available at https://www.whitehouse.gov/briefing-room/speeches-remarks/2024/07/24/remarks-by-president-biden-in-statement-to-the-american-people/.

Chapter 1

1   Declaration of Independence (US 1776).

2   Office of Public Affairs, "America's Wars," Department of Veterans Affairs, May 2021. https%3A%2F%2Fwww.va.gov%2Fopa%2Fpublications%2Ffactsheets%2Ffs_americas_wars.pdf&usg=AOvVaw2EMJPo6JuX-lH4pk9lWn45.

3   Martin Luther King quoted from "America" ("My Country 'Tis of Thee") during his "I Have a Dream" speech delivered on the steps of the Lincoln Memorial during the March on Washington for Jobs and Freedom on August 28, 1963. Full text of his speech is available at https://www.npr.org/2010/01/18/122701268/i-have-a-dream-speech-in-its-entirety.

4   Benjamin Franklin reportedly made this response to Mrs. Elizabeth Powel when she asked him outside of Convention Hall to describe the new form of government. Walter Isaacson, *Benjamin Franklin: An American Life* (New York: Simon & Schuster, 2003) p. 459.

5   Capitalization and original spelling per the National Archives transcripts are used throughout this book. "The Constitution of the United States: A Transcription," https://www.archives.gov/founding-docs/constitution-transcript, "Bill of Rights," https://www.archives.gov/founding-docs/bill-of-rights and "The Constitution: Amendments 11–27," https://www.archives.gov/founding-docs/amendments-11-27.

6   William Shakespeare, *The Tragedy of Julius Caesar*, Act I, scene 2, L 140–141.

[7] William L. Shirer, *The Rise and Fall of the Third Reich*, (New York: Simon & Schuster, copyrighted 1959, 1960, 1987, 1988, 1990, and 2011) p. 187.

[8] President Harry S. Truman signed the Economic Recovery Act of 1948 (Pub. L. 80-472, 62 Stat. 137 (1948). Known as the Marshall Plan and named for Secretary of State George Marshall, who proposed that the US provide economic assistance to restore postwar Europe's shattered infrastructure and starving population. Congress appropriated $13.3 billion for European recovery. For the US, the plan created markets for American goods and stable trading partners, and countered Soviet expansion by encouraging democratic governments in Western Europe. For more information, see "Milestone Documents: Marshall Plan (1948)," https://www.archives.gov/milestone-documents/marshall-plan.

[9] In his second Inaugural Address, President Truman described his foreign policy goals. His fourth point, now known as the Point Four Program, declared that the US would "embark on a bold new program for making the benefits of our scientific advances and industrial progress available for the improvement and growth of underdeveloped areas." The program offered knowledge and expertise instead of money or food aid. For more information, see Harry S. Truman Online Collections Research Files, "The Point Four Program," https://www.trumanlibrary.gov/library/online-collections.

[10] Under this policy, the United States was able to supply military aid to its foreign allies during WW2 while remaining officially neutral in the conflict. History.com editors, "Lend-Lease Act," History.com, November 4, 2019, https://www.history.com/topics/world-war-ii/lend-lease-act-1.

[11] Office of the Historian, United States State Department, "The Yalta Conference, 1945," https://history.state.gov/milestones/1937-1945/yalta-conf (accessed March 2022).

[12] Winston Churchill, "Sinews of Peace," presented at Westminster College on March 5, 1946, Fulton, Missouri, text available at America's National Churchill Museum, https://www.nationalchurchillmuseum.org/sinews-of-peace-iron-curtain-speech.html. For historical background, see Stephen Rogers, "Winston Churchill's Iron Curtain Speech—March 5, 1946," National WWII Museum, March 5, 2021 https://www.nationalww2museum.org/war/articles/winston-`

[13] Directorate-General for Communication, "History of the EU," European Commission, accessed August 24, 2022, https://european-union.europa.eu/principles-countries-history/history-eu_en.

[14] History.com editors, "Bay of Pigs Invasion," History.com, updated March 30, 2020, https://www.history.com/topics/cold-war/bay-of-pigs-invasion.

[15] Office of the Historian, "The Cuban Missile Crisis, October 1962," US Department of State, https://history.state.gov/milestones/1961-1968/cuban-missile-crisis (accessed August 2, 2022).

16   North Atlantic Treaty Organization, "What was the Warsaw Pact?" https://www.nato.int/cps/us/natohq/declassified_138294.htm (accessed August 2, 2022).

17   Erin Blakemore, "Cold War facts and information," *National Geographic*, March 22, 2019, https://www.nationalgeographic.com/culture/article/cold-war.

18   Union of Concerned Scientists, "Nuclear Weapons Worldwide," https://www.ucsusa.org/nuclear-weapons/worldwide (accessed August 2, 2022).

19   Martin McCauley and Domenic Lieven, "The Gorbachev era: perestroika and glasnost," Btitannica.com, https://www.britannica.com/place/Russia/Ethnic-relations-and-Russias-near-abroad (accessed March 15, 2022).

20   NPR, "Russia recognizes 2 Ukrainian regions as independent," All Things Considered, February 21, 2022, https://www.npr.org/2022/02/21/1082172502/russia-plans-to-recognize-2-ukrainian-regions-as-independent.

21   Catie Edmondson, "Annotated Transcript: Zelensky's Speech to Congress," *New York Times*, March 17, 2022, p. A8.

22   Anton Troianovski et al., "In Russia, Even the Smallest Dissent Is Silenced," *New York Times*, January 13, 2024, p. A1.

23   Arthur H. Vandenberg, "Address to the Cleveland Foreign Affairs Forum," January 11, 1947, Cleveland Ohio. Available at https://www.americanrhetoric.com/speeches/arthurvandenbergclevelandforeignaffairsforum.htm. Reprinted in 90 Cong. Rec. p. 272 (January 13, 1947).

Chapter 2

1   Declaration of Independence (US 1776).

2   The *Federalist* (the *Federalist Papers*) is a series of eighty-five essays written by Alexander Hamilton, John Jay, and James Madison and published anonymously in various New York newspapers October 1787–May 1788 to urge New Yorkers to ratify the proposed US Constitution. In lobbying for its adoption to replace the Articles of Confederation, the essays explain provisions of the Constitution in detail. Full text of the *Federalist* is available at https://guides.loc.gov/federalist-papers/full-text.

3   Although no record from that time exists for Benjamin Franklin actually saying those words, the sentiment was clearly in the minds of the delegates of the Continental Congress when they agreed to the Declaration of Independence. https://www.historycentral.com/Revolt/stories/Hang.html.

4   *Scott v. Sandford*, 60 US 393, 19 How. 393; 15 L. Ed. 691 (1857).

5   Pub. L. 88–352, 78 Stat. 241 (1964), codified at 42 U.S.C. ch. 21 as amended.

6   Civic Way, "Critical Race Theory, Fact versus Fiction," https://www.civicway.org/saving-democracy/critical-race-theory-fact-versus-fiction/ (accessed August 3, 2022).

7 Southern Poverty Law Center, "Weekend Read: The Struggle for Native American Voting Rights," https://www.splcenter.org/news/2019/11/23/weekend-read-struggle-native-american-voting-rights?gclid=EAIaIQobChMIhY6_vqur-QIVZMmUCR25cABxEAAYAyAAEgINPvD_BwE (accessed August 3, 2022).

8 Pub. L 82-414, 66 Stat. 163 66 Stat. 163 (1952), codified at 8 USC ch. 12 as amended.

9 Jennifer Schuessler, "The Complex History of the Women's Suffrage Movement," *New York Times*, August 15, 2019, https://www.nytimes.com/2019/08/15/arts/design/the-complex-history-of-the-womens-suffrage-movement.html.

10 André Munro, "Republic: government," Britannica, https://www.britannica.com/topic/republic-government, See also Thoughtco.com, https://www.thoughtco.com/republic-vs-democracy-4169936 and USHistory.org, "American Government 1c. What Is a Democracy?" https://www.ushistory.org/gov/1c.asp.

11 *In re Duncan*, 139 U.S. 449, 11S. Ct. 573, 35 L. Ed. 219 (1891).

12 James Madison, *Federalist* No. 10. (1787, 1788), available at https://guides.loc.gov/federalist-papers/text-1-10.

Chapter 3

1 Wire Services, "Melania Trump: Donald Trump's lewd talk about women is 'boy talk'," *Dallas Morning News*, October 17, 2016, https://www.dallasnews.com/news/politics/2016/10/17/melania-trump-donald-trump-s-lewd-talk-about-women-is-boy-talk/.

2 Votes for Hillary Clinton outnumbered Donald Trump by almost 2.9 million, with 65,844,954 (48.2%) to his 62,979,879 (46.1%), according to revised and certified final election results from all 50 states and the District of Columbia. For more information, see Gregory Kreig, "It's official: Clinton swamps Trump in popular vote," CNN, updated December 22, 2016, https://www.cnn.com/2016/12/21/politics/donald-trump-hillary-clinton-popular-vote-final-count/index.html.

3 Glenn Kessler, "Not just misleading. Not merely false. A lie," *Washington Post*, August 22, 2018, https://www.washingtonpost.com/politics/2018/08/23/not-just-misleading-not-merely-false-lie/.

4 Daniel Dale, "Confessions of a Trump Fact-Checker," *Politico Magazine*, October 19, 2016, https://www.politico.com/magazine/story/2016/10/one-month-253-trump-untruths-214369/.

5 Glenn Kessler, Salvador Rizzo and Meg Kelly, "Fact Checker Analysis: Trump's false or misleading claims total 30,573 over 4 years," *Washington Post*, January 24, 2021, https://www.washingtonpost.com/politics/2021/01/24/trumps-false-or-misleading-claims-total-30573-over-four-years/.

6   Jessica Estepa, "Donald Trump on Carly Fiorina: 'Look at that face!'" *USA Today*, published and updated September 10, 2016, https://www.usatoday.com/story/news/nation-now/2015/09/10/trump-fiorina-look-face/71992454/.

7   Peter W. Peterson, "A Brief History of the 'Lock Her Up!' chant by Trump Supporters against Clinton," *Washington Post*, November 22, 2016, https://www.washingtonpost.com/news/the-fix/wp/2016/11/22/a-brief-history-of-the-lock-her-up-chant-as-it-looks-like-trump-might-not-even-try/.

8   Walter Van Tilburg Clark, *The Ox-Bow Incident* (New York: Random House, 1940). Dramatized in 1942 as a film directed by William A. Wellman.

9   Joseph Thorndike, "Debate Over Trump's Taxes Sparks As Many Questions about the IRS as the Former President," *Forbes*, Dec 22, 2022, https://www.forbes.com/sites/taxnotes/2022/12/22/why-and-when-did-the-irs-stop-auditing-the-president/?sh=13a2e66125ed.

10   Casey Decker, "No, the IRS isn't legally required to audit the president," VerifyThis.com, updated January 9, 2023, https://www.verifythis.com/article/news/verify/taxes-verify/no-the-irs-isnt-legally-required-to-audit-the-president-video-trump/536-e0534e45-da7a-4484-8c5b-3f7c781a2381.

11   Tom Winter and Adam Edelman, "Trump's tax returns handed over to Manhattan prosecutors," NBC News, February 25, 2021, https://www.nbcnews.com/politics/donald-trump/manhattan-d-vance-possession-trump-s-taxes-n1258834.

12   Jonah E. Bromwich, Ben Protess, and William K. Rashbaum, "Trump's CFO Admits to Role in Tax Scheme," *New York Times*, August 19, 2022. p. A1.

13   Dan Mangan, "Trump tax returns must be given to Congress, federal appeals court says in new ruling," CNBC, August 9, 2022, https://www.cnbc.com/2022/08/09/trump-tax-returns-must-be-given-to-congress-court-says-.html.

14   Staff of the Joint Committee on Taxation, *Report to the House Committee on Ways and Means Chairman Richard Neal*, December 15, 2022, available at https://www.nytimes.com/interactive/2022/12/21/us/house-ways-and-means-trump-tax-report.html.

15   Dan Mangan, "Trump brags about not paying taxes: 'That makes me smart.'" CNBC.com September 26 2016 10:10 PM EDT updated September 26 2016, https://www.cnbc.com/2016/09/26/trump-brags-about-not-paying-taxes-that-makes-me-smart.html.

16   Emily Cochrane, Alan Rappeport and Luke Broadwater, "Trump's Orders on Coronavirus Relief Create Confusion," *New York Times*, August 9, 2020 updated December 23, 2020, https://www.nytimes.com/2020/08/09/us/politics/trump-stimulus-bill-coronavirus.html.

17   Bob Woodward, *Rage*, (New York: Simon & Schuster, 2020) pp. 232–233. See also Carol Leonnig and Philip Rucker, *I alone can fix it: Donald J. Trump's*

catastrophic final year, (New York: Penguin Press, an imprint of Penguin Random House LLC, 2021) p. 45.

18 Allyson Chiu, et al, "Trump claims controversial comment about injecting disinfectants was 'sarcastic,'" *Washington Post*, April 24, 2020, https://www. washingtonpost.com/nation/2020/04/24/disinfectant-injection-coronavirus-trump/.

19 Lloyd Doggett, "Timeline of Trump's Coronavirus Responses," Blog Post, March 2, 2022, https://doggett.house.gov/media/blog-post/timeline-trumps-coronavirus-responses.

20 JAMA 2021; 325(2):123–124. doi:10.1001/jama.2020.24865, "COVID-19 as the Leading Cause of Death in the United States," December 17, 2020, available at https://jamanetwork.com/journals/jama/fullarticle/2774465.

21 Sergei Klebnikov, "'As An American, That's My Right': Few Trump Supporters in Tulsa Wearing Face Masks," *Forbes*, updated June 20, 2020, https://www. forbes.com/sites/sergeiklebnikov/2020/06/20/as-an-american-thats-my-right-few-trump-supporters-in-tulsa-wearing-face-masks/?sh=3cc8fcd930f9.

22 World Health Organization, "Global excess deaths associated with COVID-19, January 2020—December 2021," May 2022, available at https://www.who. int/data/stories/global-excess-deaths-associated-with-covid-19-january-2020-december-2021.

23 National Institutes of Health, "COVID-19 was third leading cause of death in the United States in both 2020 and 2021," July 5, 2022, available at https://www. nih.gov/news-events/news-releases/covid-19-was-third-leading-cause-death-united-states-both-2020-2021.

24 Peter Baker, Maggie Haberman and Sharon La-Franiere, "Trump Commutes Stone's Sentence on Seven Felonies," *New York Times*, July 11, 2020, p. A1.

25 Julia Manchester, "Charlie Kirk gets first GOP convention address, calls Trump 'bodyguard of Western civilization,'" The Hill, August 24, 2020, https://thehill.com/homenews/campaign/513471-charlie-kirk-gives-first-address-at-gop-convention/.

26 An Act to Prevent Pernicious Political Activities. Pub. L. 76–252 53 Stat. 1147 (1939), codified at 5 USC §§ 7321–7326.

27 Zach Montague, "What Is the Hatch Act? Is Trump Violating It at the R.N.C.?" *New York Times*, August 26, 2020, https://www.nytimes.com/2020/08/26/us/politics/hatch-act-trump-rnc.html.

28 United States Office of Special Counsel, "OSC Clarifies its Hatch Act Role in Light of Republican National Convention." August 26, 2020, https://osc.gov/News/Pages/20-27-OSC-Hatch-Act-RNC.aspx.

29 Michelle Goldberg, "The Trump Occupation Has Begun," *New York Times*, July 21, 2020, p. A21.

30   Tom Gjelten, "Peaceful Protesters Tear-Gassed To Clear Way For Trump Church Photo-Op," NPR, June 1, 2020, https://www.npr.org/2020/06/01/867532070/ trumps-unannounced-church-visit-angers-church-officials.

31   Donald P. Moynihan, "Trump Has a Master Plan for Destroying the 'Deep State,'" *New York Times*, November 27, 2023, https://www.nytimes. com/2023/11/27/opinion/trump-deep-state-schedule-f.html.

32   Sinclair Lewis, *It Can't Happen Here* (Garden City: Doubleday, Doran and Co., 1935).

Chapter 4

1   Lincoln won the election in an Electoral College landslide with 180 electoral votes although he secured less than 40 percent of the popular vote. The Northern states with greater population controlled the Electoral College. The Southern vote split between John Breckenridge and John Bell. The results confirmed the split over states' rights and slavery, leading to eleven states seceding before Lincoln's inauguration. See History.com editors, "Election of 1860," History. com, December 1, 2017, updated June 2, 2020, https://www.history.com/topics/ american-civil-war/election-of-1860.

2   *Bush v. Gore*, 531 US 98, 121 S. Ct. 525, 148 L. Ed. 2d 388 (2000).

3   The American Bar Association published a summarized docket list as of April 30, 2021. It identifies over sixty actions by category. Available at https://www. americanbar.org/groups/public_interest/election_law/litigation/.

4   Jim Rutenberg, Jo Becker, Eric Lipton, et al, "77 Days: Trump's Campaign to Subvert the Election," *New York Times*, February 1, 2021, p. A1.

5   Proud Boys: VICE Media cofounder Gavin McInnes created the Proud Boys during the 2016 presidential election. They are self-described "Western chauvinists" who adamantly deny any connection to the racist "alt-right." They insist they are a fraternal group spreading an "anti-political correctness" and "anti-white guilt" agenda. For more information: https://www.splcenter.org/ fighting-hate/extremist-files/group/proud-boys.

6   Oath Keepers: Founded in 2009, they engage in and promote their own form of vigilante justice by voluntarily showing up armed to provide security. It claims tens of thousands of present and former law enforcement officials and military veterans as members. The group also claims to have patrolled polling locations allegedly to discourage and report voter fraud during the 2016 and 2020 elections. For more information: https://www.splcenter.org/fighting-hate/ extremist-files/group/oath-keepers.

7   Women for America First's cofounder Amy Kremer and her daughter Kylie Jane Kremer started the group in 2018 as a follow-up to her Tea Party and Trump 2016 campaign money-raising activities. The new nonprofit group's website

www.stolenelection.us appeared on posters at "Stop the Steal" protests. See https://www.motherjones.com/politics/2020/11/stop-the-steal/.

Women for America First submitted the permit application to the National Park Service for the rally along with other 501c(4) nonprofits. https://www.opensecrets.org/news/2021/01/trump-tied-to-dc-protests-dark-money-and-shell-companies/ and https://www.opensecrets.org/news/2021/10/details-of-the-money-behind-jan-6-protests-continue-to-emerge/.

8   Nicholas Reimann, "Arizona Audit Cost Trump Supporters Nearly $6 Million—Only to Assert Biden Won by Even More," *Forbes*, September 24, 2021, https://www.forbes.com/sites/nicholasreimann/2021/09/24/arizona-audit-cost-trump-supporters-nearly-6-million-only-to-assert-biden-won-by-even-more/?sh=38d95c1a2410.

9   David Folkenflik and Mary Yang, "Fox News settles blockbuster defamation lawsuit with Dominion Voting Systems," NPR, updated April 18, 2023, https://www.npr.org/2023/04/18/1170339114/fox-news-settles-blockbuster-defamation-lawsuit-with-dominion-voting-systems.

10   *Id.*

11   American Bar Association, docket list, https://www.americanbar.org/groups/public_interest/election_law/litigation/.

12   *King v. Whitmer*, Case No. 20-cv-13134, (E.D. Mich. 2021), available at https://www.michigan.gov/documents/ag/172_opinion__order_King_733786_7.pdf.

13   If a state finalizes its results six days before the Electoral College electors meet to cast their votes, Congress must accept those results as "conclusive." December 8, 2020 was the "safe harbor" deadline for states to complete vote recounts, resolve legal challenges and certify their results for the 2020 presidential election. The Electoral College voted on December 14, 2020. Established under the Electoral Count Act of 1887 (Pub. L. 49–90, 24 Stat. 373-375 [1887]). For more information see: https://crsreports.congress.gov/product/pdf/IF/IF11641.

14   Alan Freuer, "Judge Orders Sanctions against Pro-Trump Lawyers over Election Lawsuit," *New York Times*, August 25, 2021, https://www.nytimes.com/2021/08/25/us/politics/sidney-powell-election-sanctions.html.

15   *King v. Whitmer*, Case No. 20-cv-13134, Opinion and argument August 25, 2021.

16   Jim Rutenberg et al, "77 days: Trump's Campaign to Subvert the Election," *New York Times*, January 31, 2021, p. A14.

17   *Texas v. Pennsylvania* docket 22O155 (2020), appeal den. 592 US, 141 S. Ct. 1230 (2020). Docket available here: https://www.supremecourt.gov/search.aspx?filename=/docket/docketfiles/html/public/22o155.html.

18   Colby Itkowitz, "Trump and his GOP allies vow to 'fight on' after Supreme Court rejects legal challenge to overturn election results," *Washington Post*, December 12, 2020, https://www.washingtonpost.com/politics/trump-and-

his-gop-allies-vow-to-fight-on-after-supreme-court-rejects-legal-challenge-to-overturn-election-results/2020/12/12/904c719c-3c82-11eb-bc68-96af0daae72-8_story.html.

[19] Emily Davies, et al "Multiple people stabbed after thousands gather for pro-Trump demonstrations in Washington," *Washington Post*, December 12, 2020, https://www.washingtonpost.com/local/trump-dc-rally-maga/2020/12/11/8b5af818-3bdb-11eb-bc68-96af0daae728_story.html&cd=4&hl=en&ct=clnk&gl=us.

[20] Gillian Brockell, "Trump loyalists harboring martial law fantasies don't know their history," *Washington Post*, December 22, 2020, https://www.washingtonpost.com/history/2020/12/22/martial-law-trump-flynn-history/. The Brennan Center for Justice has compiled a list of sixty-eight declarations of martial law in the United States at: https://www.brennancenter.org/our-work/research-reports/guide-declarations-martial-law-united-states#war.

[21] Melanie Zanona, "House Republicans meet with Trump to discuss overturning election results," Politico, December 21, 2020, https://www.politico.com/news/2020/12/21/trump-house-overturn-election-449787.

[22] Benjamin Fearnow, "Trump Encourages 'Wild' Protests in D.C. on Date of Electoral College Vote Count," *Newsweek*, December 19, 2020, https://www.newsweek.com/trump-encourages-wild-protests-dc-date-electoral-college-vote-count-1556153.

[23] CNN, "Read the full transcript and listen to Trump's audio call with Georgia secretary of state," CNN, updated January 3, 2021, https://www.cnn.com/2021/01/03/politics/trump-brad-raffensperger-phone-call-transcript/index.html.

[24] United States Democracy Center, "Backgrounder: Fulton County Special Grand Jury Investigation Into 2020 Presidential Interference," December 9, 2022, https://statesuniteddemocracy.org/resources/backgrounder-fulton-sgj/.

[25] Katie Benner, "Trump and Justice Dept. Lawyer Said to Have Plotted to Oust Acting attorney General," *New York Times*, January 22, 2021, updated July 21, 2021, https://www.nytimes.com/2021/01/22/us/politics/jeffrey-clark-trump-justice-department-election.html?searchResultPosition=6.

[26] Clara Hendrickson and Dave Boucher, "Trump Blamed for Fake Electors," *Detroit Free Press*, January 21, 2022, p. 1A.

[27] Luke Broadwater and Alan Feuer, "Jan. 6 Panel Subpoenas 14 Fake Electors Who Submitted Certificates for Trump," *New York Times*, January 29, 2022, p. A14.

[28] Bob Woodward and Robert Costa, *Peril*, (New York: Simon & Schuster, 2021) pp. 209–211.

[29] *Id.*, pp. 228–230.

[30] *Id.*, p. 233.

[31] *Id.*, p. 239.

32 U.S. Capitol Police, "Medical Examiner Finds USCP Officer Brian Sicknick Died of Natural Causes," press release, April 19, 2021 https://www.uscp.gov/media-center/press-releases/medical-examiner-finds-uscp-officer-brian-sicknick-died-natural-causes.

33 Matthew Rozsa, "The War of 1812 vs. Jan. 6: Which was the worst attack on the US Capitol?" Salon, July 18, 2021, https://www.salon.com/2021/07/18/the-war-of-1812-vs-jan-6-which-was-the-worst-attack-on-the-us-capitol/.

34 Kat Lonsdorf et al, "A timeline of the Jan. 6 Capitol attack—including when and how Trump responded," NPR, Updated January 5, 2024, https://www.npr.org/2022/01/05/1069977469/a-timeline-of-how-the-jan-6-attack-unfolded-including-who-said-what-and-when.

35 Karen Yourish, Larry Buchanan and Denise Lu, "The 147 Republicans Who Voted to Overturn Election Results," *New York Times,* January 7, 2021, p. A10. https://www.nytimes.com/interactive/2021/01/07/us/elections/electoral-college-biden-objectors.html.

36 H.Res. 24 "Impeaching Donald John Trump, President of the United States, for high crimes and misdemeanors,"117th Congress (2021–2022).

37 The House of Representatives brings impeachment charges against federal officials as part of its oversight and investigatory responsibilities. The Committee on the Judiciary decides whether to pursue articles of impeachment against the accused official and report them to the full House. If the articles are adopted (by simple majority vote), the House appoints Members by resolution to manage the Senate trial on its behalf. These managers act as prosecutors in the Senate and are usually members of the Judiciary Committee.

38 Woodward and Costa, *Peril*, p. 342.

39 Dana Remus, "Letter from Dana A. Remus, Counsel to the President, to David Ferriero, Archivist of the United States, dated October 8, 2021," available at https://www.whitehouse.gov/briefing-room/statements-releases/2021/10/12/letter-from-dana-a-remus-counsel-to-the-president-to-david-ferriero-archivist-of-the-united-states-dated-october-8-2021/.

40 Charles Savage and Luke Broadwater, "Trump is Suing to Shield Files in Riot Inquiry," *New York Times*, October 19, 2021, p. A1. Updated November, 16, 2021.

41 Adam Liptak, "Justices Rebuff Trump's Request on Jan. 6 Records," *New York Times*, January 20, 2022, p. A1.

42 Beth Reinhard, Jacqueline Alemany, and Josh Dawsey, "Low-profile heiress who 'played a strong role' in financing Jan. 6 rally is thrust into spotlight," *Washington Post*, December 8, 2021, https://www.washingtonpost.com/investigations/publix-heiress-capitol-insurrection-fancelli/2021/12/08/5144fe1c-5219-11ec-8ad5-b5c50c1fb4d9_story.html. See also Joaquin Sapien and Joshua Kaplan, "Top Trump Fundraiser Boasted of Raising $3 Million to Support Jan. 6 "Save

America" Rally," ProPublica, October 18, 2021, https://www.propublica.org/article/top-trump-fundraiser-boasted-of-raising-3-million-to-support-jan-6-save-america-rally.

43   Woodward and Costa, *Peril*, p. 254.

44   Maggie Haberman, Alexandra Berzon, and Michael S. Schmidt, "Trump's Allies Keep Up Fight To Nullify Vote," *New York Times*, April 19, 2022, p. A1.

45   "Affidavit in Support of an Application Under Rule 41 for a Warrant to Search and Seize," Case 9:22-mj-08332-BER, US District Court for the Southern District of Florida, entered August 26, 2022, available at https://apps.npr.org/documents/document.html?id=22267188-mar-a-lago-affi.

46   "United States' Response to Motion for Judicial Oversight and Additional Relief," Case No. 22-CV-81294-CANNON, US District Court for the Southern District of Florida, entered August 30, 2022, available at https://www.pbs.org/newshour/nation/read-the-full-justice-department-filing-on-documents-recovered-from-trumps-mar-a-lago.

47   Eric Tucker, "Trump search: empty folders found," *Detroit Free Press*, September 3, 2022, p. A1.

48   Maggie Haberman and Glenn Thrush, "Trump Lawyer Told Justice Dept. That Classified Material Had Been Returned," *New York Times*, August 13, 2022, https://www.nytimes.com/2022/08/13/us/politics/trump-classified-material-fbi.html.

49   *United States v. Trump and Nauta*, 23-80101-CR-Cannon/Reinhart, S.D. Fla., Indictment, June 8, 2023. Available at https://www.scribd.com/document/651864905/US-v-Trump-Nauta-23-80101.

50   Caitlin O'Kane, "Read the full text of the Trump indictment for details on the charges against him," CBS News, updated on June 13, 2023, https://www.cbsnews.com/news/read-full-text-trump-indictment-pdf-copy-unsealed-documents-case/.

51   *United States. v. Trump*, Case 1:23-cr-00257-TSC, (D.C. Dist. Indictment August 1, 2023).

52   Kenneth Chesebro, "Memorandum Re: Important That All Trump-Pence Electors Vote on December 14," December 8, 2020, available at https://int.nyt.com/data/documenttools/chesebro-dec-6-memo/ce55d6abd79c2c71/full.pdf.

53   Maggie Haberman, Charlie Savage and Luke Broadwater, "Previously Secret Memo Laid Out Strategy for Trump to Overturn Biden's Win," *New York Times*, August 8, 2023, https://www.nytimes.com/2023/08/08/us/politics/trump-indictment-fake-electors-memo.html.

54   *Trump v. United States*, US 23-939 (2024).

Chapter 5

1   Select January 6th Committee Final Report and Supporting Materials Collection, https://www.govinfo.gov/collection/january-6th-committee-final-report?path=/ GPO/January%206th%20Committee%20Final%20Report%20and%20 Supporting%20Materials%20Collection.

2   Associated Press, "From 'an attempted coup' to chaos, searing moments of Jan. 6," *Washington Post*, July 25, 2022, https://www.washingtonpost.com/politics/from-an-attempted-coup-to-chaos-jan-6-hearing-moments/2022/07/23/4452c3ec-0a3d-11ed-80b6-43f2bfcc6662_story.html.

3   Daniel Barnes and Dareh Gregorian, "Trump probably broke the law in an effort to obstruct Jan. 6 proceedings, judge says," NBC News, March 26, 2022, https://www.nbcnews.com/politics/donald-trump/federal-judge-finds-trump-likely-not-tried-illegally-disrupt-electoral-rcna21857.

4   Luke Broadwater and Alan Feuer, "Judge Says Trump Signed Statement With Data His Lawyers Told Him Was False," *New York Times*, October 19, 2022, https://www.nytimes.com/2022/10/19/us/politics/trump-false-statement-jan-6. html.

5   *Eastman v. Thompson*, Case No. 8:22-cv-00099, (C.D. Cal. 2022), available at https://storage.courtlistener.com/recap/gov.uscourts.cacd.841840/gov.uscourts. cacd.841840.372.0_5.pdf.

6   Adam Edelman and Garrett Haake, "Republican loyal to Trump claims Capitol riot looked more like 'normal tourist visit'", NBC News, May 12, 2021, https:// www.nbcnews.com/politics/congress/republican-loyal-trump-claims-capitol-riot-looked-more-normal-tourist-n1267163.

7   Madison Hall, et al, "At least 919 people have been charged in the Capitol insurrection so far. This searchable table shows them all," *Insider*, September 21, 2022, https://www.insider.com/all-the-us-capitol-pro-trump-riot-arrests-charges-names-2021-1. Estimates of participants went up to 120,000. See also William M. Arkin, "Exclusive: Classified Documents Reveal the Number of January 6 Protestors," *Newsweek*, December 23, 2021, https://www.insider.com/ all-the-us-capitol-pro-trump-riot-arrests-charges-names-2021-1.

8   Catie Edmondson, "Jan. 6 Footage Shows Congressional Leaders Scrambling to Get Help" *New York Times*, October 14, 2022, p. A15.

9   Tom Jackman, "Capitol Police officer Caroline Edwards recounts Jan. 6 'war scene,'" *Washington Post*, June 10, 2022 https://www.washingtonpost.com/ politics/2022/06/10/capitol-police-caroline-edwards-jan6-attack-testimony/. See also NPR, "Here's every word of the first Jan. 6 committee hearing on its investigation," June 10, 2022, https://www.npr.org/2022/06/10/1104156949/ jan-6-committee-hearing-transcript.

10   Caroline Edwards, Caroline, "Was Caught in the Capitol Riot, and I Still Feel the Pain of That Day," *New York Times*, December 19, 2022, page A18.

[11]   NPR, "Here's every word of the second Jan. 6 committee hearing on its investigation," June 13, 2022, https://www.npr.org/2022/06/13/1104690690/heres-every-word-of-the-second-jan-6-committee-hearing-on-its-investigation.

[12]   NPR, "Here's every word of the third Jan. 6 committee hearing on its investigation," June 16, 2022, https://www.npr.org/2022/06/16/1105683634/transcript-jan-6-committee.

[13]   Michael Luttig, @judgeluttig, Full text of tweet available at https://twitter.com/judgeluttig/status/1346469787329646592?ref_src=twsrc%5Etfw%7Ctwcamp%5Etweetembed%7Ctwterm%5E1346469787329646592%7Ctwgr%5Edf79 36d2f94b45261c6967832214077784e0bc89%7Ctwcon%5Es1_&ref_url=https%3A%2F%2Fwww.nytimes.com%2F2022%2F06%2F16%2Fus%2Fj-michael-luttig-tweets-pence-trump.html.

[14]   Michael Luttig, "Exclusive: Read Judge Luttig's statement to January 6 committee," cnn.com, June 16, 2022, available at https://www.cnn.com/2022/06/16/politics/read-luttig-statement/index.html.

[15]   NPR, "Here's every word of the third Jan. 6 committee hearing on its investigation."

[16]   NPR, "Here's every word from the fourth Jan. 6 committee hearing on its investigation," June 21, 2022, https://www.npr.org/2022/06/21/1105848096/jan-6-committee-hearing-transcript.

[17]   *Id.*

[18]   *Id.*

[19]   Broadwater and Feuer, "Trump Pressured States to Comply on Fake Electors," *New York Times*, June 22, 2022. p. A15.

[20]   Martin Pengelly, "'I'd vote for him again': Bowers backs Trump despite denouncing 'big lie,'" *Guardian*, June 22, 2022, https://www.theguardian.com/us-news/2022/jun/22/arizona-rusty-bowers-jan-6-trump-vote.

[21]   Martin Pengelly, "Arizona Republican who defied Trump and lost primary: 'I'd do it again in a heartbeat,'" *Guardian*, August 4, 2022, https://www.theguardian.com/us-news/2022/aug/04/arizona-republican-rusty-bowers-trump-primary.

[22]   NPR, "Here's every word from the fourth Jan. 6 committee hearing on its investigation."

[23]   *Id.*

[24]   *Id.*

[25]   . Broadwater and Feuer, "Trump Pressured States to Comply on Fake Electors," p. A15.

[26]   Luke Broadwater and Alan Feuer, "Panel Ties Trump to Fake Elector Plan, Mapping His Attack on Democracy," *New York Times*, June 21, 2022, https://www.nytimes.com/2022/06/21/us/politics/trump-pressure-state-officials.html?searchResultPosition=5.

27 NPR, "Here's every word from the fourth Jan. 6 committee hearing on its investigation."

28 Broadwater and Feuer, "Trump Pressured States to Comply on Fake Electors," p. A15.

29 NPR, "Here's every word from the fourth Jan. 6 committee hearing on its investigation."

30 Broadwater and Feuer, "Trump Pressured States to Comply on Fake Electors," p. A15.

31 Todd Spangler, "Plan for fake Mich. Electors 'insane,'" *Detroit Free Press*, June 22, 2022, p. A1.

32 NPR, "Here's every word from the fourth Jan. 6 committee hearing on its investigation."

33 *Id.*

34 *Id.*

35 *Id.*

36 *Id.*

37 Josh Gerstein and Kyle Cheney, "Giuliani ordered to pay $148M for spreading lies about Georgia election workers," *Politico*, updated December 15, 2023, https://www.politico.com/news/2023/12/15/giuliani-georgia-election-workers-verdict-00132099.

38 Luke Broadwater and Katie Benner, "Jan. 6 Hearings Day 5: Trump Pressured Justice Dept. and His Allies Sought Pardons," *New York Times*, June 24, 2022, p. A1.

39 A PDF of the unsent letter is available at https://www.govinfo.gov/app/details/GPO-J6-DOC-CTRL0000014544_00012/context.

40 NPR, "Here's every word from the fifth Jan. 6 committee hearing on its investigation," June 23, 2022, https://www.npr.org/2022/06/23/1106700800/jan-6-committee-hearing-transcript.

41 Alan Feuer and Adam Goldman, "Federal Agents Seized Phone of John Eastman, Key Figure in Jan. 6 Plan," *New York Times*, June 27, 2022, https://www.nytimes.com/2022/06/27/us/politics/john-eastman-jan-6.html?searchResultPosition=5.

42 NPR, "Here's every word from the sixth Jan. 6 committee hearing on its investigation," June 28, 2022, https://www.npr.org/2022/06/28/1108396692/jan-6-committee-hearing-transcript.

43 *Id.*

44 Luke Broadwater and Michael S. Schmidt, "Enraged Trump Encouraged Violence and Sought to Join Mob, Aide Testifies," *New York Times*, June 29, 2022, p. A14.

45 NPR, "Here's every word from the sixth Jan. 6 committee hearing on its investigation."

46 *Id.*

47   *Id.*

48   *Id.*

49   Maggie Haberman, "Star Witness Is Panel's Most Powerful," *New York Times*, June 29, 2022, p. A14.

50   *Id.*

51   Broadwater and Schmidt, "Enraged Trump Encouraged Violence and Sought to Join Mob, Aide Testifies," p. A14.

52   NPR, "Here's every word from the sixth Jan. 6 committee hearing on its investigation."

53   Twitter.com has removed the tweet Cassidy Hutchinson referenced in her June 28, 2022, testimony. The tweet text is available at Brett Samuels, "Trump attacks Pence as protesters force their way into Capitol," The Hill, January 6, 2021, https://thehill.com/homenews/administration/532942-trump-attacks-pence-as-protesters-force-their-way-into-capitol/.

54   NPR, "Here's every word from the sixth Jan. 6 committee hearing on its investigation."

55   NPR, "Here's every word from the seventh Jan. 6 committee hearing on its investigation," July 12, 2022, https://www.npr.org/2022/07/12/1111123258/jan-6-committee-hearing-transcript.

56   *Id.*

57   Maggie Haberman, "Participants in Trump Meeting Describe Screaming and Insults From Rival Factions," *New York Times*, July 13, 2022, p, A16.

58   NPR, "Here's every word from the seventh Jan. 6 committee hearing on its investigation."

59   *Id.*

60   The proposed Executive Order is available at https://www.politico.com/news/2922/01/21/read-the-never-issued-trump-order-that-wold-hav-seized-voting-machines-527572.

61   NPR, "Here's every word from the seventh Jan. 6 committee hearing on its investigation."

62   *Id.*

63   Fearnow, "Trump Encourages 'Wild' Protests in D.C. on Date of Electoral College Vote Count."

64   Luke Broadwater and Alan Feuer, "Trump Intended To Send His Mob To Disrupt Count," *New York Times*, July 13, 2022, p A1.

65   *Id.*

66   Isaac Stanley-Becker and Jacqueline Alemany, "Trump hid plan for Capitol march on day he marked as 'wild', panel says," *Washington Post*, July 12, 2022, https://www.washingtonpost.com/national-security/2022/07/12/january-6-hearing-trump/.

67 Nikki McCann Ramirez, "Trump's Call for Jan. 6 March on Capitol Was PrePlanned,'" *Rolling Stone*, July 12, 2022, https://www.rollingstone.com/politics/politics-news/jan-6-trump-march-capitol-hearing-1381867/.

68 NPR, "Here's every word from the seventh Jan. 6 committee hearing on its investigation."

69 NPR, "Here's every word from the 8th Jan. 6 committee on its investigation," July 22 2022, https://www.npr.org/2022/07/22/1112138665/jan-6-committee-hearing-transcript.

70 *Id.*

71 Pub.L. 9-39, 2 Stat. 443 (1807), codified at 10 U.S.C. § 253 as amended.

72 President Lyndon Johnson used the Insurrection Act to send active duty and federalized National Guard troops into DC to quell riots that followed the assassination of Martin Luther King Jr. in 1968. President Trump deployed National Guard soldiers to stop the "rioting, looting, vandalism, assaults, and the wanton destruction of property" in Washington, DC, that followed the murder of George Floyd in June of 2020. For more information, see Scott R. Anderson, et al, "What Made Trump's Protest Response in DC Unique?" Lawfare, June 8, 2020. https://www.lawfareblog.com/what-made-trumps-protest-response-dc-unique.

73 NPR, "Here's every word of the first Jan. 6 committee hearing on its investigation," June 10, 2022, https://www.npr.org/2022/06/10/1104156949/jan-6-committee-hearing-transcript.

74 WJZ News, "'We Love You, You're Very Special': President Trump Tweets Message, Later Removed, to Rioters Storming the US Capitol," CBS Baltimore, January 6, 2021 / 11:50 PM EST, https://www.cbsnews.com/baltimore/news/its-time-to-go-home-now-president-trump-tweets-message-to-supporters-storming-the-u-s-capitol/.

75 NPR, "Here's every word from the 8th Jan. 6 committee on its investigation."

76 NPR, "Here's every word from the sixth Jan. 6 committee hearing on its investigation." Later Panel Member Elaine Luria referred to Hutchinson's testimony regarding the January 7 address during the Eighth Hearing. See NPR, "Here's every word from the Eighth Jan. 6 committee on its investigation."

77 *Id.*

78 Barbara Sprunt, "The Jan. 6 Committee has voted to Subpoena Trump. Here's what else happened," NPR, October 13, 2022.

79 NPR, "Here's every word from the 9th Jan. 6 committee hearing on its investigation," October 13, 2022, https://www.npr.org/2022/10/13/1125331584/jan-6-committee-hearing-transcript.

80 *Id.*

81 *Id.*

82 *Id.*

83 *Id.*

84   *Id.*

85   *Id.*

86   *Id.*

87   *Id.*

88   Hannah Grabenstein, "Read the Jan. 6 committee's summary of its final report," PBS updated Dec 19, 2022, https://www.pbs.org/newshour/politics/read-the-jan-6-committees-summary-of-its-final-report.

89   Select January 6th Committee Final Report and Supporting Materials Collection.

90   Laurence H. Tribe, Donald Ayer and Dennis Aftergut, "Will Donald Trump Get Away With Inciting an Insurrection?" *New York Times*, December 23, 2021, https://www.nytimes.com/2021/12/23/opinion/trump-capitol-riot-january-6th.html.

91   Michelle Goldberg Column, "The Myth of the Good Trump Official," *New York Times*, July 23, 2022, p. A21.

92   Sareen Habeshian, "Trump: Constitution should be terminated due to 'massive' election fraud," Axios, updated December 3, 2022, https://www.axios.com/2022/12/03/trump-election-fraud-constitution.

Chapter 6

1   American Civil Liberties Union (ACLU), "Block the Vote: How Politicians Are Trying to Block Voters from the Ballot Box," August 17, 2021, last updated August 18, 2021, https://www.aclu.org/news/civil-liberties/block-the-vote-voter-suppression-in-2020.

2   Amrit Cheng, "Crystal Mason Thought She Had the Right to Vote. Texas Sentenced Her to Five Years in Prison for Trying," ACLU, accessed July 18, 2023, https://www.aclu.org/issues/voting-rights/fighting-voter-suppression/crystal-mason-thought-she-had-right-vote-texas.

3   Alexa Ura, "Crystal Mason's contentious illegal voting conviction must be reconsidered, criminal appeals court says," *Texas Tribune*, May 5, 2022 updated, May 11, 2022, https://texastribune.org/2022/05/11crystal-mason-illegal-voting-texas/.

4   Center for Democracy and Civic Engagement, "Who Lacks ID in America Today? An Exploration of Voter ID Access, Barriers, and Knowledge," June 2024, available at https://cdce.umd.edu/sites/cdce.umd.edu/files/pubs/Voter%20ID%20survey%20Key%20Results%20June%202024.pdf.

5   Sam Levine, "Millions of US voters lack access to documents to prove citizenship," *Guardian*, June 12, 2024, https://www.theguardian.com/us-news/article/2024/jun/12/us-voters-citizenship-brennan-center-study.

6   William Arkin, "Exclusive: Classified Documents Reveal the Number of January 6 Protestors," December 23, 2021, https://www.newsweek.com/exclusive-classified-documents-reveal-number-january-6-protestors-1661296.

7 Jacques Billeaud, "Jan. 6 rioter who carried spear, wore horns, draws 41 months," AP News, November 17, 2021, https://apnews.com/article/prisons-arizona-capitol-siege-5c9ebf384bf936403d42e1a453c89153.

8 *Baker v. Carr*, 369 U.S. 186, 82 S. Ct. 691, 7 L. Ed. 2d 663 (1962).

9 *Reynolds v. Sims*, 377 U.S. 533, 84 S. Ct. 1362, 12 L. Ed. 2d 506 (1964).

10 *Wesberry v. Sanders*, 376 U.S. 1, 84 S. Ct. 526, 11 L. Ed. 2d (1964).

11 Pub. L. 89-110, 79 Stat. 437 (1965), codified at 52 U.S.C. § 10101 et seq as amended.

12 *Avery v. Midland County*, 390 U.S. 474, 88 S. Ct. 1114, 20 L. Ed. 2d 45 (1968). See also, *Board of Estimate of City of New York v. Morris*, 489 U.S. 688, 109 S. Ct. 1433, 103 L. Ed. 2d 717 (1989) and *Evenwel v. Abbott*, 578 U.S. ___, 136 S. Ct. 1120, 194 L. Ed. 2d 291 (2016).

13 390 U.S. 479.

14 Hendrik Hertzberg, "Alexander Hamilton Speaks Out (III): Two Senators Per State, Regardless of Population?" *New Yorker*, January 8, 2011, https://www.newyorker.com/news/hendrik-hertzberg/alexander-hamilton-speaks-out-iii-two-senators-per-state-regardless-of-population.

15 United States Census, "U.S. Census Bureau Today Delivers State Population Totals for Congressional Apportionment," page last revised March 25, 2022, https://www.census.gov/library/stories/2021/04/2020-census-data-release.html.

16 United States Census, "State Visualizations of Key Demographic Trends From the 2020 Census," page last revised August 16, 2022, https://www.census.gov/library/stories/state-by-state.html.

17 Jeff Stein, Maxine Joselow, and Rachel Roubein, "How the Inflation Reduction Act Might Affect You—and Change the U.S.," *Washington Post*, July 28,2022, updated August 15, 2022, https://www.washingtonpost.com/us-policy/2022/07/28/manchin-schumer-climate-deal/.

18 Walter J. Oleszek, "Cloture: Its Effect on Senate Procedure," Congressional Research Service, updated May 19, 2008, https://crsreports.congress.gov/product/pdf/RS/98-780.

19 Gene Lyons "Will the American people let the tyrannical minority rule?" *Santa Maria Times*, July 12, 2022, https://santamariatimes.com/opinion/commentary/will-the-american-people-let-the-tyrannical-minority-rule-gene-lyons/article_4513f55c-0bcd-5320-ba47-24db783bb690.html.

Chapter 7

1 Samuel Eliot Morison, *Oxford History of the American People* (New York: Oxford University Press, 1965) p. 404.

2 *Id*. p. 405.

3   Abraham Lincoln, "Second Inaugural Address, March 4, 1865," National Park Service, https://www.nps.gov/linc/learn/historyculture/lincoln-second-inaugural.htm (updated April 18, 2020). Text engraved on the north interior wall of the Lincoln Memorial in the District of Columbia.

4   Noah Feldman, "This Is the Story of How Lincoln Broke the U.S. Constitution," *New York Times*, November 2, 2021, p. A19. Also available at https://www.nytimes.com/2021/11/02/opinion/constitution-slavery-lincoln.html.

5   *United States v. State of Louisiana*, 225 F. Supp. 353 (E.D. La. 1963). Judge Wisdom's dissenting opinion discussed the Louisiana State constitutional requirement that an applicant for registration "understand and give a reasonable interpretation of any section" of the Constitutions of Louisiana or of the United States. See also, 380 U.S. 145, 86 S. Ct. 817, 13 L. Ed. 2d 709 (1965).

6   *Giles v. Harris*, 189 U.S. 475, 23 S. Ct. 639, 47 L. Ed. 909 (1903).

7   Christopher Ingraham, "This is the best explanation of gerrymandering you will ever see. How to steal an election: a visual guide," *Washington Post*, March 1, 2015, https://www.washingtonpost.com/news/wonk/wp/2015/03/01/this-is-the-best-explanation-of-gerrymandering-you-will-ever-see/.

8   Julia Kirschenbaum and Michael Li, "Gerrymandering Explained," Brennan Center for Justice, https://www.brennancenter.org/our-work/research-reports/gerrymandering-explained (updated August 12, 2021).

9   Kaz Welda, "The Top 10 Most Gerrymandered States in America," Rantt Media, May 25, 2017, https://rantt.com/the-top-10-most-gerrymandered-states-in-america.

10 Katharina Buchholz, "2020 Census Triggers Redrawing of Gerrymandered District Lines," Statista, April 1, 2020, https://www.statista.com/chart/21313/most-gerrymandered-districts-us/.

11 Tom Murse, "What Is Gerrymandering? How Political Parties Choose Voters Instead of Voters Choosing Them," ThoughtCo, https://www.thoughtco.com/what-is-gerrrymandering-4057603 (updated January 15, 2020).

12 Ingraham, "This is the best explanation of gerrymandering you will ever see. How to steal an election: a visual guide."

13 "Princeton Gerrymandering Project," https://gerrymander.princeton.edu/info/ (accessed November 28, 2021).

14 *Rucho v. Common Cause*, 588 U.S. ___, 139 S. Ct. 2484, 204 L. Ed. 2d 931 (2019).

15 Sean Collins, "Trump made gains with Black voters in some states. Here's why," Vox, November 4, 2020, https://www.vox.com/2020/11/4/21537966/trump-black-voters-exit-polls.

16 Kimmy Yam, "Asian Americans voted for Biden 63% to 31%, but the reality is more complex," NBC News, November 9, 2020, https://www.nbcnews.com/news/asian-america/asian-americans-voted-biden-63-31-reality-more-complex-n1247171.

17   Lys Mendez, "Latino voters were decisive in 2020 presidential election," UCLA Newsroom, January 19, 2021, https://newsroom.ucla.edu/releases/latino-vote-analysis-2020-presidential-election.

18   Pub. L. 89-110, 79 Stat. 437 (1965).

19   *Wesberry,* 376 U.S. 8.

20   Eric Griffey, "A Brief History of Texas Gerrymandering," Spectrum News 1, October 6, 2020. https://spectrumlocalnews.com/tx/south-texas-el-paso/election/2020/10/06/a-brief-history-of-texas-gerrymandering- (updated 2:25 p.m. CT October 14, 2020).

21   The U.S. Census Bureau uses the terms "Hispanic" or "Hispanic or Latino" interchangeably. In 1976, Congress enacted a joint resolution to require collection and analysis of data for "Americans who identify themselves as being of Spanish-speaking background and trace their origin or descent from Mexico, Puerto Rico, Cuba, Central and South America, and other Spanish-speaking countries," but not from Portugal or Portuguese-speaking Brazil.

Pub. L. 94-311, 90 Stat. 688 (1976) Joint Resolution relating to the publication of economic and social statistics for Americans of Spanish origin or descent.

Others have defined Latinos as people from Latin America regardless of language. For fuller discussion, see "Who is Hispanic?" by Mark Hugo Lopez, Jens Manuel Krogstad and Jeffrey S. Passel, Pew Research Center, September 5, 2023, https://www.pewresearch.org/short-reads/2023/09/05/who-is-hispanic/.

22   United States Census, "Racial and Ethnic Diversity in the United States 2010 Census and 2020 Census," August 12, 2021, https://www.census.gov/library/visualizations/interactive/racial-and-ethnic-diversity-in-the-united-states-2010-and-2020-census.html.

23   United States House of Representatives, "Directory of Representatives," https://www.house.gov/representatives (accessed October 16, 2022).

24   U.S. House of Representatives Press Gallery, "Black Americans 117th Congress as of November 4, 2021," https://pressgallery.house.gov/black-americans-117th-congress and "Hispanic Americans 117th as of June 21, 2022," https://pressgallery.house.gov/hispanic-americans-117th.

25   Alexa Ura and Carla Astudillo, "In 2021, white men are still overrepresented in the Texas Legislature," *Texas Tribune,* January 11, 2021, https://apps.texastribune.org/features/2020/2021-texas-legislature-representation/.

26   *Mobile v. Bolden,* 446 U.S. 55, 100 S. Ct. 1490, 64 L. Ed. 2d 47 (1980).

27   PL 97-205, 96 Stat. 131, (1982).

28   *Thornburg v. Gingles,* 478 U.S. 30, 48- 51, 106 S. Ct. 2752, 92 L. Ed. 2d 25 (1986)).

29   *Perez v. Abbott,* 267 F. Supp. 3d 750 (W.D. Tex. 2017); 274 F. Supp. 3d 624 (W.D. Tex. 2017).

30   *Perry v. Perez*, 565 U.S. 1090 (2011), Reported below: No. 11–713, 835 F. Supp. 2d 209.

31   *Shelby County v. Holder*, 570 U.S. 529, 133 S. Ct. 2612, 186 L. Ed. 2d 651 (2013).

32   *Abbott v. Perez*, 585 U.S. ___, 138 S. Ct. 2305, 201 L. Ed. 2d 714 (2018).

33   *Thornburg v. Gingles*, 478 U.S. 30, 48-51, 106 S. Ct. 2752, 92 L. Ed. 2d 25 (1986).

34   Abbott v. Perez, quoting Thornburg v. Gingles 33–39.

35   Id.

36   Amy Howe, "Opinion Analysis: Texas scores near-complete victory on redistricting," Scotus Blog, June 25, 2018. Https://www.scotus.com/blog/2018/06/opinion-anlysis-texas-scores-near-complete-victory-on-redistricting.

37   Ari Berman, Twitter, October 13, 2021, https://twitter.com/ariberman/status/1448298819452612616.

38   Eric Bradner, "Texas Gov. Greg Abbott approves new congressional map consolidating GOP power," CNN, https://www.cnn.com/2021/10/20/politics/texas-redistricting-senate-voting-rights/index.html (updated 5:20 p.m. ET, October 25, 2021).

39   *Voto Latino v. John Scott*, W.D. Tex. No. 1:21-cv-00965 (Complaint filed October 25, 2021).

40   Cobi Burnett, "Texas voters challenge new redistricting maps," Jurist, October 26, 2021, <u>https://www.jurist.org/news/2021/10/texas-voters-challenge-new-redistricting-maps/</u>.

41   *League of United Latin American Citizens v. Abbott* (P-21-CV-00259-DCG-JES-JVB, lead case); *Wilson v. Texas* (1:21-CV-00943-RP-JES-JVB); *Voto Latino v. Scott* (1 :21-CV-00965-RP-JES-JVB); *Mexican American Legislative Caucus v. Texas* (1:21-CV-00988-RP-JES-JVB); *Brooks v. Abbott* (l:21-CV-00988-RP-JES-JVB); *Texas State Conf. of the NAACP v. Abbott* (l:21-CV-01006-RP-JES-JVB); *Fair Maps Texas Action Comm. v. Abbott* (l:21-CV-01038-RP-JES-JVB). Two more cases were consolidated *into League of United Latin American Citizens: United States v. Texas* (3:21-CV-00299-DCG "State of Texas and John Scott" December 10, 2021) and *Fischer v. Abbott* (3:21-CV-00306-DCG-JES-JVB December 15, 2021). Available at https://thearp.org/litigation/voto-latino-v-scott/

42   *League of United Latin American Citizens*, 3:21-CV-259-DCG-JES-JVB (May 23, 2022 Memorandum Opinion and Order). Available at https://thearp.org/litigation/fischer-v-scott/.

43   Pub. L. 88–352 § 2, 78 Stat. 241 (1965).

44   Tom Murse, "What Is Gerrymandering?"

Chapter 8

[1] "Wisconsin Election Results and Maps 2020," CNN, https://www.cnn.com/election/2020/results/state/wisconsin/housedistricts-1 (updated 11:38 a.m. ET, February 17, 2021).

[2] John Johnson, "Why Do Republicans Overperform in the Wisconsin State Assembly? Partisan Gerrymandering vs. Political Geography," Marquette University Law School Faculty Blog, February 11, 2021, https://law.marquette.edu/facultyblog/2021/02/why-do-republicans-overperform-in-the-wisconsin-state-assembly-partisan-gerrymandering-vs-political-geography/.

[3] *Johnson v. Wisconsin Elections Commission*, 2022 WI 14.

[4] *Wisconsin Legislature v. Wisconsin Elections Commission*, 595 U.S. ___, 142 S. Ct. 1245 (2022) (per curiam).

[5] *Id.*

[6] *Id.*

[7] *Gingles*, 478 US 30.

[8] *Wisconsin Legislature*, 595 U.S. ___, citing *League of United Latin American Citizens v. Perry*, 548 U.S. 399, 426 (2006).

[9] *Shaw v. Hunt*, 517 U.S. 899, 910, 116 S. Ct. 1894, 135 L. Ed. 2d 207 (1996).

[10] *Wisconsin Legislature*, 595 U.S. ___.

[11] *Johnson v. DeGrandy*, 512 U.S. 997 at 1020-1021 and 1026, 114 S. Ct. 2647, 129 L. Ed. 2d 775 (1994).

[12] *Id.*

[13] *Wisconsin Legislature*, 595 U.S. ___ (dissent).

[14] Julie Bosman, "Justices in Wisconsin Order New Legislative Maps," *New York Times*, December 22, 2023, https://www.nytimes.com/2023/12/22/us/wisconsin-redistricting-maps-gerrymander.html.

[15] *Merrill v. Milligan*, No. 21-1086 Transcript, U.S. Supreme Court, October 4, 2022, Heritage Reporting Corporation, p. 58–59. Available at https://www.supremecourt.gov/oral_arguments/argument_transcripts/2022/21-1086_1pd4.pdf.

[16] Brennan Center for Justice, "Redistricting Litigation Roundup: A look at legal cases around the country challenging newly adopted redistricting plans," last updated October 12, 2022, https://www.brennancenter.org/our-work/research-reports/redistricting-litigation-roundup-0.

[17] David Leonhardt, "G.O.P.'s Full-Court Press on Voting Rights," *New York Times*, March 3, 2021, p. A17.

[18] Nick Corasaniti, Reid J. Epstein, Taylor Johnston, et al, "How Maps Reshape American Politics—Redistricting? Gerrymandering? We Have Your Answers," *New York Times*, November 12, 2021, p. A18.

[19] Michigan Independent Citizens Redistricting Commission, https://www.michigan.gov/micrc.

20   Brian Dickerson, "Populism at Its Best—Michigan's first citizens redistricting commission is honoring its pledge to put voter's interests first," *Detroit Free Press*, December 26, 2021, p. 27A.

21   Mich. Const. Art. IV § 6.

22   Nick Corasaniti, "For Elections, Michigan Maps Are a Step Toward a Fair Fight, Commission Puts End to Gerrymandering," *New York Times*, December 29, 2021, p. A1.

23   Clara Hendrickson, "Mich. Congressional districts upheld," *Detroit Free Press*, April 3, 2022, p. 4A.

24   For the People Act of 2021, H.R. 1, 117th Cong. (2021).

25   John R. Lewis Voting Rights Advancement Act of 2021, H.R. 4, 117th Cong. (2021).

26   Freedom to Vote Act, S. 2747, 117th Cong. (2021).

27   Ashley Hackett, "How Klobuchar's Freedom to Vote Act proposes to end partisan gerrymandering," MinnPost, October 13, 2021, https://www.minnpost.com/national/2021/10/how-klobuchars-freedom-to-vote-act-proposes-to-end-partisan-gerrymandering/.

28   America Votes Act of 2023, H.R861, 118th Cong. (2023).

29   *Moore v. Harper*, 600 U.S. ___ (2023) (No. 21-1271).

30   *Costello v. Carter* No. 21-1509, U.S. *cert den.* October 2, 2022. Petitioners in *Costello* had asked to be heard with *Moore*.

31   *Reynolds*, 377 U.S. 533.

32   *Wesberry*, 376 U.S. 8.

33   *Moore*, 600 U.S. ___.

34   *Id.*

35   *Allen v. Milligan*, 599 U.S. ___, U.S. 21–1086 (2023). Heard alongside *Merrill v. Milligan* (U.S. 2022).

36   *Alexander v. South Carolina State Conference of the NAACP*, U.S. 22-807 (2023). See Adam Liptak, "Justices Poised to Restore Voting Map Ruled a Racial Gerrymander," *New York Times*, October 12, 2023, p. A16.

37   Reid J. Epstein, "In Wisconsin Struggle for Power, G.O.P. Seeks to Impeach Judge," *New York Times*, September 7, 2023, p. A1.

38   *Arkansas State Conference NAACP v. Arkansas Board of Apportionment*, US App. 22-1395 (8th Cir. 2023). Available at https://www.aclu.org/documents/opinion-arkansas-state-conference-naacp-v-arkansas-board-of-apportionment. See Kelsey Jukam, "Eighth Circuit ruling limits enforcement of Voting Rights Act," *Courthouse News Service*, November 20, 2023, https://www.courthousenews.com/eighth-circuit-ruling-limits-enforcement-of-voting-rights-act/.

Chapter 9

[1] Brennan Center for Justice, "Voting Laws Roundup: June 2023," June 14, 2023, https://www.brennancenter.org/our-work/research-reports/voting-laws-roundup-june-2023.

[2] Will Wilder and Stuart Baum, "5 Egregious Voter Suppression Laws from 2021," Brennan Center, January 31, 2022, https://www.brennancenter.org/our-work/analysis-opinion/5-egregious-voter-suppression-laws-2021.

[3] Election Integrity Act of 2021, 21 LC 28 0338S S. B. 202 (2021).

[4] Stephen Fowler, "What Does Georgia's New Voting Law SB 202 Do?" Georgia Public Broadcasting (GPB), March 27, 2021 8:50 a.m. updated March 27, 2021 10:08 p.m., https://www.gpb.org/news/2021/03/27/what-does-georgias-new-voting-law-sb-202-do.

[5] Nick Corasaniti and Reid J. Epstein, "What Georgia's Voting Law Really Does," *New York Times National*, April 3, 2021, p.A12.

[6] Jamelle Bouie, "The G.O.P. Has Some Voters It Likes and Some It Doesn't," *New York Times*, March 30, 2021, p. A22.

[7] CNN, "Read the full transcript and listen to Trump's audio call with Georgia secretary of state".

[8] Brennan Center for Justice, "Voting Laws Roundup: February 2021," February 8, 2021. https://www.brennancenter.org/our-work/research-reports/voting-laws-roundup-february-2021.

[9] Brennan Center for Justice, "Voting Laws Roundup: December 2021," December 21, 2021, updated January 12, 2022, https://www.brennancenter.org/our-work/research-reports/voting-laws-roundup-december-2021.

[10] Charles M. Blow, "Voter Suppression Is Grand Larceny," *New York Times*, March 1, 2021, p. A18.

[11] *Brnovich v. Democratic National Committee*, 594 U.S. ___, 141 S. Ct. 2321, 210 L. Ed. 2d 753 (2021).

[12] Ariz. Rev. Stat. Ann. §§16–584(E) (2015).

[13] Ariz. Rev. Stat. Ann. §§16– 1005(H)–(I) (2016).

[14] *Id.*

[15] *Gingles*, 478 U.S.30.

[16] *Brnovich*, 594 U.S. ___.

[17] *Id.*

[18] *Id.*

[19] "Statement by President Joe Biden on the Supreme Court's Voting Rights Decision in Brnovich v. Democratic National Committee," Statements and Releases, July 1, 2021, https://www.whitehouse.gov/briefing-room/statements-releases/2021/07/01/statement-by-president-joe-biden-on-the-supreme-courts-voting-rights-decision-in-brnovich-v-democratic-national-committee/.

20 Clara Hendrickson, "New GOP canvasser: '20 results 'inaccurate'," *Detroit Free Press*, October 19, 2021, p. 4A.

21 U.S. Const. art. I, § 5, cl. 2.

22 Sarah A. Binder, "The History of the Filibuster," Brookings Institution, April 22, 2010, https://www.brookings.edu/testimonies/the-history-of-the-filibuster/.

23 "About Filibusters and Cloture | Historical Overview," United States Senate, https://www.senate.gov/about/powers-procedures/filibusters-cloture/overview.htm (accessed November 29, 2021).

24 "Senate Reverses a Presidential Censure," United States Senate, https://www.senate.gov/artandhistory/history/minute/Senate_Reverses_A_Presidential_Censure.htm (accessed November 28, 2021).

25 "About Filibusters and Cloture | Historical Overview," United States Senate.

26 Binder, "The History of the Filibuster."

27 "The Senate and the League of Nations," United States Senate, https://www.senate.gov/reference/reference_item/Versailles.htm (accessed November 28, 2021). See also Scott Bombay, "On this day, Wilson's own rule helps defeat the Versailles Treaty," National Constitution Center, November 15, 2017, https://constitutioncenter.org/blog/on-this-day-wilsons-own-rule-defeats-the-versailles-treaty.

28 "Fair Practice in Employment," CQ Press Editorial Research Reports, January 18, 1946, https://library.cqpress.com/cqresearcher/document.php?id=cqresrre1946011800#.

29 Pub. L. 85-315, 71 Stat. 634 (1957), codified at 42 U.S.C. ch. 20A as amended.

30 Walt Hickey, "The Longest Filibuster in History Lasted More Than a Day—Here's How It Went Down," Business Insider, March 6, 2013, https://www.businessinsider.com/longest-filibuster-in-history-strom-thurmond-rand-paul-2013-3.

31 "About Filibusters and Cloture | Historical Overview," United States Senate.

32 Lisa Mascaro, "Q&A: Filibuster, cloture and what the 'nuclear option' means for Gorsuch nomination and future of the Senate," *Los Angeles Times*, April 4, 2017, https://www.latimes.com/politics/la-na-pol-filibuster-qa-20170404-story.html.

33 Tim Lau, "The Filibuster, Explained," Brennan Center for Justice, April 26, 2021, https://www.brennancenter.org/our-work/research-reports/filibuster-explained.

34 Hunter Woodall, "Klobuchar voting rights bill stopped by Senate GOP." *Star Tribune*, October 20, 2021, https://www.startribune.com/klobuchar-voting-rights-bill-stopped-by-senate-gop/600108408/.

35 Clare Foran, Ali Zaslav, and Ted Barrett, "Senate Democrats suffer defeat on voting rights after vote to change rules fails," CNN, updated 11:38 p.m. ET, January 19, 2022, https://www.cnn.com/2022/01/19/politics/senate-voting-legislation-filibuster/index.html.

36 Oleszek, "Cloture: Its Effect on Senate Procedure." See also Christopher M. Davis, "Eight Mechanisms to Enact Procedural Change in the U.S. Senate,"

Congressional Research Service, updated December 2, 2020, https://crsreports. congress.gov/product/pdf/IN/IN10875.

37 Sarah D. Wire, "Threats against members of Congress soar, changing the job," *Los Angeles Times*, September 20, 2021, https://www.latimes.com/politics/ story/2021-09-20/threats-members-of-congress.

38 Linda So and Jason Szep, "U.S. election workers get little help from law enforcement as terror threats mount," Reuters, September 8, 2021, https://www. reuters.com/investigates/special-report/usa-election-threats-law-enforcement/.

39 *Id.*

40 Stateside Staff, "Detroit election workers describe vote counting effort amid protests," Michigan Radio, November 5, 2020, https://www.michiganradio. org/politics-government/2020-11-05/detroit-election-workers-describe-vote-counting-effort-amid-protests.

41 Breana Noble and Craig Mauger, "Shouting, confrontation at Detroit vote count center: Poll challengers barred by police," *Detroit News*, November 4, 2021, https://www.detroitnews.com/story/news/politics/2020/11/04/poll-challengers-converge-detroit-amid-close-election-results/6161484002/.

42 Erin Doherty, "RNC plans to recruit thousands of poll workers and watchers for 2024," Axios, October 11, 2023, https://www.axios.com/2023/10/11/rnc-election-integrity-2024-election-trump.

Chapter 10

1 US Const. art. 2, § 1.

2 Brian Naylor, "Read Trump's Jan. 6 Speech, A Key Part Of Impeachment Trial," NPR, February 10, 2021, https://www.npr.org/2021/02/10/966396848/read-trumps-jan-6-speech-a-key-part-of-impeachment-trial.

3 Mychael Schnell, "Pence: 'I know I did the right thing' on Jan. 6," The Hill, January 12, 2021, https://thehill.com/homenews/administration/583883-pence-i-know-i-did-the-right-thing-on-jan-6.

4 US Const, art. 6, cl. 3.

5 US Const. art. 1, § 3.

6 Congressional Record p. 142-S143, https://www.congress.gov/117/crec/2021/01/26/modified/CREC-2021-01-26-pt1-PgS142.htm.

7 Josh Dawsey, "Mitt Romney knew the storm was coming over his impeachment vote. How long it lasts will be up to Trump," *Washington Post*, February 5, 2020, https://www.washingtonpost.com/politics/mitt-romney-knew-the-storm-was-coming-over-his-impeachment-vote-how-long-it-lasts-will-be-up-to-trump/2020/02/05/cda7340c-485c-11ea-8949-a9ca94a90b4c_story.html.

8 Kyle Cheney, Natasha Bertrand, and Meridith McGraw, "Impeachment witnesses ousted amid fears of Trump revenge campaign," Politico, February 7,

2020, updated February 7, 2020, https://www.politico.com/news/2020/02/07/donald-trump-pressure-impeachment-witness-alexander-vindman-111997.

9   As an alternative to a sacred text, some have proposed using the Constitution itself since that is what the official taking the oath swears to uphold and protect. For a fuller discussion, see American Atheists, "Swearing-in," https://www.atheists.org/2013/01/swearing-in/ (accessed December 14, 2021).

10   Gerald Magliocca, "The 14th Amendment's Disqualification Provision and the Events of Jan. 6," Lawfare Institute January 6 Project, January 19, 2021, https://www.lawfareblog.com/14th-amendments-disqualification-provision-and-events-jan-6.

11   C. Ellen Connally, "The Use of the Fourteenth Amendment by Salmon P. Chase in the Trial of Jefferson Davis," Akron Law Review, Vol. 42: Iss. 4, July 2015, available at https://ideaexchange.uakron.edu/akronlawreview/vol42/iss4/12/.

12   J. Michael Luttig and Laurence H. Tribe, "The Constitution Prohibits Trump From Ever Being President Again," *The Atlantic*, August 19, 2023, https://www.theatlantic.com/ideas/archive/2023/08/donald-trump-constitutionally-prohibited-presidency/675048/.

13   Office of Legal Counsel, "Officers of the United States Within the Meaning of the Appointments Clause. Memorandum Opinion for the General Counsel of the Executive Branch," US Department of Justice, April 16, 2007, p. 78, available at https://www.justice.gov/d9/olc/opinions/attachments/2015/05/29/op-olc-v031-p0083.pdf.

14   Zach Montellaro and Kyle Cheney, "Everything you need to know about Trump and the 14th Amendment," Politico, December 29, 2023, https://www.politico.com/news/2023/12/29/trump-14-amendment-ballot-troubles-00133318.

15   Cowboys for Trump is a promotional group that staged horseback parades to spread Trump's message about gun rights, immigration controls, and abortion restrictions. Created as a limited liability corporation in an attempt to evade campaign finance transparency requirements. The New Mexico secretary of state's office prevailed in a June 2020 arbitration decision that ordered Cowboys for Trump to register, file expenditure, and contribution reports and pay a fine of $7,800. For more information, see Morgan Lee, "Appeals court: Cowboys for Trump is a political committee," ABC News, February 17, 2022, https://abcnews.go.com/Politics/wireStory/appeals-court-cowboys-trump-political-committee-82951469.

16   Erin Doherty, "Cowboys for Trump founder barred from public office over Jan. 6," Axios, updated September 6, 2022, https://www.axios.com/2022/09/06/cowboys-trump-capitol-riot-griffin-barred.

17   Ivana Saric, "'Cowboys for Trump' founder convicted for breaching the Capitol on Jan. 6," Axios, March 22, 2022, https://www.axios.com/2022/03/22/cowboys-trump-jan-6-convict.

18 Luke Broadwater and Michael Schmidt, "A Long-Shot Attempt Would Bar Trump in 2024 as an 'Insurrectionist,'" *New York Times*, September 8, 2022, p. A14.

19 *Id.*

20 H.R. 1405 117th Congress, To provide a cause of action to remove and bar from holding office certain individuals who engage in insurrection or rebellion against the United States, and for other purposes. Sponsored by Rep. Steve Cohen (D-Tennessee). Introduced February 26, 2021. For more information, see https://www.congress.gov/bill/117th-congress/house-bill/1405?r=1&s=1.

21 Pub. L. 89–554, 80 Stat. 424 (1966), codified at 5 U.S.C. § 3331.

22 Pub. L. 89–554, 80 Stat. 524 (1966), codified at 5 U.S.C. § 7311.

23 Pub. L. 89–554, §3(d), 80 Stat. 609 (1966), codified at 18 U.S.C. § 1918, as amended.

24 5 U.S.C. § 3331.

Chapter 11

1 "Kristallnacht," United States Holocaust Memorial Museum, https://www.ushmm.org/collections/bibliography/kristallnacht (accessed December 11, 2021.

2 Jennifer Rosenberg, "European Roma (Gypsies) in the Holocaust: The Story of Some of the Forgotten Victims of the Nazis," ThoughtCo, https://www.thoughtco.com/gypsies-and-the-holocaust-1779660 (updated December 4, 2019).

3 John Graham Royde-Smith, "Costs of the war: Killed, wounded, prisoners, or missing," Britannica.com, https://www.britannica.com/event/World-War-II/Costs-of-the-war (accessed December 11, 2021).

4 "Casualties of World War II," Lumenlearning.com, https://courses.lumenlearning.com/suny-hccc-worldhistory2/chapter/casualties-of-world-war-ii/ (accessed December 11, 2021).

5 "France," World Factbook, United States Central Intelligence Agency, https://www.cia.gov/the-world-factbook/countries/france/ (accessed October 1, 2022).

6 Bill Keller, "Major Soviet Paper Says 20 Million Died as Victims of Stalin," *New York Times*, February 4, 1989, https://www.nytimes.com/1989/02/04/world/major-soviet-paper-says-20-million-died-as-victims-of-stalin.html.

7 Amber Pariona, "The Deadliest Dictator Regimes in History," WorldAtlas.com, https://www.worldatlas.com/articles/the-deadliest-dictator-regimes-in-history.html (accessed August 14, 2018).

See also Kallie Szczepanski, "What Was the Long March?" ThoughtCo, updated March 10, 2019, https://www.thoughtco.com/what-was-the-long-march-195155. The Long March took place in 1934 during the Chinese Civil War. It resulted in the demise of Chiang Kai-shek's regime and the rise of communist China under Mao Zedong.

8   "Modern Era Genocides," The Genocide Education Project, https://genocideeducation.org/resources/modern-era-genocides/ (accessed December 11, 2021).

9   Erin Blakemore, "30,000 People Were 'Disappeared' in Argentina's Dirty War. These Women Never Stopped Looking," History.com, March 7, 2019, https://www.history.com/news/mothers-plaza-de-mayo-disappeared-children-dirty-war-argentina.

10   "Jamal Khashoggi: All you need to know about Saudi journalist's death," BBC News, February 24, 2021, https://www.bbc.com/news/world-europe-45812399.

11   American Civil Liberties Union (ACLU), "The Bill of Rights: A Brief History," ACLU, https://www.aclu.org/other/bill-rights-brief-history (accessed January 12, 2022).

12   "Make provision about nationality, asylum and immigration; to make provision about victims of slavery or human trafficking; to provide a power for Tribunals to charge participants where their behavior has wasted the Tribunal's resources; and for connected purposes," Session 2021-22 (22) HL Bill 152 Royal Assent April 28, 2022, https://bills.parliament.uk/bills/3023/stages.

13   Haroon Siddique, "New bill quietly gives powers to remove British citizenship without notice," *Guardian*, November 17, 2021, https://www.theguardian.com/politics/2021/nov/17/new-bill-quietly-gives-powers-to-remove-british-citizenship-without-notice.

14   *Town of Greece v. Galloway*, 572 U.S. 565, 134 S. Ct. 1811, 188 L. Ed.2d 835 (2014). See also Legal Information Institute, "Religion and the Constitution," https://www.law.cornell.edu/wex/religion_and_the_constitution (accessed December 12, 2021).

15   *McCreary County v. American Civil Liberties Union*, 545 U.S. 844, 125 S. Ct. 2722, 162 L. Ed. 2d 729 (2005).

16   *Id*. at 844.

17   *Stone v. Graham*, 449 U.S., 101 S. Ct. 192, 66 L. Ed. 2d 199 (1980). In this case, the US Supreme Court held that a Kentucky law that required the posting of the Ten Commandments on the wall of every school classroom in the state violated the Establishment Clause because the requirement was essentially religious.

18   *McCreary* at 884.

19   *Cantwell v. Connecticut,* 310 U.S. 296, 60 S. Ct. 900, 84 L. Ed. 1213 (1940).

20   Pub. L. 103-141, 42 USC §2000bb – 2000bb-4 (1993).

21   *Burwell v. Hobby Lobby Stores*, 573 U.S. 682, 134 S. Ct. 2751, 189 L. Ed. 2d 675 (2014).

22 Alexey Navalny, "Biography," https://2018.navalny.com/en/biography/ (accessed December 12, 2021) Note: most Western sources transliterate "Алексей Навальный" as "Alexei Navalny."

23 VOA News, "European Court of Human Rights Calls on Russia to Free Navalny." February 17, 2021.

24 "Russia's Navalny says prison has changed his status to 'terrorist,'" Reuters, updated October 11, 2021, https://www.reuters.com/world/europe/russias-navalny-says-his-prison-status-changed-terrorist-2021-10-11/.

25 "Alexei Navalny awarded the European Parliament's 2021 Sakharov Prize," European Parliament, October 20, 2021 https://www.europarl.europa.eu/news/en/press-room/20211014IPR14915/alexei-navalny-awarded-the-european-parliament-s-2021-sakharov-prize.

26 Tanya Lokshina, "Russian Authorities Move to Shut Down a Human Rights Giant," Human Rights Watch, November 12, 2021, https://www.hrw.org/news/2021/11/12/russian-authorities-move-shut-down-human-rights-giant.

27 Andrei Sakharov, theoretical physicist ("father" of the Soviet hydrogen bomb) and human-rights activist (1975 winner of the Nobel Peace Prize), for decades despite internal exile and house arrest, spoke out against government repression and published a series of essays worldwide to defend political prisoners held in labor camps and psychiatric hospitals. For more information, see "Andrei Sakharov 'Crystal of Morality' among Soviet Scientists," https://www.washingtonpost.com/archive/politics/1989/12/16/andrei-sakharov-crystal-of-morality-among-soviet-scientists/1b874e46-a996-432b-ae2e-09a04557489f/.

28 Tanya Lokshina, "Memory and Memorial Will Prevail," *Moscow Times*, updated November 17, 2021, https://www.themoscowtimes.com/2021/11/17/memory-and-memorial-will-prevail-a75588.

29 Chris Buckley, "Fury in China After an Outspoken Teacher Vanishes and the Authorities Keep Silent," *New York Times*, December 24, 2021, p. A21.

30 Taboo and People's Climate Music, "Stand Up / Stand N Rock #NoDAPL (Official Video)" December 2016, https://www.youtube.com/watch?v=Onyk7guvHK8. For more information, see Yale University Library, "Energy History: 'Stand Up / Stand N Rock #NoDAPL'" https://energyhistory.yale.edu/library-item/stand-stand-n-rock-nodapl.

31 "*Crown v. John Peter Zenger*, 1735," Historical Society of the New York Courts, https://history.nycourts.gov/case/crown-v-zenger/ (accessed December 12, 2021).

32 *People v. Croswell*, 3 Johns. Cas. 337 NY (1804).

33 *New York Times v. Sullivan*, 376 U.S. 254, 84 S. Ct. 710, 11 L. Ed. 2d 686 (1964).

34 *Gertz v. Robert Welch, Inc.*, 418 U.S. 323, 350, 94 S. Ct. 2997, 41 L. Ed. 2d 789 (1974).

35   *Obsidian Finance Group, LLC v. Cox*, 740 F.3d 1284 (9ᵗʰ Cir. 2014 Tanya Lokshina). See also Tim Hull, "Blogger's Speech rights Championed in the" *Courthouse News Service*, January 17, 2014, https://www.courthousenews.com/bloggers-speech-rights-championed-in-the-9ᵗʰ/.

36   Pub. L. 88–352, 78 Stat. 241, (1964).

37   Howard University, "Black Lives Matter Movement," https://library.law.howard.edu/civilrightshistory/BLM (accessed December 12, 2021).

38   National Museum of American History, "The Women's March, 2017," https://americanhistory.si.edu/creating-icons/women%E2%80%99s-march-2017 (accessed December12, 2021).

39   March for Our Lives, "Mission and Story," https://marchforourlives.com/mission-story/ (accessed December 12, 2021).

40   Daily Chart, "More than 15,000 Russians have been arrested in anti-war protests," *Economist*, March 22, 2022, https://www.economist.com/graphic-detail/2022/03/22/more-than-15000-russians-have-been-arrested-in-anti-war-protests.

41   History.com editors, "Chinese crackdown on protests leads to Tiananmen Square Massacre. This Day in History: June 4 1989," History.com, https://www.history.com/this-day-in-history/tiananmen-square-massacre-takes-place (accessed December 2021).

42   On August 12, 2017, Neo-Nazis, Ku Klux Klansmen, and other white supremacists rallied around the spot where a Robert E. Lee statue stood until the city of Charlottesville voted to remove it. The Unite the Right rally turned violent after hundreds of counter-protesters arrived. The police did not intervene until the governor declared a state of emergency and shut down the rally. The demonstrators then dispersed throughout Charlottesville. Dozens of people were injured and one killed when a Neo-Nazi drove his car into a crowd. For more information, see Debbie Elliott, "The Charlottesville rally 5 years later: 'It's what you're still trying to forget,'" NPR, August 12, 2022, https://www.npr.org/2022/08/12/1116942725/the-charlottesville-rally-5-years-later-its-what-youre-still-trying-to-forget.

43   *District of Columbia. v. Heller*, 554 U.S. 570, 639-40, 128 S. Ct. 2783, 171 L. Ed. 2d 637 (2008)(2008) (Stevens, J., dissenting).

44   *Id,.*

45   *McDonald v. City of Chicago*, 561 U.S. 742, 130 S. Ct. 3020, 177 L. Ed. 2d 894 (2010).

46   Gordon S. Wood, "The Third Amendment," National Constitution Center, https://constitutioncenter.org/interactive-constitution/interpretation/amendment-iii/interps/123 (accessed December 12, 2021).

47   *McDonald* at 780–85.

48   *Brown v. Board of Education of Topeka*, 347 U.S. 483, 74 S. Ct. 686, 98 L. Ed. 873 (1954).

49   *Loving v. Virginia*, 388 U.S. 1, 87 S. Ct. 1817, 18 L. Ed. 2d 1010 (1967). Mildred Loving, a black woman and her white husband, Richard Loving, who were sentenced to a year in prison for marrying each other and appealed their conviction. The US Supreme Court ruled that laws banning interracial marriage violate the Equal Protection and Due Process Clauses of the Fourteenth Amendment.

50   *Griswold v. Connecticut*, 381 U.S. 479, 85 S. Ct. 1678, 14 L. Ed. 2d 510 (1965).

51   *Roe v. Wade*, 410 U.S. 113, 93 S. Ct. 705, 35 L. Ed. 2d 147 (1973).

52   *Dobbs v. Jackson*, 597 U.S. ___, 2022 WL 2276808; 2022 US LEXIS 3057 (2022).

53   For a more extensive discussion of privacy and personal information protection, see "Is There a 'Right to Privacy' Amendment?" https://www.findlaw.com/injury/torts-and-personal-injuries/is-there-a-right-to-privacy-amendment.html.

54   *Riley v. California*, 573 U.S. 373, 134 S. Ct. 2473, 189, L. Ed. 2d 430 (2014).

55   Ronald Reagan, "Election Eve Address 'A Vision for America'," Ronald Reagan Presidential Library & Museum, given November 3, 1980, available at https://www.reaganlibrary.gov/archives/speech/election-eve-address-vision-america.

56   Promote the Vote Michigan worked on passage of a ballot proposal in 2018 to increase voter access to the ballot. It passed with overwhelming support. Voters Not Politicians, concluding that gerrymandering posed a threat to equal voter representation, worked on successful passage of the Proposal 2 constitutional amendment to create the Michigan Independent Citizens Redistricting Commission. See Clara Hendrickson, "Redistricting experts weigh in on results of first general election under new maps," *Detroit Free Press*, December 1, 2022, https://www.freep.com/story/news/politics/elections/2022/12/01/michigan-redistricting-commission-maps/69692417007/.

Chapter 12

1   *Marbury v. Madison*, 5 U.S. 137, 2 L. Ed. 60 (1803).

2   *Id.* at 177.

3   Bill Chappell and Daniel Estrin, "Here's why Netanyahu's court overhaul, now on hold, brought Israel to the brink," NPR, updated March 27, 2023, https://www.npr.org/2023/03/27/1166200532/israel-civil-war-netanyahu-court-control.

4   *Mapp v. Ohio*, 367 U.S. 643, 81 S. Ct. 1684, 6 L. Ed. 2d 1081 (1961).

5   *Silverthorne Lumber Co. v. United States*, 251 U.S. 385, 40 S. Ct. 182, 64 L. Ed. 319 (1920).

6 Sara J. Berman, "Arrest Warrants: What's in Them, How Police Get Them," NOLO, https://www.nolo.com/legal-encyclopedia/arrest-warrants-how-when-police-get-them.html (accessed January 9, 2022).

7 *Carpenter v. United States*, 585 U.S. ___, 138 S. Ct. 2206, 201 L. Ed. 2d 507 (2018).

8 For a fuller discussion see "Habeas Corpus," Cornell Legal Information Institute (LII), https://www.law.cornell.edu/wex/habeas_corpus (accessed December 12, 2021).

9 *Boumediene v. Bush*, 553 U.S. 723, 128 S. Ct. 2229, 171 L. Ed. 2d 41 (2008). For more information, see David Stout, "US Supreme Court backs Guantánamo prisoners' right to appeal," *New York Times*, June 12, 2008, https://www.nytimes.com/2008/06/12/world/americas/12iht-12scotus.13666865.html.

10 Congressional Research Service staff, "Capitol Unrest, Legislative Response, and the Bill of Attainder Clause," Congressional Research Service, January 22, 2021, https://crsreports.congress.gov/product/pdf/LSB/LSB10567.

11 "Ex Post Facto," Cornell Legal Information Institute (LII), https://www.law.cornell.edu/wex/ex_post_facto (accessed December 12, 2021).

12 Joanna Lampe, "Capitol Unrest, Legislative Response, and the Bill of Attainder Clause," Congressional Research Service, January 22, 2021, https://crsreports.congress.gov/product/pdf/LSB/LSB10567.

13 Findlaw staff, "How Does a Grand Jury Work?" Findlaw.com, updated November 9, 2020, https://www.findlaw.com/criminal/criminal-procedure/how-does-a-grand-jury-work.html.

14 Editorial staff, "Notice of Accusation," Justia.com, https://law.justia.com/constitution/us/amendment-06/09-notice-of-accusation.html (accessed January 11, 2022).

15 *Duncan v. Louisiana*, 391 U.S. 145, 88 S. Ct. 1444, 20 L. Ed. 2d 491 (1968).

16 *Batson v. Kentucky*, 476 U.S. 79, 106 S. Ct. 1712, 90 L. Ed. 2d 69 (1986).

17 Reporters Committee for Freedom of the Press, "Pretrial publicity's limited effect on the right to a fair trial," https://www.rcfp.org/journals/pretrial-publicitys-limited/ (accessed September 29, 2022).

18 National Center for Court Statistics, "Juror and Jury Use of New Media: A Baseline Exploration," US Department of Justice, NJC no. 240001, 2012, https://www.ojp.gov/ncjrs/virtual-library/abstracts/juror-and-jury-use-new-media-baseline-exploration (accessed September 29, 2022).

19 Administrative Office of the US Courts, *Handbook for Trial Jurors Serving in the United States District Courts*, HB100 (revised 8/12), https://www.uscourts.gov/file/2802/download, accessed September 29, 2022.

20 *Trop v. Dulles*, 356 U.S. 86, 100-101, 78 S. Ct. 590; 2 L. Ed. 2d 630 (1958). Chief Justice Earl Warren wrote that the clause "must draw its meaning from the evolving standards of decency that mark the progress of a maturing society." For

more discussion, see "The Meaning of 'Cruel and Unusual Punishment,'" https://www.nolo.com/legal-encyclopedia/the-meaning-cruel-unusual-punishment.html.

21 *Gregg v. Georgia*, 428 U.S. 153, 96 S. Ct. 2909, 49 L. Ed. 2d 859 (1976).

22 *Atkins v. Virginia*, 536 U.S. 304, 122 S. Ct. 2242, 153 L. Ed. 2d 335 (2002).

23 *Roper v. Simmons*, 543 U.S. 551, 125 S. Ct. 1183, 161 L. Ed. 2d 1 (2005).

24 George Hunter, "Worthy calls cash bail reforms for Detroit's 36th District Court 'a bridge too far,'" *Detroit News*, July 12, 2022, https://www.detroitnews.com/story/news/local/detroit-city/2022/07/12/cash-bail-reforms-set-detroits-36th-district-court-lawsuit-agreement/10034320002/.

25 For a fuller discussion, see Roger A. Fairfax and John C. Harrison, "The Fifth Amendment Due Process Clause," National Constitution Center, https://constitutioncenter.org/interactive-constitution/interpretation/amendment-v/clauses/633, and Nathan S. Chapman and Kenji Yoshino, "The Fourteenth Amendment Due Process Clause," National Constitution Center, https://constitutioncenter.org/interactive-constitution/interpretation/amendment-xiv/clauses/701 (accessed December 14, 2021).

26 Library of Congress editorial staff, "Fifth Amendment," Constitution Annotated, https://constitution.congress.gov/browse/essay/amdt5-4-1/ALDE_00000874/ (accessed October 23, 2022).

27 For a fuller discussion see "Double Jeopardy," Cornell Legal Information Institute (LII), https://www.law.cornell.edu/wex/double_jeopardy# (accessed December 14, 2021).

28 *Breed v. Jones*, 421 U.S. 519, 95 S. Ct. 1779 (1975).

29 *Miranda v. Arizona*, 384 U.S. 436, 86 S. Ct. 1602, 16 L. Ed. 2d 694 (1966).

30 Timothy B. Lee, "It's unconstitutional for cops to force phone unlocking, court rules," Ars Technica, June 24, 2020, https://arstechnica.com/tech-policy/2020/06/indiana-supreme-court-its-unconstitutional-to-force-phone-unlocking/.

31 Legal Information Institute, "Forfeiture," Cornell Law School, last updated January 2023, https://www.law.cornell.edu/wex/forfeiture.

32 *Timbs v. Indiana*, 586 U.S. ___, 139 S. Ct. 682, 203 L. Ed. 2d 11 (2019).

33 For a fuller discussion, see Constitution USA, with Peter Sagal, "Due Process Clause, Equal Protection Clause and Disenfranchising Felons,", https://www.pbs.org/tpt/constitution-usa-peter-sagal/equality/due-process-equal-protection-and-disenfranchisement/ (accessed December 14, 2021).

34 National Conference of State Legislatures, "Felon Voting Rights," June 28, 2021, https://www.ncsl.org/research/elections-and-campaigns/felon-voting-rights.aspx.

35 For a discussion and collection of cases on the presumption of innocence, see "Presumption of Innocence: Proof Beyond a Reasonable Doubt," https://www.mad.uscourts.gov/resources/pattern2003/html/patt4cfo.htm.

36   M Crim JI 1.9 Presumption of Innocence, Burden of Proof, and Reasonable Doubt.

37   Justia editorial staff, "Confrontation," Justia.com, https://law.justia.com/constitution/us/amendment-06/10-confrontation.html (accessed January 9, 2022).)

38   US Attorney's Office Eastern District of Michigan, "Victim Witness," https://www.justice.gov/usao-edmi/victim-witness, accessed July 12 2023.

39   For an extensive discussion of Compulsory Process, see Peter Westen, "The Compulsory Process Clause," 73 Mich. L. Rev. 1 (1974). https://repository.law.umich.edu/cgi/viewcontent.cgi?article=4263&context=mlr.

40   *Gideon v. Wainwright*, 372 U.S. 335, 83 S. Ct. 792, 9 L. Ed. 2d 799 (1963).

41   *Escobedo v. Illinois*, 378 U.S. 478, 84 S. Ct. 1758, 12 L. Ed. 2d 977 (1964).

42   Iryna Dasevich, "The Right to an Interpreter for Criminal Defendants with Limited English," Jurist, April 15, 2012, https://www.jurist.org/commentary/2012/04/iryna-dasevich-criminal-justice/.

43   205 U.S. 86 (1907).

44   Pub. L. 95-539, 92 Stat 2040 (1978) codified at 28 U.S.C. § 1827.

45   U.S. Courts of Appeal Administrative Office, "About the US Courts of Appeals: The Right to Appeal," https://www.uscourts.gov/about-federal-courts/court-role-and-structure/about-us-courts-appeals (accessed January 9, 2022).

46   House Hearing, 110 Congress, "H.A.S.C. No. 110–166 Implications of the Supreme Court's Boumediene Decision for Detainees at Guantanamo Bay, Cuba: Non-Governmental Perspective," July 30, 2008, https://www.govinfo.gov/content/pkg/CHRG-110hhrg45826/html/CHRG-110hhrg45826.htm.

Chapter 13

1   *Dartmouth College v. Woodward*, 17 U.S. 518, 4 Wheat. 518, 4 L. Ed. 629 (1819).

2   "An Act for the encouragement of learning, by securing the copies of maps, charts, and books to the authors and proprietors of such copies, during the times therein mentioned," Pub. L. 1–15, 1 Stat. 124 (1790).

3   U.S. Patent and Trademarks Office, "U.S. Patent Activity Calendar Years 1790 to the Present," https://www.uspto.gov/web/offices/ac/ido/oeip/taf/h_counts.htm.

4   United States Copyright Office, "United States Copyright Office Annual Report FY 2022," https://www.copyright.gov/history/annual_reports.html.

5   BRIA 23 4 a "The Origins of Patent and Copyright Law," Constitutional Rights Foundation, Winter 2008 (Vol. 23 No. 4), https://www.crf-usa.org/bill-of-rights-in-action/bria-23-4-a-the-origins-of-patent-and-copyright-law.

6   "Patents by Inventor William Gates," Justicia Patents, https://patents.justia.com/inventor/william-gates (accessed 20 December 2021).

7   "Amazon Patents – Key Insights and Stats," Insights by GreyB, https://insights.greyb.com/amazon-patents/ (updated December 8, 2021).

8   Wne Zhou, "The Patent Landscape of Genetically Modified Organisms," Harvard SITNBoston, 2015, https://sitn.hms.harvard.edu/flash/2015/the-patent-landscape-of-genetically-modified-organisms/ (accessed December 22, 2021).

9   "What are genome editing and CRISPR-Cas9?" MedlinePlus, updated September 18, 2020, https://medlineplus.gov/genetics/understanding/genomicresearch/genomeediting/.

10 Shrink wrap licenses refer to agreements that activate when the buyer removes the plastic wrap from a product such as a CD-ROM in order to use it. Click wrap agreements activate by the user's clicking "OK" on the screen to signify that they have read and agree to terms and conditions before using an application or digital media. Browse wrap agreements appear at the bottom of a web page or application start screen and come into force when the customer uses it. The user doesn't have to affirm agreement and probably doesn't notice it's there.

    For more information, see Megan, "An overview of licenses: shrink-wrap vs. click-wrap vs. browse-wrap licenses," OdinLaw and Media, February 22, 2018, https://odinlaw.com/overview-licenses-shrink-wrap-vs-click-wrap-vs-browse-wrap-licenses/.

11 Shmuel I. Becher and Uri Benenoliel, "Sneak in Contracts," Ga. L. Rev., vol. 55 p. 660 (2021).

12 "Aleksandr Isayevich Solzhenitsyn," Editors of Encyclopaedia Britannica, last updated December 7, 2021, https://www.britannica.com/biography/Aleksandr-Solzhenitsyn.

13 Justia U.S. Law, editorial staff, "National Eminent Domain Power," Justia.com, https://law.justia.com/constitution/us/amendment-05/14-national-eminent-domain-power.html (accessed January 9, 2022).

14 State Bar of Michigan, "Michigan Legal Milestones 33. Poletown and Eminent Domain," https://www.michbar.org/programs/milestone/milestones_poletowneminentdomain (accessed December 22, 2021).

15 *Poletown Neighborhood Council v. Detroit*, 410 Mich. 616, 304 N.W.2d 455 (1981).

16 *County of Wayne v. Hathcock*, 471 Mich. 445, 684 N.W.2d 765 (2004).

17 Sebastian Shakespeare, "The house guests from hell: How the military based in requisitioned country houses during WWII used Old Masters as dartboards, staircases for firewood and emptied the wine cellars," *Daily Mail*, March 22, 2018, https://www.dailymail.co.uk/home/books/article-5533701/How-military-requisitioned-country-houses-WWII.html.

18 Richard V. Adkisson, "Intellectual Property and Eminent Domain: If Ever the Twain Shall Meet," *Journal of Economic Issues*, 36 no. 1 (March 2002) pp. 41–53.

19   Paul J. Sutton, "US jurisdiction report: The lawful seizure of patent rights," *World Intellectual Property Review*, November 1, 2021, https://www.worldipreview.com/contributed-article/us-jurisdiction-report-the-lawful-seizure-of-patent-rights.

20   History.com editors, "New Deal Programs," History.com, updated October 5, 2021, https://www.history.com/topics/great-depression/new-deal.

21   Jim Probasco, "Infrastructure Investment and Jobs Act," Investopedia, updated November 19, 2021, https://www.investopedia.com/infrastructure-investment-jobs-act-5209581.

22   Pub. L. 111–5, 123 Stat. 115 (2009).

23   Diane Whitmore Schanzenbach et al, "Nine facts about the Great Recession and tools for fighting the next downturn," Brookings Institution, May 23, 2016, https://www.brookings.edu/research/nine-facts-about-the-great-recession-and-tools-for-fighting-the-next-downturn/.

24   Robert Rich, "The Great Recession," Federal Reserve, November 22, 2013, https://www.federalreservehistory.org/essays/great-recession-of-200709.

25   Jenny Gesley, "New Report on 'Regulation of Cryptocurrency Around the World' Published," In Custodia Legis Blog, December 22, 2021 https://blogs.loc.gov/law/2021/12/new-report-on-regulation-of-cryptocurrency-around-the-world-published/.

26   An Ordinance for the government of the territory of the United States North West of the river Ohio. Art. 3, Journals of the Continental Congress Volume 32, available at https://memory.loc.gov/cgi-bin/ampage?collId=lljc&fileName=032/lljc032.db&recNum=343.

27   Servicemen's Readjustment Act of 1944, Pub. L. 78–346, 58 Stat. 284 (1944) as amended.

28   Erin Blackmore, "How the GI Bill's Promise Was Denied to a Million Black WWII Veterans," History.com, June 21, 2019, updated April 20, 2021, https://www.history.com/news/gi-bill-black-wwii-veterans-benefits.

29   National WWII Museum, "History At a Glance: Women in World War II," https://www.nationalww2museum.org/students-teachers/student-resources/research-starters/women-wwii (accessed September 25, 2022).

30   Ojibwa for Native American Neteroots, "Indians 101: World War II Indian Veterans Come Home," Daily Kos, November 12, 2019, https://www.dailykos.com/stories/2019/11/12/1898727/-Indians-101-World-War-II-Indian-veterans-come-home.

31   347 U.S. 483, 74 S. Ct. 686, 98 L. Ed. 873, 38 A.L.R.2d 1180 (1954).

32   Office of Head Start, "Head Start History," US Department of Health and Human Services, current as of June 23, 2022, https://www.acf.hhs.gov/ohs/about/history-head-start.

33   Pub. L. 92–318, Title IX, § 901, 86 Stat. 373 (1972), codified at 20 USC §1681.

34 Office of Civil Rights, "Title IX and Sex Discrimination," US Department of Education, revised August 2021, https://www2.ed.gov/about/offices/list/ocr/docs/tix_dis.html.

35 "An act to close the achievement gap with accountability, flexibility, and choice, so that no child is left behind," Pub. L. 107-110, 115 Stat. 1425 (2002).

36 Alyson Klein, "No Child Left Behind: An Overview," EducationWeek, April 10, 2015, https://www.edweek.org/policy-politics/no-child-left-behind-an-overview/2015/04.

37 *Biden v. Nebraska*, No. 22-506 (US June 27, 2023).

38 *Students for Fair Admissions v. Harvard*, 600 U.S. ___ (2023).

39 *California Democratic Party v. Jones*, 530 U.S. 567, 120 S. Ct. 2402, 147 L. Ed. 2d 502 (2000), The Supreme Court ruled that a state law mandating open primaries violated the associational rights of political parties.

40 Michael McCann, "Why Private Golf Clubs Are Legally Still Able to Discriminate Against Women," SI, July 1, 2019, https://www.si.com/golf-archives/2019/07/01/private-golf-clubs-muirfield-augusta-women-discrimination.

41 *Abood v. Detroit Board of Education*, 431 U.S. 209, 97 S. Ct. 1782, 52 L. Ed. 2d 261 (1977).

42 "200+ Stores UNIONIZED and 10,600+ UNION SUPPORTERS IN SOLIDARITY!," Starbucks Workers United, https://sbworkersunited.org/ (accessed September 28, 2022).

Chapter 14

1 Carl Bernstein and Bob Woodward, *All the President's Men* (New York: Simon & Schuster, 1974). See also Woodward and Costa, *Peril*, discussing the end of Donald Trump's presidency and the beginning of Joe Biden's presidency.

2 Gerald R. Ford, "Gerald R. Ford's Remarks Upon Taking the Oath of Office as President," August 9, 1974, https://www.fordlibrarymuseum.gov/library/speeches/740001.asp.

3 *Near v. Minnesota*, 283 U.S. 697, 51 S. Ct. 625, 75 L. Ed. 1357 (1931).

4 *New York Times v. United States*, 403 U.S. 713, 91 S. Ct. 2140, 29 L. Ed. 2d 822 (1971).

5 Ivan Nechepurenko, "Belarus Imprisons 2 Journalists for the Crime of Reporting (From a Demonstration)," *New York Times*, February 19, 2021, p. A10.

6 Neil Vigdor and Ivan Nechepurenko, "Who Is Roman Protasevich, the Captive Journalist in Belarus?" *New York Times*, May 23, 2021 updated June 14, 2021, https://www.nytimes.com/2021/05/23/world/europe/roman-protasevich.html.

7 Sharyl Attkisson, "Media Bias Chart: Analysis," sharylattkisson.com, April 3, 2019, https://sharylattkisson.com/2019/04/media-bias-chart-analysis/. updated from

"Media Bias: A New Chart" published August 28, 2018, https://sharylattkisson. com/2018/08/media-bias-a-new-chart/.

8   "Media Bias Ratings," AllSides Media, https://www.allsides.com/media-bias/ media-bias-ratings (accessed December 24, 2021).

9   Ad Fontes Media, "The Media Bias Chart. Version 9.0 January 2022 Edition – Combined Web, Podcast, and TV," https://adfontesmedia.com/ (accessed February 9, 2022).

10   "Izvestiya Russian newspaper," Britannica, https://www.britannica.com/topic/ Izvestiya (most recently revised and updated by Adam Augustyn (accessed December 24, 2021).

11   "Pravda Soviet newspaper," Britannica, https://www.britannica.com/topic/ Pravda (most recently revised and updated by Brian Duignan (accessed December 24, 2021).

12   "ITAR-TASS Russian news agency," Britannica, https://www.britannica.com/ topic/ITAR-TASS (most recently revised and updated by Adam Augustyn. Accessed December 24, 2021). See also "TASS history," TASS Russian News Agency, https://tass.com/history (Accessed December 24, 2021).

13   "83 Journalists Killed in Russia between 1992 and 2023 / Motive Confirmed," Committee to Protect Journalists (CPJ), https://cpj.org/data/killed/europe/ russia/?status=Killed&motiveConfirmed%5B%5D=Confirmed&motive Unconfirmed%5B%5D=Unconfirmed&type%5B%5D=Journalist&type%5B %5D=Media%20Worker&cc_fips%5B%5D=RS&start_year=1992&end_year =2023&group_by=location (accessed July 16, 2023).

14   Benjamin Franklin Historical Society, "Poor Richard's Almanack." Franklin considered it a vehicle of instruction for common people who could not afford books, a literature for the masses. http://www.benjamin-franklin-history.org/ poor-richards-almanac/ (accessed December 24, 2021).

15   Patricia Mazzei and Frances Robles, "It's Déjà Vu in Florida, Land of Recounts and Contested Elections," *New York Times*, November 9, 2018, https://www. nytimes.com/2018/11/09/us/florida-ballots-recount-scott-nelson-gillum-desantis.html.

16   American Bar Association, docket list.

17   In June 2013, Barton Gellman at the *Washington Post* and Glenn Greenwald at the *Guardian* broke stories about National Security Agency surveillance activities conducted on US citizens and foreign officials. Their source was Edward Snowden. Both newspapers shared a Pulitzer Prize for their articles. For more information: https://www.brookings.edu/blog/brookings-now/2014/10/20/ ten-noteworthy-moments-in-u-s-investigative-journalism/.

18   David Bloom, "Love It Or Hate It, The Trump Show Has Been Very Good For Media Business," *Forbes*, November 5, 2018, https://www.forbes.com/

sites/dbloom/2018/11/05/happy-election-season-media-donald-trump-has-been-very-good-for-you/?sh=319407ab3abd.

19 Ashley Lutz, "These 6 Corporations Control 90% Of The Media In America," Business Insider, June 14, 2012, https://www.businessinsider.com/these-6-corporations-control-90-of-the-media-in-america-2012-6.

20 Adam Levy, "The Big 6 Media Companies," The Motley Fool, updated December 19, 2021 and January 3, 2022, https://www.fool.com/investing/stock-market/market-sectors/communication/media-stocks/big-6/.

21 Whitney Joiner and Alexa McMahon, "The Lost Local News Issue," *Washington Post Magazine*, November 30, 2021, https://www.washingtonpost.com/magazine/interactive/2021/local-news-deserts-expanding/.

22 Mason Walker, "US newsroom employment has fallen 26% since 2008," Pew Research Center, July 13, 2021, https://www.pewresearch.org/fact-tank/2021/07/13/u-s-newsroom-employment-has-fallen-26-since-2008/.

Chapter 15

1   Reid J. Epstein, "Losing Faith in Government, Many Americans Say it's Time to Change the System," *New York Times*, July 14, 2022, p. A13.

2   Thomas Elias, "Will abortion decision revive Calexit?" California Focus, *Santa Maria Times*, July 12, 2022.

3   Abraham Lincoln, "A House Divided," presented at Springfield, Illinois, June 16, 1858, The Civil War Research Engine at Dickinson College, https://housedivided.dickinson.edu/sites/teagle/texts/lincoln-house-divided-speech-1858/.

4   Gary Wills, *Lincoln at Gettysburg: The Words That Remade America* (New York: Simon & Schuster, 1992) dustjacket text.

5   American Battlefield Trust, "Gettysburg," https://www.battlefields.org/learn/civil-war/battles/gettysburg (accessed February 11, 2022).

6   Abraham Lincoln, "Gettysburg Address," November 19, 1863, National Park Service, https://www.nps.gov/linc/learn/historyculture/gettysburgaddress.htm (updated April 29, 2021). Punctuation and capitalization per the Bliss version engraved on the south interior wall of the Lincoln Memorial in the District of Columbia. It is one of only five known manuscript copies and the only one with Abraham Lincoln's signature.

7   William Shakespeare, *Hamlet* Act I, scene iii, L 55-81.

8   Doris Kearns Goodwin, *Team of Rivals: the Political Genius of Abraham Lincoln* (Simon & Schuster, 2005).

9   Laurence H. Tribe, Donald Ayer and Dennis Aftergut, "Will Trump Get Away With Inciting an Insurrection?"

10 The US Constitution (Article II Section 1) and the Presidential Succession Act of 1947 (Pub. L. 80–199, 61 Stat. 380 (1947)) outline the presidential order of

succession: Vice President, Speaker of the House, President Pro Tempore of the Senate, followed by other Cabinet officers in the order of their agencies' creation. For more information, see https://www.usa.gov/presidents.

[11] Lincoln, "Second Inaugural Address." https://www.nps.gov/linc/learn/historyculture/lincoln-second-inaugural.htm.

[12] Lincoln, "Gettysburg Address," https://www.nps.gov//linc/learn/historyculture/gettysburgaddress.htm.

[13] Feldman, "This Is the Story of How Lincoln Broke the US Constitution."

Appendix A

[1] Pub. L. 82-414, 66 Stat. 163 (1952) codified at 8 U.S.C. § 1401, as amended. Also known as the McCarran–Walter Act.

[2] Social Security Administration, "How the Americans with Disabilities Act (ADA) Protects People with Mental Illness," May 28, 2015, https://choosework.ssa.gov/blog/how-the-americans-with-disabilities-act-ada-protects-people-with-mental-illness.

[3] Federal Reserve, "The Fed Explained," Board of Governors of the Federal Reserve System, updated October 6, 2021, https://www.federalreserve.gov/aboutthefed/the-fed-explained.htm.